THE SOCIAL WELFARE FORUM, 1970

Wilbur J. Cohen

THE
SOCIAL WELFARE
FORUM, 1970

OFFICIAL PROCEEDINGS, 97TH ANNUAL FORUM

NATIONAL CONFERENCE ON SOCIAL WELFARE

CHICAGO, ILLINOIS, MAY 31 TO JUNE 5, 1970

 Published 1970 for the

NATIONAL CONFERENCE ON SOCIAL WELFARE *by*

COLUMBIA UNIVERSITY PRESS, *New York and London*

ISBN: 0-231-03473-3

Library of Congress Catalog Card Number: 8-85377

PRINTED IN THE UNITED STATES OF AMERICA

The Contributors

WERNER W. BOEHM, Dean, School of Social Work, Rutgers—The State University, New Brunswick, N. J.

EVELINE M. BURNS, Professor of Social Work, New York University Graduate School of Social Work; Professor Emeritus, Columbia University School of Social Work

ALAN K. CAMPBELL, Dean, Maxwell Graduate School of Citizenship and Public Affairs, Syracuse University, Syracuse, N.Y.

WILBUR J. COHEN, Dean, School of Education, University of Michigan, Ann Arbor; President, National Conference on Social Welfare

DAN W. DODSON, Director, Center for Human Relations and Community Studies, New York University, New York

VIRGINIA R. DOSCHER, Staff Associate, American Public Welfare Association, Chicago

DANIEL M. FOX, Principal, Organization for Social and Technical Innovation; Assistant Professor of History and Public Administration, Harvard University, Cambridge, Mass.

FLORENCE HORCHOW, free-lance writer, Columbus, Ohio

BARBARA JORDAN, State Senator, State of Texas; member, President's Commission on Income Maintenance Programs

REV. ROBERT P. KENNEDY, Director, Social Action Division, Catholic Charities of Brooklyn, Brooklyn, N.Y.

GEORGE MCGOVERN, United States Senator, State of South Dakota, Washington, D.C.

ROBERT R. MAYER, Associate Professor, Department of City and Regional Planning, University of North Carolina, Chapel Hill

VICTOR OBENHAUS, Professor of Christian Ethics, Chicago Theological Seminary, Chicago

HOWARD E. PRUNTY, Field Consultant, Child Welfare League of America, Inc., New York

ALVIN L. SCHORR, Dean, Graduate School of Social Work, New York University, New York

T. GEORGE SILCOTT, Executive Director, Wiltwyck School for Boys, New York

JOHN D. TWINAME, Administrator, Social and Rehabilitation Services, United States Department of Health, Education, and Welfare, Washington, D.C.

The National Conference on Social Welfare

THE NATIONAL CONFERENCE ON SOCIAL WELFARE is a voluntary organization of individual and organizational members whose major function is to provide a national forum for the critical examination of basic problems and issues in the social welfare field.

These annual forums furnish a two-way channel of communication between paid and volunteer workers, between social welfare and allied fields, and between the service organizations and the social work profession.

Since 1874, through its annual forums and its comprehensive publications program, the National Conference has reflected the history and dynamic development of social welfare in this country. Its national office serves as headquarters for state conferences in social welfare; as the secretariat for the U.S. Committee of the International Council on Social Welfare; and as a clearinghouse for educational materials for use on local, state, national, and international levels.

Among the newer services developed by the Conference in recent years is its insurance program and information services, including a library of unpublished Annual Forum manuscripts; its document retrieval program, of which the data-processed production of the KWIC Index of its publications since 1874 is a part; and its Selected Bibliography service.

Foreword

THE BEGINNING OF THE DECADE of the 1970s finds the nation struggling with a number of critical social dilemmas, endemic to the history and value orientation of this society. Yet the ongoing character of the social problems created by these dilemmas seems highly inconsistent with the great progress made in solving the many technological problems of infinite complexity. At this juncture in time, little progress on these issues of critical concern to the human condition are indicated.

The decade of the seventies finds the nation almost irreconcilably divided on how to end a most unpopular war, one which most agree should be terminated yet incessantly continues. A second dilemma relates to the failure of the national commitment made in 1964 to achieve greater economic justice in this economy of high abundance by bringing an end to poverty. Although few deny that we must diminish the effects of poverty, major controversies exist about the proposals advanced and the amounts of resources to be allocated. The third major issue is that of social justice for nonwhite ethnic groups which Myrdal so aptly defined many years ago as the most significant of all the American dilemmas. Despite the seminal commitment to "equality" and "liberty and justice for all" the value system of this nation has consistently been in conflict between the ideal of social justice on one hand and racism on the other.

The first two dilemmas, serious and significant, seem somewhat capable of fairly immediate resolution. Although conflicting values underlying these issues might very well resist an oversimplified solution, the resources and decision-making apparatus are readily apparent. The war can be terminated immediately, and a swift end to poverty is possible. Racism seems to be infinitely more complex, woven intricately into the fabric of the total societal ethos and programmed into the emotional status of an overwhelming part of our population.

In both the formal and informal arenas of the 1970 Annual Forum, these three major American dilemmas were in constant focus. Social welfare leaders of this nation addressed their attention to these issues constantly in Forum presentations. In the opening address, the Conference President, Wilbur J. Cohen, comments clearly on the critical nature of what he calls "the gigantic problems of war, poverty, and race relations . . . in the face of the great capacity of the country for meeting the basic needs of all its people." In a keen analysis of the crisis at hand, Cohen offers cogent recommendations for priorities in the 1970s.

Seven papers are focused on both theoretical and practical concerns of President Nixon's welfare reform, the Family Assistance Plan. Hailed by some as the most innovative program in public welfare since the Social Security Act of 1935, it is criticized by others as a most limited approach to the solution of the problem of income redistribution and income security.

Other papers deal with decision-makers in social policy, institutional racism in social agencies, social change and service delivery, neighborhoods and social policy.

The section entitled "Confrontation, 1970" summarizes the opening and closing General Sessions, representing highly dramatic and meaningful scenes where social problems were discussed and debated in highly emotional terms. The report of the Opening General Session, by T. George Silcott, and that of the Closing General Session, by Virginia R. Doscher, provide valuable insights. Like all written reports, they can only capture a bit of the flavor of the human interaction which took place in these major confrontations. The report entitled "Chicago Scene I," by Werner W. Boehm, describing the political confrontations which took place between membership groups in the newly emerging social welfare groupings and the Conference "establishment" offers important historical perspectives. Similarly, Howard E. Prunty's report as a participant, in "Chicago Scene II," gives the insight of one close to the many volatile situations. It describes the variety of informal activities which provided such a great deal of the important learning experiences of the Annual Forum in 1970.

A companion volume, *Social Work Practice, 1970,* will be published separately by Columbia University Press. The Chairman extends his deep thanks to the members of the Editorial Committee, who contributed a great deal of time and energy in reading and selecting papers for publication in the two volumes: Delwin M. Anderson, Kathryn Close, Jeannette Hanford, Rachel Marks, and Jay Roney.

The Editorial Committee wishes to record its gratitude to Joe Hoffer, Sara Lee Berkman, and Mabel Davis, of the Conference staff, for their continuous help as well as to Dorothy M. Swart, of Columbia University Press.

ARTHUR KATZ
Chairman, Editorial Committee

Greetings to the Conference

from PRESIDENT RICHARD NIXON

THE NATIONAL CONFERENCE ON SOCIAL WELFARE represents a timely and promising forum in a crusade for reform which we cannot afford to lose.

I believe that there is no proposal I have sent to Congress more central to my own philosophy of fairness and progress for all the American people than the Family Assistance Plan. It places the United States on the way to end poverty as we know it within ten years, and it makes us true partners in creative progress toward social welfare.

It offers new hope to the helpless by providing help equally to every dependent family in every State. It offers new fairness to the working poor, by helping them to lift themselves out of poverty. And it offers the taxpayer light at the end of the tunnel, by providing new incentives and job training to get people off welfare rolls and onto payrolls. It combines realism with idealism.

I know that we can count on the support and cooperation of those represented at this meeting, and I welcome your assistance as well as your advice.

National Conference on Social Welfare Distinguished Service Awards

THE NATIONAL CONFERENCE ON SOCIAL WELFARE AWARDS were established by Executive Committee action in 1954 to accomplish a twofold purpose by calling attention to the significant social problems of the times, and by recognition of the outstanding achievements of individuals or organizations in helping to solve them. The first Award was presented at the 1955 Annual Forum in San Francisco.

Conditions of the Awards and procedures for selection of recipients adopted by the Executive Committee specified that awards would be given only when outstanding candidates were submitted; that up to three awards might be given in any one year in recognition of outstanding contributions in administration, research, practice, or, in exceptional cases, for long and sustained achievement in the advancement of social welfare, but not solely for long service; and that recipients need not be members of the Conference or of the social work profession.

Final selection of recipients is made by the National Board of the Conference from nominations and supporting background material submitted by the members.

No Distinguished Service Awards were presented in 1970.

1955 EDITH M. BAKER, Washington, D.C.
FEDELE F. FAURI, Ann Arbor, Mich.
ELIZABETH WICKENDEN, New York

1956 TIAC (Temporary Inter-Association Council) PLANNING COMMITTEE, New York

1957 THE REVEREND MARTIN LUTHER KING, JR., Montgomery, Ala.
WILBUR J. COHEN, Ann Arbor, Mich.

1958 THE HONORABLE JOHN E. FOGARTY, Rhode Island
LEONARD W. MAYO, New York

1959 ELISABETH SHIRLEY ENOCHS, Washington, D.C.
OLLIE A. RANDALL, New York

1960 LOULA DUNN, Chicago
RALPH BLANCHARD, New York
HELEN HALL, New York

1961 THE HONORABLE AIME J. FORAND, Rhode Island

1962 THE ATLANTA *Constitution,* Ralph McGill and Jack Nelson, Atlanta, Ga.
JOSEPH P. ANDERSON, New York
CHARLOTTE TOWLE, Chicago

1963 HARRIETT M. BARTLETT, Cambridge, Mass.
ERNEST JOHN BOHN, Cleveland
FLORENCE G. HELLER, Glencoe, Ill.
Special Award: Television Documentary, "The Battle of Newburgh," IRVING GITLIN and the NATIONAL BROADCASTING COMPANY, New York
Special Citation (Posthumous): ANNA ELEANOR ROOSEVELT, "First Lady of the World"

1964 DR. ROBERT M. FELIX, Bethesda, Md.
Special Citation (Posthumous): JOHN FITZGERALD KENNEDY, "Man of Destiny"

1965 JAMES V. BENNETT, Washington, D.C.
SIDNEY HOLLANDER, Baltimore, Md.
CORA KASIUS, New York

1966 REPRESENTATIVE WILBUR D. MILLS, Ark.

1967 THE HONORABLE HUBERT H. HUMPHREY, Washington, D.C.
PLANNED PARENTHOOD–WORLD POPULATION
Special Awards (Posthumous):
RUTH M. WILLIAMS, New York
HOWARD F. GUSTAFSON, Indianapolis

1968 LOMA MOYER ALLEN, Rochester, N.Y.
KENNETH BANCROFT CLARK, New York

1969 THE HONORABLE ELMER L. ANDERSEN, St. Paul, Minn.
HARRY L. LURIE, New York
IDA C. MERRIAM, Washington, D.C.

1970 No awards were presented

Contents

Confrontation, 1970

Abstracts

BOEHM, WERNER W.
"The Chicago Scene I: Conference Report"
Events in Chicago were centered basically on two issues: "the $35,000 misunderstanding" deriving from NWRO's contention that non-payment by the Conference constituted a "broken promise" voted by the New York Annual Meeting of Members; and pressure to convert the Conference to an action body. Major thrust of Emerging Social Welfare Interests (SSW) was to deny the relevance of NCSW structure and program in response to the needs of the poor and the solution of urgent social problems; to persist in forcing adoption of a social action function in substitute for its educational role.

BURNS, EVELINE M.
"Welfare Reform and Income Security Policies"
Our ultimate objective must be to remove as many as possible from our present dependency-creating system; to reduce the gap between defined standards of living and defined family resources. The demo-grant would involve a sizable redistribution of national income and would risk employables living on the guaranteed income; it would avoid the impossible administrative task of individual evaluation and the polarization of society into two groups—one receiving benefits, the other paying the costs. It has the advantage of making universal, taxable, nondiscretionary payments, simply and cheaply administered through the tax system and leaving "gap-filling" at a minimum.

CAMPBELL, ALAN K.
"Decision-Makers in Social Policy"
Social policy is too often the by-product of legislation passed for other purposes by those more interested in rewards of the system than in policy output. Where power resides in the majority, minorities, or coalitions of minorities, the new "managers of society," the social scientists have failed in the area of politics where decision-making relies on the views and prejudices of the public at large. Development of new social policy needs substantial background research to avoid fragmentation, and to create a comprehensive framework capable of winning majority support in a major shift in public attitudes.

Cohen, Wilbur J.
"Social Welfare Priorities for the 1970s"
The social welfare community must provide the courageous leadership needed to redefine social goals, to redirect our priorities toward the solution of our urgent domestic needs. We have the resources and mechanics in our economic and political system. We lack the willingness to work together, the determined statesmanship needed to change the misconceptions and attitudes of our institutions; to provide increased revenues through revised tax structures; to eliminate waste in existing programs; to divert military expenditures to adequate income and national health insurance plans; to revise education and training programs.

Dodson, Dan W.
"Institutionalized Racism in Social Welfare Agencies"
White racism is an indictment of our society; voluntarism, a panacea for the powerful to serve the powerless, adopting the mythologies of our society and attempting the socialization of blacks into our white system. Blacks, through confrontation, conflict, and disruption of power groups, demand restructuring to give visibility to consumers at every stage of operation. Agency survival will depend on elimination of the rationalizations of racism which exclude minorities from full participation in power structures, in agency control, in development of new programs and work methods using the program skills of minority consumers in shared power.

Doscher, Virginia R.
"Where Are Solutions?"
Divergent opinions about the unsolved problems of our society were expressed from four viewpoints: (1) "We are fighting the capitalistic system. The economic system must change to solve the problems of the poor." (2) "Change must be massive, comprehensive, and fast to create institutions offering alternatives to transformation of society from the black perspective." (3) "Change must come through elimination of legislation and regulations reducing the discretionary powers of political bodies and government." (4) "Change effected by revising and refocusing social welfare programs through the legislative process."

Fox, Daniel M.
"Neighborhoods and Social Policy: Continuities and Discontinuities with the Past"
Neighborhood community development is historically rooted in the struggle for power by ineffective and dehumanizing social institu-

tions and bureaucracies dealing with fragmented sections of society traditionally excluded from participation. Militant citizens in a frustrating decade of effort to improve their condition, by rearrangement of structural preconditions, are demanding a share in the struggle for power affecting their lives. They will continue to force the issue of public responsibility and for structural innovation in effecting change in human condition and redressing the wrongs to minorities.

JORDAN, BARBARA
"Income Security Policies—the Heineman Commission Proposal"
Rationale of the primary Heineman Commission proposal was compromise, favoring prompt implementation of an annual income allowance of $2,400, recognized as inadequate, for a family of four as an essential preliminary move in the direction of eliminating poverty. The Commission, seeing this as a "feasible first step" politically and economically toward bringing the poor into our operative economic community, provides for a permanent federal review board for continuing systematic evaluation of the program; for increases in the level of benefits as conditions and experience allow; and for market incentives, not compulsion, as a basis for employment and training.

KENNEDY, REV. ROBERT P.
"Moral and Ethical Issues in Income Maintenance II: a Catholic Viewpoint"
The Catholic view and the view of all moral and ethical systems accept man's right to life, to bodily integrity, and to a decent standard of living. Income maintenance is a part of the State's obligation to insure man's right to life and a share in the goods of society with justice, equity and dignity. Man's obligation to society is to make God's creation more useful and adaptable to human needs—to greater perfection in his society and development of his own capabilities. His obligation to work stems from human dignity, not from his obligation to society.

McGOVERN, GEORGE
"A Critique of the Family Assistance Plan"
A nation's greatness is not measured by its wealth or weapons, but by its wisdom and compassion. Poverty has many causes, requiring many-pronged preventions. The family assistance plan carries the seeds of yet another failure in providing for the poor. Its basic payment level is inadequate; its administrative structure and work incentive requirements are both archaic and unrealistic, providing no clear relationship between welfare and food reform programs. It is

but a timid step in the development of a national system to secure the health and well-being of all our people.

MAYER, ROBERT R.
  "Social Change or Service Delivery?"
Social structural change is a means of eliminating the undesirable in a social system—a methodology for problem-solving, not an answer to all social problems. Components of the proposed model include a sustained pattern of interaction among individuals; a determination of boundaries to eliminate elements outside the system and to determine interaction of individuals; tools to evaluate aspects of the system responsible for undesirable behavior; and methods of intervention to change systems of social relationship through planned social change.

OBENHAUS, VICTOR
  "Moral and Ethical Issues in Income Maintenance I: a Protestant Viewpoint"
The issue of income maintenance has brought sharp conflict with American values evolved from the Hebrew-Christian tradition and closely identified with property, the concept of individuality, and the deeply imbedded conviction that help is given where there is need and that the individual should work for what he receives. Our increasing concern for the dignity of man as evidenced by the proposed income maintenance plans has established income as a right, not a privilege, and questions the Protestant ethic concept of work in the realization that assurance of minimum security may provide incentive for creative and productive activity.

PRUNTY, HOWARD E.
  "Chicago Scene II: Report from a Participant"
A small group, representatives of "emerging interests" who went to Chicago with a sense of mission—to make the Conference relevant to the issues of racism and poverty, to force it to become more political and action-oriented—were disappointed. Strategies of direct confrontation, disruption, Conference-wide participation, and quiet diplomacy failed to change white attitudes of hostile resignation, of passive resistance to responsible change. NCSW needs both groups if it is to continue as a viable organization.

SCHORR, ALVIN L.
  "Income Maintenance and the Social Security Ideology"
The social security concept has been payment of "income-by-right" to large identifiable groups of potentially poor—a form of "income-test-

ing" as opposed to "means-testing." Critics object that it attempts two essentially incompatible objectives—the maintenance of wages and the prevention of poverty—and that its proportionate diversion of income to the poor does not do enough to prevent poverty. Our national attitudes will determine whether future income maintenance plans will merely provide income to meet a predetermined standard, or will succeed in a basic redistribution of national income to give the poor a just and larger share.

SILCOTT, T. GEORGE
  "Social Welfare Priorities—a Minority View"
Reactors from Emerging Social Welfare Interests in response to the Presidential Address condemn the Conference, the Annual Forum, social welfare agencies, and the profession as irrelevant to our social ills; as grossly inadequate in their service to the needs of mankind. NCSW leadership is challenged to "push the seemingly reluctant membership into taking action in solving problems of people" and to join a unified front of blacks, Puerto Ricans, Chicanos, and American Indians in their demand for an action-oriented conference to replace the traditional "talk conference."

TWINAME, JOHN D.
  "The Family Assistance Plan—the Nixon Proposal"
The income strategy behind the President's proposal is a bold but not an ideal or ultimate solution to the welfare trap caused by our past efforts to end poverty. It provides an opportunity for a major advance in social welfare, a restructuring of national priorities, a redirection of our resources, a change in social theories behind our federal programs. The family assistance plan supplemented by job training and work incentives by extension and expansion of social services reorganized from the viewpoint of the consumer, and with his participation, is a start in the eradication of poverty and fuller realization of human potential.

THE SOCIAL WELFARE FORUM, 1970

Social Welfare Priorities for the 1970s

WILBUR J. COHEN

THIS IS A MOST CRITICAL TIME in our nation's history. Our country is in a grave crisis. Growing divisiveness and frustration grip the nation. There is a lack of understanding in high places of our urgent needs and priorities. There is a lack of courageous leadership at the federal, state, and local levels. There is often rhetoric when it is least helpful.

The gigantic problems facing us mount: the war, poverty, race relations, the cities, slums, unemployment, inflation, pollution; in the face of affluence and the great capacity of the country for meeting the basic needs of all its people, there are inequalities and inequities.

We need vigorous leadership and intelligent action to end the war. We must continue to press President Nixon and the Congress to end the war; not only this war, but all wars. Escalation of military expenditures must be ended. We must oppose the antiballistics missile system and the supersonic transport. These are unnecessary and undesirable expenditures of funds that must be allocated to meet our domestic welfare needs.

But it is clear that the withdrawal of armed forces from Vietnam will not solve our domestic problems automatically. To redirect our priorities will take time, effort, and statesmanship. We must begin this task immediately. A council of social advisers should be established to define our social goals and priorities.

Unfortunately, there are still among our fellow citizens many who believe that poverty is an inevitable condition of mankind, that segregation is desirable, that increased unemployment is healthy, that poor people are lazy, that more and bigger automobiles are a sign of economic growth, that long hair is a sign of radicalism, and that problems on the college campus can be solved by replacing the college president. There are those who believe that all taxes paid in the public sector are bad, but any price paid in the private sector is acceptable and that the federal government is an evil worse than any foreign totalitarianism.

We must continue to point out that these simplistic notions are out of date in a complex economy. Most of all, we must strive to elect to public office men and women who have the insight and the courage to counter these views which retard our progress and inhibit the reordering of priorities to meet the needs of our people.

The social welfare community has a special responsibility to draw attention to our compelling needs and potentialities. That is one of the values of the Annual Forum of the National Conferences on Social Welfare: it provides an opportunity to voice our convictions and explain our programs for making the United States of America a more perfect Union.

The right to vote is an inalienable right and should be guaranteed and protected. Residence laws for receipt of welfare payments have been held invalid by the Supreme Court of the United States. Residence requirements for voting in national elections are equally unsound. Every otherwise eligible individual should be entitled to vote in national elections for congressmen, senators, and the President. And we must encourage everyone to do so.

The right to education, medical services, a job, and a home. without regard to race, creed, color, or sex must be assured. There is no ethical distinction that can be justified between *de jure* and *de facto* segregation or discrimination. Our political leaders must not hide behind constitutional niceties but must take the moral leadership to help eradicate the cancer of discrimination and racism from the body politic. The elimination of racial discrimination would increase incomes by some $15 billion a year and would aid in the reduction of poverty and the increase in productivity and in the enhancement of individual dignity and self-reliance. Racial discrimination of any kind must be abolished.

Poverty is a blight upon our nation. It is clear that we could eradicate poverty from the length and breadth of this land of ours. We have the resources. We have the institutional mechanisms. But there is a lack of insight, determination, and leadership.

Yet, much has happened in the last several years to give us some hope that we are on our way to reducing the extent of poverty. The report of the President's Commission on Income Maintenance Programs, headed by Ben Heineman,[1] and the report on public welfare of the Committee on Economic Development show an increasing awareness by business and community leaders that we can and must conquer poverty. I believe that we should make the elimination of poverty one of our urgent national goals—now.

A broad and comprehensive income-supplement program is necessary. It must be broader and much more adequate than the family assistance program now pending in the United States Senate. Not only must the levels of payment be increased, but a commitment must be made that the federal government will finance and administer the system 100 percent. We should support amendments in the Senate toward these objectives. We must have an adequate income plan now. It must cover both individuals and families.

Social security benefits should be substantially increased. In addition to the 15 percent increase in benefits which took place in 1970 we must increase benefits another 35 percent to bring them up to a minimum level of adequacy. The 12 percent increase in total benefits which has passed the House of Representatives is a good second installment payment, but it can and should be improved in the Senate.

An increase in social security payments will benefit not only the aged, but the disabled, widows, and dependent children.

The disabled and the widows and children who receive social

---

[1] *Poverty amid Plenty: the American Paradox* (Washington, D.C.: U.S. Government Printing Office, 1969).

security benefits should be included in the Medicare program. Their incomes are low and their needs are great. They should have health insurance protection, which should include coverage of prescription drugs for them as well as for the aged.

There are some 40 million persons in the United States who have no health insurance coverage whatsoever. Millions of others have incomplete or inadequate coverage. A national health insurance program covering everyone in the nation is necessary—and inevitable.

There are many persons who believe that we must wait for a complete restructuring of our health system before we extend health insurance to the millions who have no protection. Certainly, we need a basic reorganization of our health services. We need incentives to economical and efficient delivery of services. But the poor and the disadvantaged should not be asked to wait for full access to health services until the perfect solution of a national health delivery system is in effect.

We can and we must take some steps now in the direction of both the extension of health insurance coverage and the reorganization of services.

Neighborhood health centers should be established in all major metropolitan areas; maternal and child health services, including family-planning services on a voluntary basis, should be available to inner-city residents; and a broad training program should be carried out to facilitate new careers in medical care for persons living in the inner cities.

We must take steps to eradicate hunger and malnutrition in the nation. As one step in this effort, the amendment to the welfare reform bill, sponsored in the Senate by Senator George McGovern, should be adopted. It provides for automatic delivery of food stamps to each welfare recipient without the advance payment now required. It would substantially reduce the administrative cost of the present cumbersome plan and make food stamps available to millions of persons who do not now receive them.

We need a comprehensive program of nutrition and health education which will adequately inform individuals of the ways in which they can prevent malnutrition and ill-health.

Our unemployment insurance system requires major improvement. The Congress is considering legislation to extend the coverage of the program, but much more fundamental changes are needed. While many unemployed individuals receive inadequate weekly payments and other unemployed individuals exhaust their benefits, there is $12 billion in the unemployment insurance reserves. It is clear that the funds are actually available to improve substantially the amount of benefits and to extend the benefit period.

It is a striking anomaly that the welfare reform legislation providing for minimum federal benefit standards is endorsed by the Administration and the House Committee on Ways and Means, but minimum federal benefit standards are opposed by both so far as unemployment insurance is concerned. I can see no difference in principle. As a matter of fact, both Houses of Congress this year approved federal standards in unemployment insurance relating to various restrictive policies that affect benefits. We must continue to press for federal minimum benefit standards for the amount and duration of unemployment insurance. Since the President recommended federal minimum benefit standards in welfare, we must press him to recommend such standards in unemployment insurance as part of an immediate attack on our growing unemployment problem. We should support proposals to convert both unemployment insurance and the employment service to a federal system.

Farm employees should be covered under unemployment insurance. Moreover, farm employees should be covered under the National Labor Relations Act so that they will have the right and protection to bargain collectively.

A public employment program must be established which will assure individuals of employment in public service jobs irrespective of their education, background, or experience. Training programs should be related to employment assurance. The need for personnel in hospitals, nursing homes, libraries, schools, recreation facilities, and other community facilities should be given priority.

Several recent Supreme Court decisions have clearly established the applicability of the Fourteenth Amendment of the

Constitution to welfare payments and procedures. The constitutional guarantees of equal protection of the laws and due process must be assured to every person, rich or poor, black or white, brown or yellow, student or adult, child or senior citizen. Continued support should be given to the program of legal aid to the poor, and lawyers should be encouraged to handle cases which contest the validity of any law which transgresses the constitutional guarantees, including any legislation which invades the home by authorizing "no-knock" entry by the police.

We must have more effective programs to deal with alcoholism, drug abuse, and child neglect.

State laws relating to abortion must be liberalized. State programs relating to the protection of women and children must be reexamined and brought up to date. States must strengthen their services to children, the aged, and other groups requiring special help, such as the mentally retarded and the mentally ill. Federal funds should be substantially increased to achieve these objectives.

To accomplish the social objectives that are necessary during this decade we must obtain increased revenues. Some additional funds can be obtained from substantial reductions in military expenditures, by elimination of waste and inefficiency in existing programs, and elimination of unnecessary agricultural subsidies, particularly in tobacco.

In addition, we must close the loopholes in the federal and state tax structures. There are still several states that do not have a state income tax, yet no state can provide the services necessary for its people today without an income tax.

To expand education and to provide the disadvantaged with appropriate educational services, there must be a significant increase in funds for education during the decade of the seventies. The property tax on homes which is a basic source of revenue for elementary and secondary education is no longer a sound and dynamic source for the financing of schools. The property tax on homes must be reduced, and eventually eliminated, as a basis for financing schools. State and federal income taxes must provide the major source of revenues for the schools of the future.

Our educational system must be made more relevant to the needs and aspirations of our young people. Vocational education should be broadened and extended. Early childhood education should be available in every community. The advantages of the Head Start program should be available to all children. Parents and the community should be involved in the educational system. The teacher certification system should be reexamined and modified to enable more individuals from minority groups to become teachers.

Our higher educational institutions must enroll more individuals from minority groups. Schools of social work and schools of education have been leading the way and should further accelerate their efforts in this area. Student financial aid, institutional aid for tutorial services and for expansion of recruitment and job placement must be provided to attain greater minority enrollment.

We view with great concern the failure of the Administration to recommend additional federal appropriations for the nation's education and health programs. We urge the Congress to take affirmative and prompt action to increase the appropriations for programs of importance to the disadvantaged, the poor, and minority groups.

Federal support of medical research, mental health, and medical manpower should be expanded.

Those of us in social welfare who believe that the public sector must take a greater role in improving social conditions are frequently criticized for this advocacy on the grounds that it weakens individual, family, and private responsibility. The fact of the matter is that increased public responsibility is necessary because of the apparent inability of private action to bring about needed changes.

There is much that the private sector can and must do, and we should bend every effort to make the private sector take a more effective role in promoting human welfare. Among the significant steps that could be taken are: elimination of any kind of discrimination in employment or promotion; on-the-job training for the disadvantaged, with emphasis on new careers; extension of credit to welfare recipients; and appointment of

minority group representatives to boards of directors of corporations, foundations, and educational institutions.

I believe that important modifications are necessary in our
economic, political, and social system. I believe that our political
system permits improvements to be made in a way which the
establishment can and will accept, namely, through the ballot
box. Let us work toward changes which will be constructive and
useful. Let us not be among those who advocate a "benign
neglect" of our major problems.

Changes in social policy first develop in the hearts and minds
of men and women. Social action first requires an understanding
of new needs and a willingness to modify attitudes and institutions to meet these needs. There are those critics who say talk
is meaningless and ineffective. But any change in social policy
first must be built upon talk and a meaningful dialogue among
all those who play a role in a democratic society.

We need at this moment in history the determination to make
modifications and to chart a course in a new direction of social
policy. We can do so if we work together.

Many people are frustrated, alienated, and depressed about
our ability to move ahead in a constructive manner. I do not
share this view. There are vast opportunities today for men and
women of good will to lead the way to improving our institutions. There are opportunities all around if we would but take
advantage of them—in our neighborhoods, in our communities,
at the city and state level, in Congress, and in urging the Administration to modify basic policies.

We have had grave crises in our national life before. We will
have others in the future. Let us show a determination now to
move ahead in social welfare. I believe we can and must chart
new priorities for the 1970s.

The Family Assistance Plan— the Nixon Proposal

JOHN D. TWINAME

This is a crucial moment for the social welfare movement—and not in the United States alone. Instead of again adapting schemes employed by our European friends, we have within our grasp the possibility of restructuring the welfare system in a way that is new; an approach based on some common sense about poverty that has had to be hammered into us by the inadequacy of our attempts in the past.

In 1969, there was broad concern that fundamental welfare reform was needed. In August, 1969, President Nixon showed his determination to get at the cancer of poverty by prescribing surgery—not just more band-aids. He announced the Administration's proposals, and we hope that by August of 1970 the Congress will have passed them, to open up a new era for public welfare by enactment of the Family Assistance Plan—keystone of the new income strategy toward the elimination of poverty in this society.

We have tried to listen, and we have tried to learn—from the poor, the professionals, the general public, and from history itself. We started out with a pure services strategy, with the emphasis on changing the behavior of sick citizens. Then money was finally provided directly to those who were clearly dependent, and therefore somehow deserving, but with all the strings attached to confirm the very dependency that the public somehow thought was being relieved. Fortunately, in the 1960s the poor became visible. This may have been the best outcome of the war on poverty, because still we were pursuing a strategy whereby predominantly we taxed the poor to pay salaries of people like us to help relieve the increasing poverty of those who remained untouched by the expanding economy.

We offered services of training, but too often jobs were just not there at the completion of training. Moreover, the tax on earnings of the welfare poor still ran from 67 percent to 100 percent. Social workers were given the task of strengthening family life; the system was built to reward family desertion.

The final handcuffs for workers in public welfare were the demands for service coupled with impossible administrative requirements. We provided too little income and too little service to too few people, and thus made sure that we perpetuated the very situation we hoped to eliminate. If there has been a failure, it is the failure of most of the nonpoor in America; for they have made the wrong assumptions, held on to the old myths. Really, we in the establishment have needed the poor more than they have needed us.

There is no other way out of the welfare trap than to change the body of social theory behind the federal programs. The Administration is trying to do this. Many social workers have said that services are of little value until there is adequate income to assure at least minimum economic security so that a person can begin to reach out, to risk the steps beyond survival to improve the quality of life.

This brings us to the common-sense answer: since the basic characteristic of poverty is lack of money, added income is the only cure. Thus the income strategy must involve not only insuring a minimum national income for those in need, but provide added income opportunities through training and jobs that give rewards for working.

A major step toward a total income strategy was the proposal that the federal government stop taxing persons whose income is below the poverty level. The income strategy would rightly leave this money, estimated at $650 million, in the hands of the poor who earned it rather than use the revenue to finance some new program. This is what the Administration proposed. Quite significantly, Congress agreed, signaling a fundamental change of heart in the country as well. To enhance this departure, a series of new income proposals to update old programs followed in the areas of minority enterprise, the benefit period of unemployment insurance, and minimum wage coverage.

The cornerstone of the income strategy, the most significant piece of social legislation offered in the past decade, and perhaps since 1935, came in August, 1969, in the form of the Family Assistance Plan. This is not an improvement of an old program, but a wholly new direction in social processes. Its principles are simple. First, income assistance is not to be conditioned on dependency. It is a program that will help people through those times when they are not self-sufficient, and it assumes that most recipients are neither aged nor disabled; thus, the assistance for most recipients will be temporary.

Second, it provides incentives to work and incentives for family stability, reducing the discrimination against male-headed families and the working poor.

Third, it provides for a national minimum support level to all families on welfare, minimizing the discrepancies between states.

Fourth, it aims toward simplified eligibility determination and administration to reduce administrative costs while at the same time doing more to preserve the dignity and integrity of public assistance recipients.

The income strategy also requires a major commitment to job training and job development because common sense also tells us that this economy cannot at present generate income adequate to give children a real chance to break the poverty cycle unless the family has a working member. This earned income must be a parental responsibility as well as a responsibility of our society to make earned income possible for everyone who can work.

This income strategy and the Administration's proposals, while bold, are not offered as ideal or as ultimate. Some inequities remain, and the minimum income is not adequate. But we must begin where we can, and we can begin by appropriating annually sufficient funds to enable this program to reduce the poverty gap in America by 60 percent.

Some criticize the proposal because it does not go far enough. I do not think they take into account the absolute necessity to keep our economy in balance. The control of inflation exacts a price; but the price is paid primarily by the poor.

Some hesitate, and a majority of the President's advisors did, because the cost looks too high. They do not take into account the fact that under the present system we are going to pay the cost anyway, but the situation will then be so desperate that we will find it difficult to restructure the process. The calendar and the spiraling costs continue to work against us.

The Senate Finance Committee has pointed out some remaining problems due to the income penalties imposed by other programs, including medicaid, food stamps, and public housing. In other words, if a person who is on welfare achieves a certain income level because of his additional earnings, he may forfeit substantial benefits from programs that are based on need. We agree that the so-called "notch effect" of these other programs should be smoothed out, and we have given them further study. The Administration has offered a number of amendments to the Senate, but it will undoubtedly take more planning and further legislative changes in the next year or so to adjust satisfactorily the incentives inherent in other programs.

Now, as we have learned, a service program can do little to help an individual or a family in the absence of adequate income, and no income-maintenance program alone can enable individuals to achieve the objectives of self-support, family stability, or improved capacity for self-care. The problems of dependency are far too complex. While income support is critical, it must be joined with an effective service program if the overriding goal of reducing dependency is to be achieved. Consequently, since the introduction of the Family Assistance Plan the Administration has proposed a complementary social service amendment to the bill before the Congress.

Most public attention will be focused on the income-maintenance aspects of welfare reform, but I believe that the new premises for social services constitute every bit as important a turning point in social welfare. I hope that the National Conference on Social Welfare will stimulate constructive thinking that will lead to concrete program development.

The social service proposal has these principal features:

1. There should be administrative separation of income-maintenance activities from the delivery of social services. People trained in social service should have the opportunity to give full time to social work, and their work deserves to be free from the stigma of investigating welfare-payment eligibility. Social services would be free to all poor people regardless of their eligibility for money payments. People with incomes above the poverty level would also be eligible for social services, paying fees based on income. In this way, services can be brought to those in need of them, regardless of income.

2. Services should be community-based, with participation in their design and delivery by the people who need and want them. This means more local flexibility and responsibility and less emphasis on arbitrary requirements that services be uniform throughout the state. Needs in a city are different from those in a rural community and should be serviced differently.

3. Social services should be offered on a voluntary basis, with the exception of certain necessary interventions, as in cases of child abuse. The helping profession can do more for the consumer who asks for help than for the one who does not welcome it.

4. The consumer should be more than recipient or client or patient. An expanding choice of services is needed by the consumer, with a voucher or credit card system which would allow him to choose his day care or homemaker service. Such a system would also attract voluntary and even profit-making enterprises to fill the service gaps within prescribed quality standards.

We must move to a clearer articulation of specific services in order to gain public understanding. Social welfare has suffered too long from vagueness. If we want expanded support we have to be able to communicate results. With this in mind, the Social and Rehabilitation Service (SRS) will enumerate with wide latitude the basic list of core services that should be federally supported and ask the states for an annual plan that emphasizes program objectives rather than arbitrary measures, such as worker-client ratios.

Two of the important social services that need more federal support are foster care and adoption services, and the SRS, with state cooperation, intends to improve their quality and scope, especially with regard to hard-to-place children.

The Administration would like to provide incentives for consolidating services so that delivery systems may be organized at the state and local levels more from the point of view of the consumer and less from the point of view of our bureaucratic jurisdictions. Specific incentives toward this end are provided in the social services amendment. The coordination of programs within the SRS is one of our primary goals, and the increasing cooperation of the heads of our seven interrelated programs is now moving us to this objective.

Over all, this legislative proposal offers the opportunity to take a major leap forward in social welfare, with the goal of raising the caliber of services and shifting the focus from purely remedial and curative to preventive and developmental services.

All this will come about only with sound planning, progressive management of resources, and selfless dedication at all levels of the social welfare system. The debate is very much alive, and the creative thinking and active support of the social work profession is needed. But the clock is running out, and there is danger that the Administration's proposals may be hung up in committee. This is unthinkable.

It is unthinkable for some 25 million of our fellow citizens in poverty. It is unthinkable when we realize what their alienation means to the stability of our democracy.

It seems to me that this reform in social welfare is a key to America's crisis in self-confidence. The young are not the only Americans who are asking the questions: Can't we change our institutions within the system? Is it not within our power to improve the quality of life for all Americans?

If this debate finds us bickering over the small details, protective first of our assumed prerogatives and organizational structures, if we propound unrealistic alternatives to attract attention, or mount opposition out of ideological or political instincts, we may find our legislators coming home to say that in the confusion, the chance to change welfare's collision course somehow passed us by.

Income Security Policies—the Heineman Commission Proposal

BARBARA JORDAN

On JANUARY 2, 1968, President Lyndon B. Johnson established the Commission on Income Maintenance Programs, popularly known as the Heineman Commission. In doing this, he made the following statement:

The welfare system in America is outmoded and in need of a major change . . . Look into all aspects of existing welfare and related programs and make just and equitable recommendations for constructive improvements wherever needed and indicated. We must examine any and every plan, however unconventional, which could promise a constructive advance in meeting the income needs of all the American people.

Ben Heineman was named chairman of the twenty-one member commission. For twenty-two months through field visits, public hearings, technical studies, and official briefings, the Commission members visited with the poor and reviewed the operations of welfare and related programs. We listened, and we heard the sounds of the poor. We tried to feel their social isolation. We did smell poverty and see the devastation it has wrought. We were confronted by anger and frustration and a cutting cynicism at the presence of one more group on the scene to study poverty and its implications. On November 12, 1969, the Commission submitted its final report to President Nixon. It was unanimously approved by the Commission with six individual members making supplementary statements.

The main recommendation of the Commission is for the creation of a universal income-supplement program financed and administered by the federal government, making cash payments to all members of the population with income needs. We proposed that the program be initiated at a level providing a base income of $2,400 per year for a family of four with no other income. Benefits should be scaled to pay $750 per adult and $450 per child to families with no other income. The basic payment would be reduced by 50 cents for each dollar of income from other sources. Families of four with other income up to $4,800 would receive some supplementation.

I fully understand that there is room for disagreement with the level recommended. The dollar amount was thoroughly discussed and made the subject matter of individual supplementary statements by certain Commission members. The inadequacy of the level of benefits chosen is recognized in the body of the report. We state:

Since an income of $2,400 for a family of four is below the poverty line, the basic benefit level proposed would not meet the full needs of families with no other source of income. *This level has not been chosen because we believe it to be adequate, but because it is a level which can be implemented promptly.*[1]

The Commission recommends that once the program is launched, the level of benefits be raised as conditions and experience allow. In further recognition of the need for future modifications it is recommended that the legislation establishing the income-supplement program create a permanent review commission in order to provide for continuing systematic evaluation of the program as conditions and opportunities change.

The question may logically be raised as to why the Commission would recommend an inadequate benefit level if it did in fact believe it to be inadequate. We were perhaps caught in our own pragmatism. We believe that our recommendations should become law. Laws are still enacted by the United States Senate and the House of Representatives and signed by the President. With images in mind of the House Ways and Means Committee and the Senate Finance Committee and their diverse membership, we

[1] *Poverty amid Plenty: the American Paradox*, the report of the President's Commission on Income Maintenance Programs (Washington, D.C.: U.S. Government Printing Office, 1969), p. 58.

were guided in part by practical economic and political implications. The estimated net added cost of the recommended program to all levels of government would be $6 billion in 1971. This amount would be the increase in the disposable income of the 10 million households (36 million people) receiving payments under the plan. We could have recommended a guarantee of $3,600 per year for a family of four. The break-even income level would be $7,200, at a cost of over $20 billion and over 20 million households, or over 74 million persons, would receive some federal supplementation. Such a cost, we feel, would have weakened the credibility of our recommendation.

We feel strongly that enactment of a universal income-supplement program is essential. It is clear to the Commission that such a program is needed in the United States to assist persons excluded from existing programs and to supplant other programs. We state in our report:

It is time to design public policy to deal with the two basic facts of American poverty: The poor lack money, and most of them cannot increase their income themselves. These conditions can be remedied only when the Government provides some minimum income to all in need.[2]

Our primary recommendation does move us in the direction of eliminating poverty. It will begin to lead us out of the bankruptcy of the present welfare system.

Edmund K. Faltermayer observes:

Seldom has a nation governed by rational men created an institution so erratic in its operation, and so perverse in some of its social effects, as the U.S. welfare system. In a period of prolonged prosperity and shrinking poverty, welfare payments have zoomed past the $5-billion-a-year level. About nine million Americans are now on some form of the dole—the largest number since the great depression of the 1930's. Yet some of the most deserving poor have received no help at all; the rules work to exclude them. And for those it does cover, the system appears to be counter productive. It has done almost nothing to rehabilitate people and put them to work, and far from promoting the cohesiveness of family life, it has tended to encourage the breakup of families, with particularly disastrous results in the Negro slums.

2 *Ibid.*, p. 57.

Along with these effects, the welfare system—an amalgam of state and local programs operated with matching federal aid—is an unbelievable administrative mess, with standards differing widely from place to place. Complicated by mountains of paper work and millions of annual house-to-house calls, administrative overhead amounts to about 10 cents for every dollar that is paid to the poor.

In *Fortune's* view, the only objective that makes sense is an across-the-board attack on the whole problem of welfare dependency. By now it is widely accepted that this nation is rich enough to provide a minimum level of subsistence to those who have missed the train of the U.S. Economy. This means supplementing the incomes of everyone genuinely in need, through a system that is efficient and dignified, and that contains built-in incentives for families to stay together and for the able-bodied to seek work.[3]

I quote that portion of Faltermayer's article because it points out some of the rationale of the Commission's primary recommendation. In addition to our concern for adequacy of benefit level, we felt that the recipient of the supplement should know clearly his rights and entitlement to the supplement. Federal administration, according to objective eligibility criteria, would in large measure replace the discretion and action by whim or vindictiveness now exercised by local administrators. Benefit amounts and appellate procedures would be the subject of federal Law and regulations. The recommended program successfully meets the test of equity in that it would narrow and ultimately eliminate the inequitable differences between those eligible for categorical programs and those not eligible.

We are aware of the power of the work ethos in America. We know that any program which provides income without work may affect work effort. The Family Assistance Act of 1970 pending in the Congress takes notice of this fact in the provision which requires every member of a family receiving family assistance benefits, with specific exceptions, to register with an employment service for training and employment. This act, further, would terminate benefits for an individual who refuses training, "suitable employment," or rehabilitation services. The Commission rejects any idea of a work requirement. Given the level of

3 Edmund K. Faltermayer, "A Way out of the Welfare Mess," *Fortune Magazine,* July, 1968, p. 62.

the basic income-support program, we believe that "the disincentive effect will not be powerful." Work will always produce increased income. This will give the recipient the financial inducement to work.

> We do not think it desirable to put the power of determining whether an individual should work in the hands of a Government agency when it can be left to individual choice and market incentives. . . . Unless jobs were abundant and the training programs had adequate capacity, any requirement that unemployed recipients of income support accept training would be meaningless. The Commission believes that market incentives and not compulsion should be the basis for accepting both employment and training.[4]

The Commission takes the foregoing position on work incentives versus possible disincentive effects of the proposed program only after careful analysis and thought. There is not much evidence which clearly indicates the impact the program would have on labor force participation. There is evidence, however, which shows that the plethora of manpower and training programs has yielded uneven results. While some people have benefited from the training programs, some of the chronically poor have been left untouched by them.

The administrative costs of the program recommended by the Commission are estimated to be less than 3 percent of the federal payments to recipients, or approximately $200 million. This cost compares favorably with the approximately 15 percent under current public assistance programs.

What does the major recommendation of $2,400 per year for a family of four with no other income really offer to the poor? What does the break-even level of $4,800 at the 50 percent rate mean in terms of the quality of life of the poor? What does the universality of payments portend for the morass of federal, state, and local programs? These are bothersome questions which, in my judgment, only experience can definitely answer. The experience which can provide creditable answers is the experience of the poor. The Commission believes that the plan offers a way out of a disastrous condition. Half of the income needs of

4 *Poverty amid Plenty* . . . , pp. 59–60.

the poor would be met by the program. Is that enough and if not, what is enough? We believe that we have recommended "a feasible first step," both politically and economically.

The Commission makes several subsidiary recommendations which would improve the effectiveness and operation of the basic income-supplement program. It is recommended that federal participation in existing public assistance programs be terminated and that federal matching funds be made available for a new, locally administered, noncategorical, temporary assistance program. We have earlier alluded to the inequities which prevail in present programs. Every recent study of the welfare system has pointed up its problems. The Commission recognizes the need for continued short-term emergency assistance locally administered. We can anticipate the necessity for interim stopgap measures in individual instances before the income supplement could be started. Dr. Margaret S. Gordon, a Commission member, indicates a different approach in a supplemental statement to the Commission report:

I agree with the majority recommendation that Federal participation in existing categorical Public Assistance programs be terminated, once the proposed universal income supplement program becomes effective. However, I believe that a new program of Federal grants-in-aid should be adopted to encourage states to provide income supplements to *augment* the Federal Universal income supplements in a manner consistent with the objectives of our proposed income supplement program.[5]

The pending Family Assistance Act of 1970 requires most states to supplement federal assistance payments to maintain the January 1, 1970, level of payment in the state with a 30 percent federal cost share of state supplementation costs. Amendments have been offered that provide for a phased increase in federal cost share of state supplementation to 50 percent and in another to range from 50 percent to 83 percent.

It would appear that there is a reluctance or an unwillingness on the part of our lawmakers to have the states get out of the welfare field. The Commission was aware of regional variations

5 *Ibid.*, p. 83.

in the cost-of-living and the level of public assistance payments. We were unable, however, to devise a method of payment which would take such variations into account. We encourage high-payment states to maintain that level and we do see savings to states in the federal income supplement. We feel strongly that public assistance programs as we now know them should be dismantled.

The recipients of public assistance payments who testified before us almost uniformly expressed a negative attitude toward the social welfare caseworker. The view was frequently expressed that the worker's role was to meddle, interfere, or police the recipient's activity. No sensitivity to the inordinate caseload of the average social worker was shown. We can see the need for the continued provision of certain social services but we feel that they should bear a direct relationship to the need which is individually expressed. We cannot envision a circumstance in which the use of social services should be a requirement or a condition for receiving the proposed income supplement.

The poor stand on the outside of America's orbit. The working poor stand farther away than the unemployed poor. In a sense, they are penalized because they work. Can we bring all of the poor into the operative economic community? The Commission believes that we can. We can if our system of welfare has not become the victim of entropy. "Entropy" is defined as a mathematical expression of the degree to which the energy of a thermodynamic system is so distributed as to be unavailable for conversion into work, in other words, the irreversible tendency of a system toward increasing disorder and inertness. Has the energy of social workers, agency administrators, and the American people been so dissipated by present welfare concepts and structures that it is lost to the citizen who needs attention? Has the necessity of filling out budgetary forms and administering payment programs consumed the time and intellect of those most capable of providing creative ideas and innovation? Is poverty to be an enduring fact of life in our country?

Senator Abraham Ribicoff, of Connecticut, in offering amendments to the family assistance program of 1970 had this to say about the Commission report:

The recent report of the President's Commission on Income Maintenance Programs—the Heineman Commission—has warned us that the increasing affluence of our society, by itself, offers no hope for the poor. Those who have assumed that as the average income moved higher, the poor were getting a bigger share, are wrong.

The result is that today, completely alien life styles are developing among the poor in the ghettos of our cities and the poorest rural counties of our Nation. In a future which promises greater riches for many but continued poverty for some, these differences threaten to become unbridgeable chasms.

As the Heineman Commission points out, in these chilling words:

In these trends is the potential for social division unparalleled in our country.[6]

Senator Ribicoff urged the Congress to commit the nation to the complete eradication of poverty by 1976. He points to the lack of national commitment as the primary reason for our inactivity and our failure to erase poverty from the face of our nation.

The President's Commission on Income-Maintenance Programs offers a program designed to move us in the direction of the eradication of poverty.

The poor have been x-rayed, dissected, examined, probed, accused, belittled, isolated, and brutalized. We have done everything to them except give them their humanity. Their plight is an indictment of every American whose stomach is full. We try to hide the poor under the freeways and behind billboards and bury them in bureaucratic red tape, but their presence cannot be denied. They are developing vocal and articulate spokesmen, and the poor will be heard.

What will be their forum?

6 Abraham Ribicoff, Amendments to Welfare Reform Proposal, *Congressional Record*, 91st Congress, Vol. 116, No. 62, April 20, 1970.

A Critique of the
Family Assistance Plan

GEORGE McGOVERN

TODAY, MORE THAN EVER, Americans look for wise and compassionate leadership: leadership that unites, not divides; leadership that inspires, not debases; leadership that knows American security must rest on something other than the number of troops we have in other peoples' countries and the billions of dollars we spend on armaments.

It is time to realize that the true measure of this nation's greatness is not its wealth or its weapons but its wisdom and its compassion—how it cares for its deprived and its elderly, its widows and orphans, its physically handicapped, mentally retarded, and emotionally disturbed.

More than two centuries ago, a great English biographer wrote, "A decent provision for the poor is the true test of civilization." Today, America, the richest nation in the world, fails that test. Today, America, almost alone among advanced industrial nations, stands out as a country that punishes its poor instead of providing for them.

It fails, not because it lacks the resources, but because it misdirects and wastes them. It fails because it takes pride and power rather than humility and common humanity as signs of greatness and strength.

Until a few weeks ago, along with millions of other Americans, I believed that, however slowly, we were finding our way out of war and toward peace. I believed, at long last, that we might redirect our resources toward rebuilding our own society— toward ending hunger; toward providing a system of public welfare, at once dignified and adequate; toward providing every

American child with a decent education; toward restructuring our outmoded and inefficient system of health care; toward reclaiming our despoiled environment and elevating our national spirit.

Then came the sickening, and I believe illegal, decision to invade Cambodia, and everything changed. Suddenly, instead of coming home, America is sucked deeper into the morass of a foolish and impossible crusade in Asia that has nothing whatever to do with this country's national security, much less with promoting "the general welfare."

Our national interest demands an intelligent balance between foreign policy and internal policy. But with respect to Vietnam, Laos, and Cambodia, the tail is wagging the dog. Befuddled and deceitful policy protects the security of military dictatorships at the expense of the real security of the American people.

Time and again, the opportunity to lead America away from fear and the discredited commitments of the past has been lost. Is it any wonder that millions of Americans now question the fundamental legitimacy of our national institutions and the men who direct them?

That is why, at this time, it is so important for one of those institutions, the Senate, to respond to those questions by reasserting its right to take part in the awesome decisions of war and peace, life and death. That is why I sponsored the amendment in the Senate to share responsibility with the President for bringing this tragic conflict to a close.

This amendment to end the war says that after 50,000 dead and 275,000 wounded, and the waste of $125 billion on killing and destroying, America has done enough and it is time to come home.

This amendment provides that after December of 1970, funds may only be spent to bring our men home, and that is to be completed by June of 1971. It is not a hastily drawn measure. It provides authority to protect our troops as they withdraw, to arrange for an exchange of prisoners and asylum for Vietnamese who feel threatened by our departure.

Finally, if the June date should prove impractical, the President may request a joint resolution of Congress to extend that date, an action I am sure the Congress would take if it were proved necessary.

Until America's part in this war is ended, none of us will really be able to devote our attention and resources to what matters most to us—the human needs of our own people. Instead of looking forward to the dividends of peace, we will continue to suffer the deficits of war. If America is to begin to heal herself, her part in the war must end, and her energies be committed to the resolution of our social ills.

Decisions being made in the Department of Health, Education, and Welfare and at the White House could have a profound impact on the course of the health of our people and our society. They reflect this Administration's pledge to eradicate hunger, stimulate jobs, reform public assistance, and otherwise lead toward a realization of our potential and the utilization of our wealth. I speak of the Administration's welfare reform proposal. I am anxious about this proposal because of the limitations the Administration has put on its commitment. Time and again, legislation offered to eradicate hunger in this rich land has met resistance from the Administration. The poor are pitted against measures to "economize" and, inevitably, they lose.

The money is in Asia when it should be in America. It is in ABM, SST, nuclear carriers, and multiple warheads. And that is why all who are concerned with hunger and with housing, with health and education and a clean environment, are doomed to disappointment in what we seek for America.

I have praised the Administration's initiatives in offering welfare reform. Its objectives are substantial and laudatory; unfortunately, the proposal to accomplish the desired ends is not. It carries within it the seeds of yet another failure to really provide for the poor, of promises that raise hopes only to dash them once again.

Let me be specific about my reservations regarding the family assistance proposal.

Whenever a benefit has depended on proving that a man does not have and cannot get enough money, in the end that man has

waited hours on a hard bench to see a doctor, has been pa-
tronized by his caseworker, has been told that Congress never
appropriated the money for the apartment he needs. The programs to which I refer—medical care in public clinics, public assistance, and public housing—all were started by reformers with
high hopes and all have turned out badly. These programs illustrate the axiom that "programs for poor people tend over
time to become poor programs."

This occurs because our society still regards poor people as
lazy, as incompetent, as stupid or irresponsible, and bad. Theirs
are the first programs scapegoated when we need money for
war or to fight inflation. We know that record well. Programs
are established in a burst of reformist zeal only to founder on
the difficulty of keeping them well-financed and properly administered. In the desperate competition for tax dollars and
voter sympathy, but without powerful allies, poor people's programs inevitably fail.

The Administration's family assistance proposal is a poor
people's program par excellence. And the traditional problems
of designing such programs are compounded by its unitary
design. Although social workers have long sought a single criterion for eligibility for assistance—need—they have not always
argued for a single solution. Poverty is made up of many causes;
it requires many-pronged prevention. The man who is severely
disabled and lives alone has different needs and problems from
the mother with several small children. The requirements of the
aged widow are not the same as the unemployed youth's, and
few make the mistake of thinking so.

When we examine the population in poverty, we notice two
things: the absolute number of persons counted as poor has de-
clined in recent years, and the poverty population is more than
ever represented by female-headed families. This is explained by
the fact that intact families are able to climb out of poverty in a
time of economic growth, when jobs and overtime and moon-
lighting are available for fathers and part-time jobs for their
wives. But, then as now, the female-headed family is and remains
poor. A program which relies on employment-related income

incentives to eradicate poverty will leave those families once again untouched. The family assistance proposal is such a program.

The longing for a simple and unitary solution has produced another type of confusion. Poverty is treated as a lack of money that can be mathematically calculated and meted out. So we find treated together in a single program those who cannot work, who do work, who might work, and who can only work occasionally. It is this structural arrangement that creates the problem of "work incentives." It is difficult, perhaps impossible, to provide through a single formula an adequate payment for those who cannot work and allowances that provide incentive to those who can or may work. Those who cannot work get too little (accounting for the family assistance proposal's $1,600 level), while to Congressmen and the public those who can work seem to get too much.

It was this dilemma, and the Senate Finance Committee's determination that full-time workers should do better than those who worked part-time or not at all, that led to the demand for substantial revision of the family assistance proposal. Within the proposal's design, the simplest solution would have been to provide more generous payments for the working poor, but that was not possible within the cost that the Administration was willing to bear. Instead, state supplementation for intact families with an unemployed parent was eliminated.

Another solution rejected by the Administration was the provision of more jobs at decent pay. Those who can and do work would do better with reasonable pay and steady work than by inclusion in a welfare program.

A similar set of observations might be made about the aged and the disabled. They do not need welfare-type programs to change their conditions so much as they need recognition that their conditions will not change. The old cannot become young again nor the permanently disabled whole. They should be spared the ignominy of means tests or income tests and the necessity to patch together a bare subsistence out of welfare, charity, and minimal social security. The Advisory Council on

Social Security in 1965 supported the view that low-paid workers ought to get benefits high enough to eliminate the need for public assistance. I have proposed that we absorb most of those now in the adult catagories into the social security system, and eliminate welfare status for these groups.

We are not ignorant of the causes of poverty. They are well known: age, disability, childhood, and limited employability. With thoughtfully planned social security programs, virtually no one who is aged or disabled would need to look to a welfare-type program for aid. We would be left then with the problem of poverty largely limited to families with children. To meet that problem, we require a new program of subsidies for children—a program of progressively taxed children's allowances to replace the income tax deduction for children. While not limited to poor children, such a step would favor them most and solve the problem that the minimum wage does not adequately support a family with more than one or two children. That, by the way, *is* the problem of the working poor.

A system of children's allowances would avoid the "work incentive" dilemma of the family assistance proposal. There would be no means test. The working man would not need to reduce his resources in order to qualify. Yet such a program would make it unnecessary for most of the working poor to present themselves for welfare—a condition despised by most of them. Such a program would do as much for those who are just above the poverty line as for those just below, providing that small margin that young workers so desperately need.

We are not in a position to abandon programs that provide jobs enough and social insurance enough to prevent most forms of American poverty. Thus I too will support attempts to improve the proposal put forward by President Nixon in his family assistance program, but only as one element of a broader anti-poverty strategy.

I reject the idea that the family assistance proposal is the single, long-term, antipoverty device for this country because I believe it involves a divisive approach which cannot help but fail. For the limited ends of relieving those forms of poverty which cannot be prevented through employment or social insurance, I support the Administration's proposal with reservations.

I have four particular concerns with the proposal. First, I am concerned that there be federal assumption of costs and administration. Shared administration in public assistance has not worked, and detailed regulation of state and local personnel is neither possible nor desirable.

Second, I am concerned that there be clear movement toward adequate levels of assistance. If there are insufficient funds in 1970, that should not prevent our writing a program of staged increases into this bill. It should not excuse discouraging high-cost states from providing payments above the poverty line, nor should it excuse reverting to policies that penalize intact families.

Third, I am concerned by the lack of clarity around administration of the employment services. For example, they will decide who should be trained for employment and what constitutes a refusal to work. It is precisely this type of discretion that is used now to exclude people from assistance; the proposed legislation offers little reassurance on these points. In the end, the capacity of the poor to work depends less on the administration of welfare programs and more on fiscal and manpower policies which determine the availability of work. Public employment, missing entirely from this proposal, is a necessary complement to proposals for welfare reform.

Finally, I am concerned about food assistance. Until basic welfare payments provide enough income for needy families, food assistance must be administratively tied to welfare payments. I would gladly forego food stamps tomorrow if America's poor had income enough to meet their basic needs. Until that time, it is folly to give up one of the most important programs we have enacted. We must not let the crusade against hunger be overshadowed today by the promise of welfare reform in the indefinite future.

I am convinced that if our government fought as hard to see the hungry fed as it fights to see the ABM's, MIRV's and SST's fly, malnutrition would soon be only a bad memory. If America can subsidize a corrupt dictatorship in Saigon, if it can subsidize wealthy oil men and millionaire investors in municipal bonds here at home, it can afford to subsidize millions of its poor.

If we lack the moral fiber to do that, then the meaning of America, to herself and to the rest of the world, will have undergone a serious change, and the very foundations of the nation will have been severely undermined. It is time for America to come home, home from death to life, home from destroying to rebuilding, home to the sure principles that gave her birth.

Income Maintenance
and the Social Security Ideology

ALVIN L. SCHORR

On one side, it is said that we are now about to depart from an ill-conceived, poorly rationalized system of supporting the income of some people. We are to take the first small step toward a uniform program that will protect all people in the United States against poverty. On the other side, it is said that this step is itself ill-conceived. It is interesting rhetorically and it may be brilliant politically—that remains to be seen—but the President's welfare program is exactly in the poor law tradition; which is to say that it is 400 years older than a departure is entitled to be.

I see no giant step for mankind here, and not even much of a first small step. I see a *potential* reform of public assistance. I value it as such, for even modest reforms of public assistance are hard to come by. I stress *potential* reform because the proposed program was framed by careful Calvinists and careless reformers. It is not yet self-evident that a final bill will represent real net progress.[1]

Frankly, I believe that our conversation about the Family Assistance Plan has tended to be either too grand or too petty. We have been grand when we said that we wanted to guarantee income or wipe out poverty and that the rest was technical. Surely, Congress or somebody else in Washington could work that out. We have been petty in getting caught up in details of various welfare proposals. We discovered arithmetic, and acted as if the difference between disregarding 50 percent or 30 per-

[1] See Alvin L. Schorr, "The President's Welfare Program and Commission," *Public Welfare*, XXVIII (1970), 26–32.

cent of earned income held the key to a centuries-old problem. We discovered economics, and acted as if jargon like "tax rate" and "notch problem" solved dilemmas that the jargon of social work could not.

Between the grand decision and the minutiae lie the old dilemmas: how to pay enough to live on without appearing to interfere with the wage structure; how to deal equitably with those whom we want to work, with those who plainly cannot work, and with those about whom we have mixed feelings; how to pay anything at all on the grounds of poverty without distrusting and controlling. If there are solutions to these dilemmas, they must lie somewhere between magic wands and arithmetic—in those reaches where intelligence and understanding are meant to operate.

Regardless of how the current welfare proposals fare, I believe that events in the next decade hinge on our view of an old dilemma that has been resolutely ignored by experts and professionals, including the social workers who ought to know most about it. That issue is the desirability of means-testing or income-testing. The terms have been used rather differently by respectable authorities.[2] For my purposes, "income-testing" applies to any program in which benefits are provided only to applicants who have less than a specified income. "Means-testing" is the form of income-testing in which the applicants' inadequate income must be established in case-by-case examination. By these definitions, public assistance as it was practiced in the 1960s was a means-tested program. As it would be practiced, if it relied largely on declarations of income, it would be an income-tested program. The President's Family Assistance Plan, as apparently it is intended to be administered, would be income-tested but not means-tested.

In general, our ideology from 1935 until recently may be characterized as a social security ideology. At each point we identified the major risks to income—old age, disability, widow-

[2] Eveline Burns, for example, uses "means-testing" to mean programs that test both income and resources, while "income-testing" means programs that test only income. For another definition, see George Hoshino, "Can the Means Test Be Simplified?" *Social Work*, X, No. 3 (1965), 98–103.

hood, being orphaned, unemployment—and devised a program that would guard against each risk. Public assistance was to be a device for people with special, temporary needs and, in a sense, was itself to be a temporary program. If any large group of people should require public assistance for considerable lengths of time, that fact would highlight the need for improving or augmenting social security and so keep public assistance small. In this total system, obviously, income-testing does not loom large. Still, the social security ideology was meant to prevent poverty, and it does. Over half of OASDHI benefits go to people who would otherwise have been poor.[3] In 1965, OASDHI alone kept 3.5 million households out of poverty.[4]

The social security ideology is only a manner of thinking, and not even such an old one in the United States; reasonable men may question whether it is still appropriate. Indeed, there has been a good deal of questioning of social security ideology in the Western world in the last decade. In countries like Great Britain and Canada, the social security concepts of poverty prevention and income-by-right have been under fire by proponents of income-testing.[5] The outcome of the debate probably will for a time be in doubt. Holland appears to have moved substantially into income-testing; France has rejected it.[6]

Undoubtedly, debate elsewhere has fueled the questioning here, but somehow the central issues concerning social security have not been openly joined. Joseph Pechman and his co-authors wrote a book setting forth criticisms of social security, but the book is technical and no one has troubled to reply.[7] The Presi-

[3] Robert J. Lampman, "Transfer Approaches to Distribution Policy," American Economic Association, 1969.

[4] Ida Merriam, "Welfare and Its Measurement," in Eleanor Sheldon and Wilbert E. Moore, eds., *Indicators of Social Change* (New York: Russell Sage Foundation 1968), pp. 721–84.

[5] For selections from the British debate see *Social Reform in the Centrifugal Society*, a New Society pamphlet (London: New Science Publications 1970); Richard M. Titmuss and Michael Zander, *Unequal Rights* (London: Child Poverty Action Group, 1968); and Sir John Walley, "Decay of the System Designed to Prevent Poverty," London *Times*, April 6, 1967.

[6] For a French point of view on this, see Pierre Laroque, "Human Rights, Social Work, and Social Policy," in *Social Welfare and Human Rights* (New York: Columbia University Press, 1969), pp. 72–87.

[7] Joseph A. Pechman, Henry J. Aaron, and Michael K. Taussig, *Social Security, Perspectives for Reform* (Washington, D.C.: Brookings Institution, 1968).

dent's Commission on Income Maintenance Programs (the Heineman Commission) made recommendations that would move us away from the social security ideology,[8] but it dealt ambiguously or not at all with the considerable issues that are involved. Much of the public debate about welfare reform has carried an implied criticism of social security as inefficient, but the criticism has been almost offhand, as if it were not connected with other serious issues. Meanwhile, public assistance has grown steadily, presenting us by the late 1960s with the fact of an income-tested program that is not temporary or residual in any sense. Willy-nilly and unconsciously, our social security ideology has begun to adapt to that fact.

Three major criticisms have been lodged against the social security approach. First, the so-called "social insurance" programs, OASDHI and unemployment insurance, have dual objectives that are, some would say, incompatible. That is, on the one hand the programs are intended to prevent poverty, and on the other hand they are wage-related; in other words, they pay out according to the size of contributions. Strictly wage-related benefits do most for those who have earned the most and thus paid in the most. Conversely, the more that the program does for people who are poor, the less it seems to be related to prior earnings or payments.

An example may help. At the beginning of 1970, retirement benefits were raised by 15 percent for all social security beneficiaries. The $55 a month received by the poorest beneficiaries was increased by $7 or $8; but $30 was added to the benefits of those who were already receiving $200 a month. There is nothing much there for poverty prevention. On the other hand, a provision was dropped from the same bill that would have raised the minimum payment for any beneficiary from $55 to $100 a month. Two thirds of the $2 billion cost would have wound up in the pockets of poor people. To be sure, benefits would have appeared somewhat less related to prior contributions than before the change. In this tension between wage-relatedness and

---

8 *Poverty amid Plenty: the American Paradox,* report of the President's Commission on Income Maintenance Programs (Washington, D.C.: U.S. Government Printing Office, 1969).

poverty prevention, critics say, both objectives are clouded and the program does not do well for either.

The second criticism is related to the first. In thirty-five years of social security we have not done enough about preventing poverty. It would be better to turn social security into a frankly wage-related program, letting it do what it might for those who have moderate or even quite good incomes, and construct a proper income-tested program to meet the needs of the poor.

Third, it is said that social insurance is not efficient in poverty alleviation. A program is "efficient" when a high proportion of its cost goes to poor people. The suggested $100 minimum in social security may serve as an example. It would be regarded as 66 percent efficient—the poor would get two thirds of the cost—and was dismissed in the report of the President's Commission as inefficient.

Let me make rejoinder to these criticisms. The ambivalence between wage-relatedness and poverty prevention is deliberate. The programs were designed to provide money to types of people who are likely to be poor, but without leading them to *think* poor. Although most old people may be poor, for example, *all* old people are (or will soon be) entitled to retirement payments, and obviously that includes many who are not poor. That is intentional. It is meant to build a system in which all people have adequate incomes to which they feel entitled. Those who want to test the real meaning of the system might query beneficiaries on such a question as; "If you will give up your rights to social security, I will declare you entitled to an Old Age Assistance (OAA) payment that is 20 percent higher. Yes or no?"

Ambivalent objectives are, of course, reflected in the fact that social security is designed to give some advantage to those who are poorest. They do not receive as much as those who earned more, neither do they receive as little as a strictly proportional system would dictate. Yet, social security is not a game in which the rich must lose because the poor gain. Society makes an investment in social security that quite compensates wealthier beneficiaries for any advantage the poorest are receiving. I am not really pointing at the cost advantages in a universal, government-administered program. They are substantial but are swamped by the government's unspoken commitment (soon, perhaps, to be spoken) to improve social security benefits regularly to keep pace with rising costs and productivity. The result is that most beneficiaries, including the wealthiest, receive far more in benefits than private insurance would have paid in return for the same contributions. No one at any time receives less than private insurance would have paid.

The criticism that the social security approach has failed to do enough about poverty, is difficult to argue to any useful conclusion. It has been indicated that OASDHI reduces by a fifth the number of households that are poor.[9] Obviously, it could do better; it *should* do better. But if we thought that the program should not be oriented to poverty prevention, it would do worse. About three fourths of the aged who get social security benefits are poor or would be if it were not for social security.[10] Should a program dealing with so many poor people be made *less* effective for them because it has not been *more* effective? In any event, whether social security has done well enough is involved with whether we would have invested enough money in any programs, regardless of their ideology. As I say, it is difficult to argue this point to a useful conclusion. The criticisms reflect well-founded irritation and impatience. Saying that hardly tells us in what direction to go.

Third is the efficiency criticism. Social insurance programs tend to be inefficient; income-tested programs are efficient. Although the statement sounds plausible, it is in fact misleading. When income-tested programs deal with the so-called "working poor," the issue of incentive to work arises. One solution is to set assistance standards so low that assistance never competes with possible income from employment. I assume that we reject such a solution. Another solution is to develop an incentive scale for disregarding income, such as is incorporated in the Family Assistance Plan or the President's Commission's proposed in-

9 Merriam, *op. cit.*
10 Robert M. Ball, "Policy Issues in Social Security," *Social Security Bulletin,* XXIX, No. 6 (1966), 3–9.

come supplement. But such programs require that payments be made to people whose incomes are well above the level that is set as minimum, and efficiency declines rapidly with rises in the minimum level. For example, the Commission's income supplement would, if it assured income at the poverty level, be 36 percent efficient.[11] That is, it would be markedly less efficient than OASDHI. Moreover, if an income-tested program were accompanied by withdrawing from poor people the advantage they now enjoy in calculating social insurance benefits, they would lose in two ways. It would turn out that an income-tested program at decent levels was not efficient after all, and they would lose out in the rest of social security as well.

I have dealt so far with criticisms of the social security ideology and rejoinders that must be made to those criticisms. Apart from criticisms there are two major purposes that a social security ideology supports and that widespread income-testing would undermine.

One has to talk first of stigma, or its converse, income by right. When a third of the nation was poor, by standards even more stringent than we use today, experts cast about for ways to provide income as a matter of right. As it has turned out, many rights would serve—a history of work, contributions to a fund, payment of a government tax, old age, veteran status, and so forth. Social security was, in this sense, a product of widespread revulsion against income-testing. More recently, Medicare precipitated a struggle on the same issue. The American Medical Association and others argued that medical care should be provided on the simplest demonstration of need. At some risk of getting no program at all, old people opposed a program that would apply an income test. On one occasion, Wilbur J. Cohen explained: "We need a system which creates no invidious distinctions based on income—one where an individual is entitled to receive benefits on the basis of his general contributions to society." [12] In the end Congress was persuaded.

Need or want is the only quality that we have not by itself converted into a right or been able to feel as a right. It is not,

11 *Poverty amid Plenty* . . . , Table 5–5, p. 62.
12 Michigan News Service, May 12, 1960.

in truth, for lack of trying. Aid to Dependent Children was conceived in the 1930s in a deliberate attempt to protect children from the humiliation and inadequacy of general relief. If mothers' aid or children's aid could be singled out, people like Edith Abbott argued, assistance would be provided as a matter of right to those who could demonstrate need.[13] History has offered a bitter rebuttal to that fond hope. Review for a moment the other income-tested programs designed for poor people: public housing, medical care in public clinics, commodity and food stamp programs. It is impossible to consider them without seeing American attitudes toward poverty at work on their financing, benefit levels, and the flavor of their administration.

I am properly respectful of what at least some people intend when they talk about a large-scale move to new, income-tested programs. However, I do not think that the stigmatizing programs we have were designed by hypocrites and damned fools alone. I think they were designed by reformers and politicians whose work, however decent or sanitary, suffered the fate of all income-tested programs for the poor in the United States. Anyone who has watched Congress at work on the family assistance program has had a small taste of this process. Step by step, Congress has written stigma into a comparatively sanitary bill: pursuit of deserting fathers; no appeal to courts; ambiguity about confidentiality; a requirement to accept virtually any work. And so far that is only Congress—not local officials.

Those who criticize the social security approach and advocate new income-tested programs are asserting, in effect, that we will prevent stigma by an act of will. They do not think that programs should be stigmatizing and they will not have it so. I am saying that our repeated failures to achieve exactly this end must lead us to regard the problem as a deeper one. If income-tested programs do not begin badly, we make them bad. We add the features that stigmatize.[14] We begin with income-testing but

[13] Edith Abbott, "Acceptance Speech at Presentation of Survey Award," in *The Social Welfare Forum, 1951* (New York: Columbia University Press, 1951), pp. ix–x.

[14] For a small study of this process at work, see George Hoshino and Mary K. Ruth, "The Administration of 'Selectivity' in the Breakfast Program of a Public Elementary School," School of Social Work, University of Pennsylvania, 1970 (processed).

become suspicious and apply means-testing. These are not arguments against reforming public assistance; public assistance cries out for reform. They are arguments against catching up in the net of public assistance or income-testing a larger portion of the population than is absolutely necessary. Perhaps we may feel differently when somewhere we can point to an income-tested program applied to people of working age that we can call a decent program.

Let me turn to the second broad social consequence of a social security ideology. Although it is a complicated system, addressed to various categories of people and needing to be rationalized, it is in conception addressed to all the American people. The alternative that is being advocated is a two-part system: one part like private insurance for the bulk of Americans; the other part designed for, and carefully limited to, poor people. The symbolic meaning of this alternative at this particular time need hardly be elaborated. But the choice has consequences reaching far beyond the symbolism of one nation or two.

No program in the United States is a good program merely because it started out well; it requires regular improvement in benefit levels and monitoring of administrative quality. Programs with powerful constituencies are regularly expanded and liberalized, but poor people's programs may even be cut back. Witness the fate of OEO and the ceiling on Aid to Dependent Children when the country was at war. It is difficult, perhaps impossible, for programs limited to poor people to do well over the long run. By contrast, the social security ideology allies the poor with those who have more. They have differences, as allies always do, but they share a broad interest in program improvement—and in the end the poor do better. We need not deal with this matter entirely theoretically. The aged poor now receive half of social security benefits and all or almost all of OAA benefits. How would it be if there had been no retirement insurance and its original cost had gone into OAA? Would OAA pay more to the aged than it does now? Would it pay nearly as much more as the aged poor now get from social security?

The issue of which ideology will place more money in the

hands of poor people opens up the most serious underlying question: Are we seeking to provide enough money to meet some momentary standard, or do we mean to make a deeper redistribution so that poor people will have a larger *share* of national income? It is beginning to be noticed that the so-called "poverty level" as it is defined at any one time is meaningless.[15] People judge themselves by their relationship to what seems average. That is why what is considered poverty level in the United States would be considered a decent income in Great Britain. That is why a modest income in the United States today will be poverty in ten years. That is why proponents of income-testing are able to make happy predictions that their programs will decline in cost over the years. As national wealth rises and even the poor benefit, naturally it will take less to meet their deficit. Meanwhile, we will all have come to define poverty at a higher level, a point that tends not to be faced by advocates of income-testing. Their objective is more modest.

If we really mean to eliminate poverty, we must seek not only more money but a larger *share* of money for those who have least. It is a difficult goal to achieve, but on the face of it not an impossible one. We already have a vast system that transfers income from one family to another in order to meet social objectives. Its mechanisms include social security, income, wage, and sales taxes, veterans' benefits, and so on. Well over $100 billion a year changes hands; income transfers already provide more than half the total income of poor people.[16] So the problem is to make that system more powerful over time. The fifth of the population with the least income has for years received about 5 percent of national income, and, I suggest that we try to double that percentage.[17] However, the precise percentage is not im-

15 For example, see Alvin L. Schorr, *Poor Kids* (New York: Basic Books, 1966), pp. 88–90; Victor R. Fuchs, "Redefining Poverty and Redistributing Income," *Public Interest,* No. 8 (1967), pp. 88–95; S. M. Miller and Pamela Roby, *The Future of Inequality* (New York: Basic Books, 1970), pp. 35–44; and *Poverty amid Plenty.* . . .

16 Robert J. Lampman, "Transfer and Redistribution as Social Process," in Shirley Jenkins, ed., *Social Security in International Perspective* (New York: Columbia University Press, 1969), pp. 29–54.

17 Alvin L. Schorr, "The Free Society," Canadian Conference on Social Welfare, 1970.

portant. Important is whether or not we understand that our aim is to increase the income share of those who have the least.

The social security ideology lends itself to this goal and income-testing does not. I offer these reasons for the assertion. First, as I have indicated, programs that cut across income lines are more potent politically than those that do not. They have a built-in dynamic for self-improvement. Second, income-tested programs absorb the attention of poor people and their supporters in a small portion of the arena to which they ought to be attending. They fight for a better welfare program but tend to overlook the sums of money being dealt out elsewhere. On the other hand, the social security ideology by its nature directs attention to all income-transfer programs. It directs attention to the need for "human subsidies."

The point was illustrated during the last session of Congress. The attempt to set a minimum social security benefit of $100 per month (worth $1.3 billion to our poor people) was allowed to go down to defeat without a murmur from poor people or liberal Congressmen. The income tax exemption for dependents was increased over several years to $750. This was regarded as a victory for liberals, for it will help people with moderate incomes more than would an across-the-board tax reduction. At an ultimate cost of $5 billion it still will put no money at all in the pockets of poor people. As James Tobin pointed out in an irate letter to the New York *Times,* measures could easily have been devised that would give poor people a share in the windfall. Those two measures, losing about $6 billion that the poor should have had a chance at, went through Congress in a matter of days. Meanwhile, all the country debates a $3 or $4 billion welfare reform for months; and when a bill is finally passed, it will be supposed that poor people should be satisfied for some little time. So we are already paying the cost of the prominence of income-testing. It is already evident that OASDHI is being skewed to give the poor a smaller share in benefits than they have had.[18]

In short, the choice between the social security ideology and income-testing is, in part, a choice between objectives. If we

18 Robert J. Lampman, "Transfer Approaches to Distribution Policy."

mean for those with the least income to have a larger share, we will develop permanent mechanisms that assure that. If we do not mean that or are neutral about it, we will develop programs that fill a gap *after* people are poor. I am tempted to say that the latter is efficient not because of intrinsic efficiency, but because poor people will be allocated less in that fashion. As I have said, they will be able to apply less power and the matter will be defined in a way that absorbs their energy in winning comparatively small gains.

To summarize, at play not far beneath current discussions about welfare is a fundamental choice of direction about income maintenance. If we continue to build on the social security ideology, we will perfect the programs we have and consider new ones; children's allowances and federal long-term unemployment insurance seem to be reasonable candidates. Without doing serious violence to their rationale we will bend these programs so that they will be more serviceable to poor people. We will also reform public assistance; that is not at issue. If we move toward income-testing, we will bend our present social security programs toward those who are not poor. We will make some major experiment in reforming public assistance, and see how it turns out.

It is a desperately important decision. One is always tempted to say that the fate of the nation hinges on the decision. Let me put the point more modestly. On that decision, in my view, hinges whether or not we will stigmatize or scapegoat large numbers of poor people. On that decision hinges whether we will for the first time set out to redistribute national income in favor of poor people. If we do not, we will surely awaken in eight or ten years to the realization that, by some new definition, a fifth of the population is poor. The spread of stigmatization and the persistence of poverty would powerfully affect the fate of the nation. Conversely, if we really begin to reduce poverty and to give all our citizens reason to have a feeling of dignity, we may shape quite a different fate. Social workers have not only to choose, but to explain to the nation what the choices are.

Welfare Reform and Income Security Policies

EVELINE M. BURNS

Everyone today seems to be in favor of welfare reform. There appears to be general agreement that our welfare (or public assistance) programs are gravely deficient in many respects. By and large, the payments do not bring people above the poverty line. A large number of clearly needy people are excluded, among whom, ironically, are the working poor. These programs discourage initiative by deducting every dollar of earnings from the assistance payment, or, as the economists would put it, by taxing at 100 percent the earnings of welfare recipients. They encourage family breakdown by, in effect, offering a financial inducement to fathers to desert their families. They threaten, if not destroy, the applicants' dignity and self-respect by the procedures used in the determination of eligibility and the amount of the payment and, on occasion, go so far as to invade the recipients' civil or constitutional rights. They treat people in similar circumstances in very different ways according to their age, the cause of their need or where they live, and as a corollary are believed to encourage people to move from less liberal to more liberal jurisdictions.

In accordance with this diagnosis, current proposals for reform include some or all of the following policies:

1. Raising the standard of living to be attained by every eligible person

2. Narrowing the resources to be taken into account in determining whether an applicant is in need

This has taken the form of limiting the range of relatives held responsible for the support of their kin, excluding certain kinds or amounts of property in determining resources in the hope of encouraging thrift and, most recently, exempting from consideration some fraction of current earnings, in the hope of encouraging efforts at self-support.

3. Broadening eligibility to include the working poor

4. Changing the method of determining eligibility and the amount of the payment to avoid deterrence and undue interference with the privacy and rights of the applicant

5. Involving the federal government in the program to a greater extent in order to make possible a more uniform minimum guarantee level in all states.

This process of modifying the character of the nation's ultimate safeguard against income inadequacy has, of course, been going on for a long time. Our welfare programs belong to the family of income security measures best described as "gap-filling." The family includes the old poor law, current public assistance programs, the income-conditioned pension, and the recent babies, the negative income tax (N.I.T.), the little "preemie," the Nixon Family Assistance Plan, the income supplement plan of the President's Commission on Income Maintenance Programs (the Heineman Commission), and the McCarthy bill. All of them aim to fill all or part of the gap between the defined target standard of living (the minimum income guarantee) and the individual's or family's available resources as defined. All are dominated by not wholly compatible objectives: to provide income to all those in need but not to pay money to those who are not needy; to adjust the payment to the precise income gap of each individual applicant but to have a system that is speedily responsive to the changing circumstances of each individual case and is yet administratively simple; to include inducements to self-support and thrift and to spend as little money as possible.

The different members of the family have tried to achieve these objectives in various ways. The old poor law defined the target standard of living very austerely by use of the "less eligibility" principle and defined available resources very broadly to include a wide relative responsibility requirement, deduction of all earnings from the payment, and exhaustion of all savings and property as a condition of eligibility. The scope of the program was kept down by rigorous verification and investigation of the family circumstances coupled with various deterrent conditions attached to the receipt of aid, such as payment in kind or loss of certain civic rights, performance of arduous work, or residence in a workhouse or poor law institution.

Modern public assistance programs are somewhat more liberal. Assistance is given in the home and in cash. The target income is somewhat higher though far from generous, and people are permitted to retain some kinds or fractions of their property; in many states the scope of relatives' responsibility has been narrowed; and for certain groups of needy people some fractions of earnings may be disregarded. There is a trend toward simplifying the process of eligibility determination, including in a few cases the use of an affidavit in place of the detailed investigation and verification of resources. But each case is still dealt with individually.

In the income-conditioned pension, there is some departure from this highly individualized adjustment of needs and resources. All those whose resources, as legally defined, fall below some specified level are eligible for the full basic payment. Only above this level do resources involve a reduction of the pension by some defined amount until a point is reached at which no public payment is receivable. This system prevails in Australia and New Zealand and is found, in principle, in our veterans' pension system.

The latest member of the "gap-filling" family, the negative income tax in its many forms, including the Nixon plan, the income supplement of the Heineman Commission, and the McCarthy bill, perpetuates the individualized determination of the money payment and differs from its relatives mainly in the specifics of the program. The N.I.T. approach does indeed provide for a national minimum. But although in principle it aims "to fill the poverty gap," all current proposals except the McCarthy bill fall far short of this. Indeed, the Nixon Family Assistance Plan even reverts to payments in kind, by relying on food stamps to provide a sizable fraction of the guarantee. Coverage would be wider than that of the other gap-filling programs. First, because it is a federal system, it would avoid the inequities and anomalies of the eligibility conditions and administrative policies of the states and jurisdictions. Second, it would cover also the working poor. However, even in this last respect, it does not differ from the policies in New York and a few other states which already supplement earnings.

The provision for disregarding specified amounts of income in the hope of encouraging initiative is again not novel or revolutionary. For some years, the federally aided Aid to the Blind program has been required to disregard specified amounts of earnings, and the states have been permitted to do the same thing for recipients of certain other federally aided programs, although by no means have all of them taken advantage of the opportunity. But the N.I.T. would universalize this policy, though it remains to be seen whether the specific sums to be disregarded in determining eligibility will prove to be more liberal than the provisions in some of the states which also permit a deduction from assessable earnings to allow for the costs of earning.

Probably the most novel feature of the N.I.T. is the proposal to eliminate the detailed investigation and verification of needs and resources and substitute a simple income declaration. Here again, however, the policy has precedents. In a few states, the affidavit is already in use so that what is new is again a universalizing of something already being done. The program is to be administered and policed by some federal authority (although the Nixon proposals envisage the possibility of agreements to permit the states to carry out this function on behalf of the federal government). Already, however, the idea that administration could be handled by the internal revenue authorities has been abandoned. Nor does the Social Security Administration want it, understandably, for the more one examines the details of the plan, the more evident it is that a large amount of administrative discretion is involved. It remains to be seen whether the new agency, dealing as it will only with "the poor," will be able to free itself from welfare ideology.

It can be readily granted, however, that the N.I.T. is, in principle, the most liberal of almost all gap-filling programs. It thus provides an opportunity for assessing the social potential of the gap-filling approach to income security.

Does it meet need?

Assuming that meeting need means bringing all persons above the poverty line, the answer, of course, depends on the level of the guarantee. Both the Family Assistance Plan and that of the Heineman Commission fall short of this standard, though the latter is much more nearly adequate. The states will indeed be required to supplement the $1,600 cash Nixon guarantee, which is below that of all except eight states, up to their current level of payments; but it is noteworthy that they will not be required to supplement income of the working poor or to be as liberal as the basic plan in their treatment of earnings for supplementation purposes. It may be doubted whether the proposed extraordinarily drastic penalties on the states for noncompliance will be embodied in the final legislation, especially in view of uncertainties about the degree to which the program will, in fact, relieve of their financial burdens the states paying more than $1,600. To the extent that under either proposal, needy people will require supplementation from their states (and at least in the Nixon plan they are likely to be in the majority), there is no assurance that the process of determining supplementation eligibility will be any improvement over that which currently prevails under the state public assistance programs. In addition, applicants may even suffer the inconvenience of having to deal with two administrations.

The Heineman proposals do indeed recognize the unlikelihood that any gap-filling program that operates on the basis of anticipated income or income received in a previous period can deal with unanticipated departures from the income reported in the declaration, and provide for a supplementary emergency relief program, which they anticipate will be small. Yet, in fact, the population for whom assurance of immediate income assistance is most vital, the very poor, are a group characterized by highly fluctuating income. The turnover on current general assistance and AFDC programs is considerable, though we do not have figures for the country as a whole. But it is perhaps significant that in Great Britain, the Supplementary Benefits Commission, which administers what is essentially a negative income tax program (although it does not supplement full-time earnings), reported in 1966 that out of 3.5 million applications (of which 14 percent were rejected), only 34.3 percent resulted in continuing weekly payments, while over 50 percent were for single payments.

Will gap-filling encourage incentive?

Undoubtedly, the permission to retain some fraction of earnings without a corresponding reduction in the guaranteed payment will remove some of the present discouragement to employment. But our knowledge of the stimuli to initiative is too limited to permit forecasts of the extent to which a disregard of some fraction of earnings will serve as a positive inducement to employment, especially if the guarantee is high enough to assure at least the poverty-level income. Much would seem to depend on whether people place emphasis upon the amount of earnings left to them or on the share that is taken by Uncle Sam. If the latter is decisive, then anything short of permitting people to retain 100 percent of their earnings will fail to encourage earning. The OASDI experience seems to suggest that people do not make a great distinction between a policy that reduces payments one dollar for every two dollars earned and one that reduces payments dollar for dollar. The big drop in beneficiary earning comes at the point at which the one-dollar reduction for each two dollars earned begins. This would seem to suggest that if the "disregard" policy is retained, there would be more inducement to earn by allowing people to keep the whole of some stated sum (as is proposed in the Nixon plan) than by a percentage reduction starting from the very first dollar of earnings (as is proposed by the Heineman Commission).

In any case, it is important to note that the policy of building incentives to earn into the payment system itself by the device of disregarding some fraction of earnings has two unfortunate consequences. Unless the "disregard" is at least as high as 100 percent minus the lowest income tax bracket tax rate, the assistance recipient is taxed at a higher rate than all other income-receivers, and the lower the percentage of earnings disregarded, the greater the discrimination against the assistance recipient. Second, to avoid discriminating against the earner whose income is immediately above the guaranteed minimum (the so-called "notch problem"), it has been held necessary to extend the disregard up the income scale. But this necessarily greatly enlarges the numbers who will be entitled to some N.I.T. payment. Even the niggardly Nixon program proposes to make some payments up to the $3,920 income level.

Will gap-filling help the working poor?

Inclusion of the working poor will indeed remove the inequity of discriminating against those who are making every effort to support themselves and will avoid the anomaly that persons "on relief" may be better off than some of those in full-time employment. But this policy runs the risk of subsidizing, and this encouraging, low-wage employment. It is indeed ironical that in a century and a half we have come full circle. Not only has that historical bogeyman, the Speenhamland system, been reinstated and hailed as a desirable reform, but its most vocal exponents are the very professionals who years ago were most instrumental in criticizing and abolishing Speenhamland, namely, the economists.

Commitment to a policy of subsidizing earnings requires an equal commitment to a statutory minimum wage and the provision of publicly assured jobs at standard wages, if it is not to act as a wage depressant.

Will it remove inducements to move to more liberal or rich states?

To the extent that people do move to areas with more liberal welfare programs, a gap-filling program that was national in scope and guaranteed an income at least up to the poverty line would remove this inducement. But no proposed program other than the McCarthy bill will do this, for none places the national guarantee at so high a level. As a result, even under the Heineman proposals, there will be some states where, as a result of state supplementation, payments will be above the national guarantee, and to this extent, the alleged inducement to move will remain. The Nixon proposals are particularly inadequate in this respect, since all but eight states currently have standards above the $1,600 level.

Will it remove incentives to family breakup?

To the extent that fathers leave home in order to make their families eligible for assistance, a national gap-filling program will indeed lessen incentives to family separation. But since, under the N.I.T. type of guarantee, the *amount* of the payment is dependent on proof of income inadequacy on the part of an individual or family, there will still be financial advantage to a family to split up whenever the wage earner's income exceeds the additional costs of living apart from his family, plus his share of the guarantee. For the family's net income would then be the sum of the father's net earnings plus the N.I.T. that the technically incomeless "deserted family" would receive. Having said this, it is only fair to point out that we know practically nothing about the extent to which decisions to form or dissolve a family are affected by considerations of financial advantage. However, it seems clear that any gap-filling program may facilitate family breakup by enlarging the freedom of women, who no longer will have to put up with unsatisfactory husbands merely because they are dependent on them financially.

Is it an efficient system?

Probably the most impressive claim that is made for the gap-filling approach, as compared, for example, with social insurance or a demogrant, is that it is efficient, meaning thereby that it makes payments only to those in need and does not subsidize those who are better off. One gets more poverty-removing bang for each buck. But the more eager we are to build in meaningful incentives in the form of disregards of earnings, the less efficient the system becomes, for as already pointed out, it necessarily involves including in the program more and more higher income earners.

How great this extension can be is illustrated by the experience of New York City, where over one in eight of the population is now on welfare. It is not generally recognized that for some years New York has operated, through its public assistance system, a gap-filling program of the N.I.T. type. The standard of living assured is approximately at the poverty level, there are sizable disregards of earned income, the scope of relatives' responsibility has been narrowed, the working poor can claim supplementation of earnings from general assistance, there is a move toward a flat-grant system, and the process of determining eligibility has been greatly liberalized and in some cases even replaced by the use of an affidavit or declaration. The numbers on assistance would be still larger if the same earnings disregards were applied to those seeking wage supplementation as are applied to those already on relief; in any case they are likely to rise as knowledge of the existence of a relatively liberal non-deterrent system becomes more widespread.

The Heineman Commission has estimated that in the nation as a whole, with a plan that would guarantee an income of $3,600 for a family of four, some 20.5 million households, or 74.6 million people, would be receiving payments. With a guarantee of $4,000 the corresponding figures would be 24.2 million and 88.3 million.

Can we contemplate as our ideal a system in which almost half the population would be in continuous touch with governmental authorities to receive payments whose amount will be determined on an individual basis by a process from which official discretion cannot be wholly removed? I confess that the prospect fills me with acute distaste. It will be said that even now, every income receiver has to make quarterly returns to government to determine how much he owes in the way of income tax. But it is psychologically quite another thing to have to affirm every quarter that one is unable to support one's family above the poverty line and needs some supplement from the government. This would perpetuate the dependent status about which we show so much concern when contemplating the rise in welfare rolls. What this gap-filling approach would do, even at its best, is enormously to expand the dependent population. Far from eliminating the welfare system, we would be extending it.

THE OBJECTIVES OF REFORM

Given the basic similarity of the N.I.T. approach in any of its forms to all other members of the gap-filling family, it is astonishing to be informed by John Twiname, speaking for the Administration, that the Nixon Family Assistance Plan "is a revolutionary change . . . it is the keystone in a new income strategy pointing in a whole new direction." Still more astonishing are the ecstasies of Daniel Moynihan in contemplating his brain child. The family assistance plan, his asserts,

reflects the social initiative that will almost certainly define the beginning of a new era in American social policy. . . . With it, the United States takes its place as the leading innovator in the world in the field of social policy. . . . It is a program utterly without precedent. . . . It will cause future generations to regard us as a . . . people who were somehow touched with glory.

If we are indeed seeking a "revolutionary" new policy or even if we are serious about welfare reform, surely our objective must be to remove as many people as possible from this essentially dependency-creating program. Some gap-filling on an individual basis will, of course, always be necessary; for no program dealing with millions on a more formal basis and on the basis of averages, can hope to meet the emergent needs and special circumstances of all families. Our aim must be to keep this type of program to a minimum by dealing with people's needs for income in other, less highly individualized ways.

The most drastic but also the most effective method of limiting the role of gap-filling would be to utilize the demogrant. Under the demogrant, everyone would receive a payment equal to the defined guarantee, regardless of income, resources, or family status. The demogrant would, in principle, be taxable, though obviously people whose total income was no more than the minimum guarantee would not pay any income tax.

This is indeed a revolutionary, and perhaps at first sight a shocking, proposal. But the advantages of such an approach are many. Assuming that the guarantee is at least equal to the poverty line, it would meet need more certainly than any gap-filling program because, being paid out automatically, it would be nondiscretionary and predictable. There would be no problem of administrative delays in adjusting payments during the year to unexpected changes in income status. Incidentally, it would be much simpler and cheaper to administer.

It would thus reduce the role of gap-filling to a bare minimum, concerned primarily with emergencies such as loss of home and effects due to fire or theft or with special circumstances of families with unusual or nonrecurrent needs. Because it would be paid to individuals, adults and children, regardless of family status, it would remove any financial inducement to "fiscal desertion" by fathers, though like the gap-filling measures it would make it possible for some wives, now tied to their husbands by financial dependency, to separate and become independent.

Furthermore, the demogrant approach would have the advantage of treating the poor in regard to motivation and initiative in exactly the same way as the rest of us are treated. Society leaves us, the nonpoor, free to decide how much or how little we shall work, though we know full well that some fraction of our earnings will be claimed by Uncle Sam at the end of the year. But we do not trust the poor to behave that way. We insist on work requirements and build in incentives which have the incidental result of taxing the earnings of the poor, those who are receiving welfare payments, at a higher rate than that applied to many of the rest of the population. This anomaly would be avoided by the demogrant.

In sum, the demogrant would relieve the income-guaranteeing system of the onerous task of dealing with people individual by individual, and from trying to solve the problem of initiative. It would utilize the tax system as the single instrument for determining who among the population should contribute toward the costs of government and how much.

Such a program would, of course, involve a very sizable redistribution of income; for the net cost to be recouped from those with total incomes above the guarantee would be very large, though it must be recalled that their incomes too would have been increased by the demogrant. But we must face the fact that any program, gap-filling or other, that truly guarantees an income above the poverty line to all will call for a large measure of income redistribution. If we are unwilling to face this unpleasant truth, we should stop talking about abolishing poverty.

Payment of a demogrant would indeed run the risk that some employable people might be content to live upon the guaranteed minimum, and this may be a price we shall have to pay for the abolition of poverty. How large this group might be and therefore how high the price, we do not know, for our knowledge about initiative is still primitive. We base current policies largely on what folklore tells us was true of people at the beginning of the nineteenth century. I suggest that in the meantime, even if, as some believe, the Protestant work ethic has lost some of its force, there have been two major changes of which we have failed to take account in our concern about initiative. First, as a nation, we are much better off and can offer a sizable differential between the level of a realistic minimum guarantee and the income that can be secured by working. The "bait" can therefore be significant. Second, we have a literate population and are equipped with a magnificently effective advertising system, so that through television, newspapers, magazines, and other communications media, as well as window shopping, our people are constantly stimulated to further acquisitiveness and dissatisfaction with their current standard of living.

Where the demogrant approach compares least favorably with gap-filling is in regard to the efficiency objective, the desire for a system that does not make payments to those who are not needy. Yet even this disadvantage is less serious than appears at first sight. First, as already pointed out, the urge to build incentives into gap-filling programs involves making payments to people who are considerably above the poverty level. Second, it is possible to utilize the tax system to recoup all or part of the payments from those who are deemed not to need them. There is indeed every reason why we should make more use of the tax system to determine who shall receive social benefits "for free" and who should pay something for them. For we are rapidly becoming an income-tested society. We have income tests for medicaid, for subsidized housing, for day care, for scholarships, for school meals, for surplus foods and stamp plans. And the nature and level of the income test differs irrationally from program to program.

In any case, the concept of efficiency, so beloved by the economists, is restricted to a purely financial calculus. There are also social efficiencies and inefficiencies to be considered. Programs that deal only with "the poor" run the danger not only of being poor programs, but also of polarizing society into two groups, the poor and the nonpoor, with one receiving benefits and the other footing the bill. There is growing evidence of a rising resentment on the part of those just above the poverty line that everything is being done for the poor while they are neglected. A program that perpetuates this popularization is inefficient in my book. So is one that puts people in the position of applicants, dependent in some degree on administrative discretion. So is one that applies different theories of motivation to the poor and the nonpoor.

Even if at the present time we are not prepared for so drastic a policy as the universal demogrant, there are still many program changes we could adopt, bearing in mind that our overriding objective is to remove as many people as possible from the gap-filling system. We could utilize the demogrant on a more limited scale by paying it only to the aged, the totally disabled, and, above all, to children through a children's allowance program. This latter would have the great advantage of redressing the balance of social provision which now so shamefully neglects children or treats them less favorably than it does the aged. Even if we could remove only 50 percent to 75 percent of children from poverty through a children's allowance program rather than by gap-filling that would be a great step forward.

In any case, I suggest that we must abandon the will-o-the-wisp hunt for a single all-embracing income security measure. Even the demogrant would need to be complemented by a program of publicly assured jobs at standards wages, by training and retraining and relocation programs, by measures to remove the financial barrier to receipt of needed medical care, and by intensified efforts to promote family planning. What is needed is the development of a well-integrated series of measures, each directed toward one of the major causes of income insecurity. Thus, where the problem is loss or interruption of earning power (due to old age, disability, or temporary unemployment), social insurance with broadened coverage and more adequate benefits is an appropriate remedy. The needed changes would be more readily accomplished if, through the payment of a demogrant to the aged and a children's allowance, the social insurance system were relieved of the burden of providing minimum security for the aged and dependents' allowances, and could concentrate on replacing some fraction of previous earnings.

Where the problem is due to submarginal earnings, the remedy is minimum wage legislation and the provision of publicly supported jobs at standard wages. Where the cause of income inadequacy is size of family, a children's allowance is the obvious answer. Where income inadequacy is due to heavy, and usually temporary, drains on family income because of the cost of medical care, the remedy is a health insurance or national health service program. Where poverty is attributable to family breakdown, a children's allowance plus a mothers' allowance should be the answer. A mothers' allowance would rid us of our present ridiculous attitude toward the contribution of housewives to the gross national product. For it is not work to which we attach value, it is *paid* work. If a woman cares for someone else's husband and/or children for pay, she is "working" and praiseworthy; if she cares for her own husband and/or children, she is not.

The fact that we have to attack the problem on many fronts should not dismay us. We have perhaps been overhasty in dismissing the categorical approach to income security because of its inappropriateness when applied to gap-filling public assistance programs. Yet if the programs are devised to deal with categories that reflect the causes of income inadequacy, there are real advantages to categorized programs. They permit us to devise measures appropriate to the circumstance of identifiable classes of insecure people. Above all, by identifying the costs attributable to each type of threat to security, they increase the likelihood that we shall devote more effort to eradicating the causes and adopting preventive measures.

I am aware that not all of the reforms I am advocating will be accomplished overnight. But I conceive it to be the task of a conference of social workers to take the longer-run view and to give policy leadership. What is important is that we should be clear as to the direction in which we want to move. What is our ultimate objective? I insist that gap-filling programs are not the answer to prayer. We can indeed do much to improve the lot of those currently dependent on welfare by adopting a federal program that embodies some of the features of the negative income tax, such as a realistic federal minimum, wholly federally financed and administered, and this we should press for. The main objective of policy, nevertheless, must be to remove as many people as possible from contact with an essentially individualized, discretionary, and dependency-creating system that, however liberalized and by whatever name called, cannot escape the conflicting aims and fundamental weaknesses of all gap-filling programs.

Moral and Ethical Issues in Income Maintenance

I. A PROTESTANT VIEWPOINT

VICTOR OBENHAUS

O NE SERIOUS PROBLEM in providing subsidy for those in need is the apprehension that they will be corrupted by not having to work for what is received. Perhaps the obverse side of that coin is the resentment on the part of those who are engaged in work of any sort that someone else is receiving something without having to expend a corresponding amount of effort comparable to his own. The Nixon Family-Assistance Plan reveals both phases of our concern, presumably protecting those who are now working by giving the assurance that others are not going to be rewarded for failing to do so. The reasons for our apprehension are far too complex and deeply embedded in the human psyche to warrant an attempt at analysis here. From the theological perspective, this raises the whole question of human pride and sin. Suffice is to say, however, that there is a genuine element of justice in the complaint. Surely it goes even further back than the time when the Apostle Paul contended in his letter to the Thessalonians that he who does not work shall not eat.

A new continent waiting to be settled provided excellent opportunity for the manifestation of that Biblical injunction. Social work in America has been heavily influenced by this same philosophy. It probably did not originate in the Scriptures, but the Scriptures proved very helpful in putting pressure on the indolent. The indolent, of course, are those who do not have money, the nonworkers. Those who have been endowed either by family or by some lucky strike in real estate or who have won the Irish sweepstakes, or have achieved security by some other means, do not seem to be subject to the same indictment. In other words, we seem not to have a similar concern for those who do not *have* to work.

For whatever reason, then, we are deeply apprehensive of those who fail to exert the energy of which they are capable in order to merit assistance from either public or private sources. This becomes a moral issue because of the consequences to the nonworker and it exhibits a fundamental aspect of distributive justice. A Harris poll indicates that 28 percent of the American people favor giving income without work and 60 percent oppose it.

This anxiety about people getting something for nothing and the corresponding corruption of their capacities for creativity through the resulting indolence is frequently held up as a prostitution of the Protestant ethic. Incidentally, the Protestant ethic has little to do with Protestantism, the Bible, or the Reformation, which was the vehicle of Protestantism. As Roger Shinn has suggested, it was a creative cultural force for a certain epoch of history.[1] Max Weber is responsible for our use of the term in this sense.[2] Actually, this is, I believe, a perversion of what Weber was actually talking about. I doubt whether he would use the term in the current sense were he dealing with the issues before us. I have no desire to defend the term "Protestant" in this instance, but as Philip Wogaman has pointed out,[3] the term "Protestant ethic" is a distortion of both Protestantism and ethics. The true half of it lies in the concept of the importance of work, but the false half is that of establishing whether people are deserving of what God has given them and the subordination of man to work. Work was something man did to the glory of God. There was nothing in the concept that said that effort in art, song, sculpture, or what not might not also be to that glory. This is obviously no more Protestant than Catholic or Jewish,

1 Roger Shinn, "Ethical Perspectives on the Guaranteed Annual Income," *Social Action*, XXXIV, No. 3 (1967), 43.

2 Max Weber, *The Protestant Ethic and the Spirit of Capitalism* (New York: Charles Scribner & Sons, 1930).

3 Philip Wogaman, *Guaranteed Annual Income: the Moral Issues* (New York: Abingdon Press, 1968), p. 78.

Somehow in our evolution as a new nation we became insepar-
ably tied to the notion that productivity was money-making.
Therefore, he who vigorously pursued the practices involved in
adding to his income was presumed to fit within the Protestant
ethic. America's two best illustrations are Andrew Carnegie and
John D. Rockefeller. The latter could say with complete sincerity, "God gave me my money."

Ideas or acts are moral or ethical depending on the standards
against which they are evaluated. We are a people torn between
several sets of values. The so-called "American way of life" has
given us one set of values which places conformity to the ongoing
economic patterns and its consequent conduct over against
another set of values even more deeply embedded in our Western
culture. These have been derived from our Hebrew-Christian
rootage. They include the consequences to individual life from
the patterns of conduct and activity conventionally prescribed.
Generally speaking, most economists seem to have devised their
models within such a framework.

To many it is axiomatic that an individual who is not working
at something which is contributing to the economy is really not
working. What we are now confronted with, obviously, is the fact
that work itself is having to be largely rethought.

We are suspicious, and not without some reason, of the fact
that a person who is paid for doing nothing conventionally productive may take advantage of this and become a drag on society
at large. At the same time, we "know" that the economy at
present cannot use many of the persons whom we would rather
not pay for not working. Actually though, do we really know
this? Many women who would be provided income maintenance
would probably drop out of such employment as they now have
in order to provide more adequate care for children at home. A
look at the long-range ethical implications provides a substantial
answer here, but we have not been disposed to look at the long
range. What would society gain if many children who are now
unattended at critical years were to be afforded the supervision
and attention that every child requires? The forestalling of
family disintegration and warped lives is a basic ethical concern.

Quite apart, however, from the additional care which might be provided for youth by those who are taken off the conventional labor market there remains the widespread apprehension growing out of our work ethic that individuals would take advantage of the busy bees in society and would themselves live as drones. This, of course, overlooks the fact that we simply do not know what individuals would do if they had some freedom of choice. The Heineman Commission's report comments:

Our observations have convinced us that the poor are not unlike the nonpoor. Most of the poor want to work. They want to improve their potential and to be trained for better jobs. Like most Americans the poor would like to do something with their lives beyond merely subsisting.[4]

It goes on to say:

Exaggerated fears of massive work disincentive effects often have influenced discussions of income maintenance. Though those effects could be important, our fears should not lead us to forget the crippling effects of poverty. Men and women who are poor cannot afford to take risks. They are seriously impeded in making plans. They usually are precluded from accepting opportunities that require the investment of time or money. Most of their time and energies are absorbed in survival on a day to day basis. Once the poor are assured a minimum stable income they will be in a much better position to use other antipoverty programs.[5]

We did not require Karl Marx to inform us that a person is in a large measure shaped by his work. More definitive studies of attitudes and the consequences of our labors have indicated that relationship. If indolence were the principal outcome of a society without traditional work the consequences would, of course, be tragic. Is the opportunity for self-fulfillment worth the experiment? Obviously, we do not know the answer. We have not passed this way before. We are apparently moving in the direction of a substantially new conception of the meaning of work.

[4] *Poverty amid Plenty: the American Paradox,* the report of the President's Commission on Income Maintenance Programs (Washington, D.C.: U.S. Government Printing Office, 1969), pp. 59–60.
[5] *Ibid.,* p. 60.

INCENTIVES

Today we assume that a minimum education is the right of every person; so are certain political rights, those incorporated in our most hallowed national documents, such as life, liberty, and the pursuit of happiness. Though there is no theological justification for these rights spelled out in our documents, nevertheless they have been arrived at both by generations of experience, including great injustices, and by an increasing understanding of the dignity of man. Coming to grips with the moral and ethical issues involved has facilitated this accomplishment even though there are still some persons who are denied these rights through the pride, or ignorance, or sheer malice of other people. Is it not possible, then, that just as these rights have come to be accepted because they are morally and ethically justified, we may likewise come to accept basic economic existence as a right? When this is accomplished the question of incentives will be seen in a new light. Erich Fromm contrasts a psychology of scarcity which produces "anxiety, envy, egotism" with a psychology of abundance which "produces initiative, faith in life solidarity." He contends that "for the first time the guaranteed income would free man from the threat of starvation and thus make him truly free and independent from any economic threat. . . . It will also establish a principle rooted in western religious and humanist tradition; man has the right to live regardless!" [6]

We simply do not know what will provide incentive for creative and productive activity for the poor unless they are first assured minimal security. We do know that people who have had opportunity for training and who have been assured freedom from other activities can turn their attention to artistic creativity. I noted in a visit to Israel several years ago the way in which children of poverty who gave indication of skills were singled out and given the freedom to develop talents which otherwise would have gone unrecognized and unnourished. We cannot imagine the vast reservoir of talent untapped in America

[6] Erich Fromm, "The Psychological Aspects of the Guaranteed Annual Income," in Robert Theobald, ed., *The Guaranteed Income* (New York: Doubleday, 1965), p. 176.

because of the strangulation of poverty. The figures seem to indicate that from 15 to 30 million children may be restricted in their creative capacities simply because of their parents circumstances of poverty and deprivation. Surely the restriction on the fulfillment of potential in these children constitutes in itself a great moral and ethical issue, to say nothing of the consequences to their parents living in anxiety and fear beneath the poverty line.

It is interesting that the Administration's family-assistance plan is very sensitive to this matter of incentives. By its stipulation of work requirements it has sought approval from the skeptics who believe that only poverty or some kind of pressure is necessary to bring out innate capacities the fulfillment of society's demand for productivity.

It would be inaccurate, if not actually wrong, to suggest that payment for nonwork is the only alternative. A fundamental issue is the provision of work itself so that there is opportunity to go beyond the basic minimum which some authorities on family need may have stipulated. Many of the protest movements, even riots, have taken place not over relief allotments but over the lack of opportunities for work. Getting into the responsibility for providing jobs and the economics of work is beyond the limits of this presentation. I am simply affirming that any moral and ethical consideration of the problem of income maintenance must incorporate the question of incentives and the realization that we do not know what kinds of incentive are most effective in a system where the minimal essentials are assured. We do have substantial evidence, however, that people who live in fear and want and are treated as inferiors in the body politic are incapable of contributing constructively to society.

THE WELFARE STIGMA

Every person who works with the poor knows the consequences of the restrictions placed upon them by the limitations of income. In one sense, of course, we all face this. Less measurable and perhaps far more drastic are the defeat and humiliation with the consequent deterioration of spirit which go along with this implied inferiority. Any one of the many options of income maintenance may not eliminate this sense of restriction which comes with limited income. What it could do for the releasing of the human spirit we cannot estimate. Here, certainly, is the moral issue. The sense of degradation and inferiority which goes with having to accept alms has undercut the emotional vitality of a large segment of the nation. Not the least aspect of making a program of income maintenance available is the freedom of those who possess some conscious or unconscious sense of guilt for contributing to, or even being aware of, the deprivations of others. Granted that this may not be a very weighty or profound experience, it is a component of the total picture. Income maintenance may do something for others than the recipients.

There is more than a taint of suspicion that the poor have been kept poor to sustain the status structure in the nation. Perhaps this is more true of the Blacks, but it has implications for other segments of our society as well. The seeming necessity for supporting our social stratification system has contributed to humiliation and subsequent defeatism for many. Some form of income maintenance becomes a *sine qua non* to break this structure.

Up to this period in our national life we have assumed that: (1) our economy cannot support the amount which would be required to lift the people now in poverty above the poverty level; (2) we must not contribute to the disintegration or demoralization which would follow from allowing individuals to be supported by the rest of the economy even if work is not available for them; and (3) it is unfair to those who are engaged in productive work to have to sustain those who are unable to find work or who might take advantage of the new freedom if they were relieved of the necessity of working.

These are in part economic problems, but they are also philosophical, ethical, and moral problems. Up to now we have been primarily concerned with the economic aspects and the denial of distributive justice as it seemingly injures those who carry the burden of providing for the nonworkers. It may be all too easy to "cop out" on the economic aspects of this issue, but actually it must be reaffirmed that these are not primarily economic problems in an economy such as ours. Were we not engaged in a war which has consumed so large a portion of our nation's resources, we might be able to give more adequate attention to the fundamental ethical and moral issues involved.

We have arrived at a degree of humanization and economic achievement where we can insist that every child shall be reared in such circumstances of family security and educational opportunity that, barring physical or mental disability, he will be able to provide for himself at maturity. This is the new watershed of American accomplishment; its assumption simply awaits the recognition of moral and ethical responsibility.

Finally, for those who have at least some measure of religious orientation, there is the issue which underlies all others and which determines the moral and ethical aspects of income maintenance. It is the question of the nature of man himself. For those committed to the Hebrew-Christian tradition this implies that man has an ontic relationship, that he is a part of the very essence of life. The implication of this fact for man's identity and his social relationships lift the moral and ethical issues to the foremost place in consideration. Of course, this has implications for the economy, the utilization of resources, and distributive justice. It assumes that man is but a tenant on the space ship Earth and that the arrangements he makes for his existence take full cognizance of his fellow passengers. Income maintenance may contribute constructively toward assisting individuals to fulfill their potential in this relationship.

II. A CATHOLIC VIEWPOINT

REV. ROBERT P. KENNEDY

PERHAPS IT MIGHT BE WELL to list the issues:
1. Has a man a right to income maintenance?
2. If he has, whose is the duty to guarantee that right?

3. To what level of income maintenance is he entitled?

4. How does this relate to his obligation to work?

5. In what way is a man who receives income maintenance subject to the provider?

6. What right to reputation remains to one who receives income maintenance?

7. How is the right to income maintenance related to future development?

1. *The right to income maintenance.* The logic is simple. A man has a right to life. Income maintenance is part of that right to life. Therefore, a man has a right to income maintenance. The proof is more complex.

The fundamental right to life is acknowledged by all moral and ethical systems. In the tradition of Catholic social teaching, this right is always connected with a fuller development of what makes up the parts of this right.[1] There is also a very ancient and continuous tradition that links God's purpose in creation with this right to life and the duty of others to support this right through distribution of the goods of creation.[2]

So far as creation is concerned, God is the Master of Creation; therefore, creation is to be shared by all men according to their need, and the ownership of property, including the means of production, land, and wealth, is conditioned by an obligation to stewardship in regard both to God and their fellow men.[3] Property ownership is never an absolute right but one that is conditioned by, and subject to, the rights of others and of society in general.[4] Any economic system, therefore, must tend to maximize production until an optimum level is achieved and then, at least equally important, arrange for the distribution of the wealth created in as equitable a way as possible. Rewards are to be given to those who contribute the most to production of wealth, but all are to have an opportunity to share in the consumption, as determined by family needs.[5]

1 Pope John XXIII, "Peace on Earth," par. 11.
2 "The Church in the Modern World," in Walter M. Abbott, ed., *The Documents of Vatican II* (New York: Gill Press, 1966), par. 69, p. 278.
3 Pope Paul VI, "On the Development of Peoples," par. 23.
4 *Ibid.*, par. 22.   5 Pope John XXIII, *op. cit.*, par. 56.

This is important and must be stressed. It is man as the head of his family who must be considered in assaying his rights to income maintenance. Normally, family needs are to be taken care of by the wages that the worker earns, but when this cannot be done, income maintenance and family maintenance are intimately connected.[6]

2. *The responsibility to provide income maintenance.* Basically, all men have this responsibility, but the responsibility of all is the responsibility of none. As it is an essential element of the common good that men survive, it falls upon the State to take care of income maintenance.[7] If this action does not take place, conditions only worsen.[8]

It is through the State that society regulates the rights and duties of men so that the common good will be achieved. Therefore, it has a function of ordering both production and consumption so that the greatest good for the greatest number of people is achieved within a framework of justice and equity. It has an obligation to use its power to help those members of the population who are least able to help themselves.[9] Traditionally, these have always been the economically disadvantaged as well as those who because of mental, physical, or emotional disabilities can no longer provide for themselves, or those who because of social disadvantage or sickness or age no longer participate in the economic life of society. The State has a definite obligation to make sure that citizens share in consumption of the goods of society in relationship to their needs. Therefore, ethics demands that the State take the necessary steps and make the necessary arrangements to bring this about. Income maintenance and the necessary attendant health, education, and welfare services are an important part of the State's obligation.[10] If private groups, motivated by charity, were willing and capable of supplying these things to individuals and families, the State would be free

6 United States Bishops' Pastoral Letter, "On the Christian Family," 1949, in John F. Cronin, S.S., *Social Principles and Economic Life* (Milwaukee: Bruce Publishing Co., 1959), p. 202; Pope Pius XI, "On Christian Marriage," par. 127.

7 Pope Pius XI, "On Atheistic Communism," par. 133.

8 Pope John XXIII, *op. cit.,* par. 63.

9 Pope Leo XIII, "On the Conditions of Workers," par. 60.

10 Abbott, *op. cit.,* par. 75, p. 278; John XXIII, "Christianity and Social Progress," par. 59.

of its obligation. There is no evidence that this is so, and therefore the State must see to adequate income maintenance because it is tied with the right to life that the State is to protect for each of its citizens.

3. *Level of income maintenance.* The question of the level of support is a more difficult one to treat without involving oneself in the toils of the "dismal science" of economics and its statistical tables. Perhaps the descriptive note attached to the Bureau of Labor Statistics Lower Living Standard Budget is sufficient. The level of maintenance should allow "the maintenance of health and social well-being, the nurture of children and participation in community activities." [11] The budget figures that as of the spring of 1969, it cost $6,771 for a family of four living in New York–northeastern New Jersey to reach this level.

4. *Income maintenance and the obligation to work.* The question of how income maintenance relates to a man's obligation to work is perhaps the most difficult to answer. In one sense, the obligation to work is independent of a man's receiving income. Man is obliged to work, for he is the fulfillment of creation. It was not until man was created that God could see that His work was exceedingly good. The task of man in to complete the work started by God by making God's creation more useful and adaptable to human needs.[12] Man does this by impressing upon nature the mark of his personality, and in this way he shares in both the duty and the function of creation. Also, because man forms society, he works so that society may achieve a certain level of perfection, and thus his work has social implications since it is to be in the service of his fellow men. He works also to develop his own personality and to bring it to the full richness of his capability. He also works so that the future may become better and the city of man gradually develop into a higher likeness to the city of God.[13]

Because of the great dignity of human labor it cannot be re-

11 *Regional Labor Statistics Bulletin,* December, 1969, p. 15; Pope Pius XII, "Address to Italian Workers," June 13, 1943, in John F. Cronin, S.S., *Catholic Social Principles* (Milwaukee: Bruce Publishing Co., 1950), p. 304.

12 Abbott, *op. cit.,* par. 34.

13 *Ibid.,* par. 67, p. 232.

duced to an economic factor or forced into the framework of the law of supply and demand.[14]

Normally, family needs are to be taken care of by the wages that the working man earns. However, his obligation to work flows from human dignity and nature and not from his obligation to society.[15] Society's role is to enable him to exercise his rights and to guarantee him employment and security.[16]

The State has a serious obligation to foster those conditions in which each person can make a contribution to the furthering of creation by work. The State is to allow and foster the full development of each of its citizens. In a complex technological society where only some of the citizens are involved in production, the State might become a large-scale employer in the service part of the economic society.[17] Also, so that people will be able to express their creativity and service to their fellow men by making available a whole gamut of social services in education, art, and health, the State will supply income for such creative people since the law of supply and demand cannot set an economic value on their work.[18] There is a problem here which gives rise to the next issue.

5. *In what way is a man who receives income maintenance subject to the provider?* What is the morality of work requirements in relation to income maintenance?

Each individual should make a contribution to the society in which he lives. It is not enough to grant rights to income maintenance; all men must work together to produce a sufficient supply of goods and to carry on the many undertakings that modern civilization makes possible and demands. Able-bodied men have an obligation to perform work, and the State has an obligation to make work available and to insist on participation. The future of

14 United States Bishops' Pastoral Letter, "The Church and Social Order," 1940, in Cronin, *Catholic Social Principles*, p. 343.
15 Pope Pius XII, "La Solennità della Pentecote," June 1, 1944, in Cronin, *Social Principles* . . . , p. 165.
16 Pope Pius XII, "Pentecost Sunday," 1941; Pope John XXIII, "Christianity and Social Progress," par. 41.
17 Pope Pius XII, "To Catholic International Congresses for Social Study and Social Action," June 3, 1950, in Cronin, *Social Principles*. . . , p. 45.
18 Pope Pius XI, "The Reconstruction of the Social Order," par. 71; Pope Pius XI, "On Atheistic Communism," par. 75.

a society depends on its children, and despite the dismay of the Women's Liberation Front, the function of child rearing is still the mother's role in our society. Therefore, no other demand can be made on her but the fulfillment of her obligation to her children.

In general, the State should work to bring about a climate in which full employment is possible, and serve as an employer of last resort rather than use coercion. Today it is commonly agreed that the common good is best maintained when personal rights are safeguarded. It is better to safeguard liberty of action than to work out elaborate schemes of forced work. The myth of the idle, undeserving poor has almost no factual basis and often seems to be a psychological projection of those who are unwilling for the State to fulfill its obligation.[19]

6. *Right to reputation.* Allied to this is the issue of the right to his reputation that the recipient of income maintenance has. Unfortunately, those who receive income maintenance are fair game at every cocktail party, congressional hearing, or gathering of so-called "concerned" taxpayers. Traditional morality has always protected the right of a person to his good name and so held detraction to be more serious than theft since a good name is better than wealth. Calumny adds the further injustice of lack of truth in the accusation.[20] Both require that the harm done be repaired in an efficacious and positive way. This is true even if one is talking about a class of people rather than an individual.[21]

The Roman Catholic bishops of New York State discussed this subject in a joint pastoral letter in December, 1969:

What is most disturbing to us is that rather than address ourselves to the root causes of poverty, to direct our energies to a just and equitable distribution of the goods of creation, we tend to engage in invectives about the poor and the maligning of their moral character. The dependency of the poor is becoming a source of divisiveness

19 Pope John XXIII, "Peace on Earth," par. 11-38, 46-66.
20 For an example of traditional treatment of detraction and calumny, see Henry Davis, S.J., *Moral and Pastoral Theology*, L. W. Geddes, S. J., ed. (7th ed.; New York: Sheed and Ward, 1958), XI, 417-20.
21 *Ibid.*, pp. 332-34.

rather than an opportunity for working together to remedy the fundamental causes of poverty and to find in sharing, the meaning of brotherhood.[22]

In brief, people have a right to be helped and a right to be understood and a right not to be talked about.[23]

7. *Income maintenance and the future.* A final issue is to determine how the right to income maintenance affects the future. There is the present crisis that must be taken care of, but future development must be provided for as well.[24]

The answer to this serious problem cannot be found in some new order that is to be established. It is not really practical to hope that by a better use of technology in the near future, prosperity for all men will automatically happen and lead to a constantly raised standard of living and full employment. The lesson of history must force us to be skeptical. There is no necessary connection between a high degree of productivity and the realization of human values. Every plan or program must be inspired by the principle that man can never be just an object that he must be a subject, that is, the guardian and promoter of human values, and as such he is more important than mere things.[25]

There is hope that in the long run the economy will solve its problems and overcome technological unemployment. However, as a famous economist said, in the long run we are all dead. No country can face the inevitable increase of technological unemployment without doing something about it. We cannot sacrifice the present generation for the advantages that might come to future ones.[26] The whole question of how a man receives money for his livelihood requires a new approach. New criteria will have to be adapted to estimate the value of a man and establish new definitions of just what work is and how man makes a

22 Joint pastoral letter of the Roman Catholic bishops of New York State, *Brooklyn Tablet*, November 26, 1969, p. 1.

23 Pope Pius XII, "To 'Stations de Plein Air' Movement," May 3, 1957, in Cronin, *Social Principles . . .* , p. 228; Pope Pius XII, "Christmas Message," 1952, in *Selected Addresses and Letters of His Holiness Pope Pius XII*, arranged by Maurice Quinlan (London: Pan Books, 1959), p. 134.

24 Abbott, *op. cit.*, par. 70, pp. 79–80.

25 Pope Pius XII, "Christmas Message," 1952, in Quinlan, *op. cit.*, p. 134.

26 Pope Pius XII, "To Christian Union of Executives and Businessmen," March 7, 1957, in Cronin, *Social Principles . . .* , p. 203.

contribution to society. We have to look at just what must be done about the whole relationship of human need and income distribution. Human need must be considered the most important factor and what is a fair share must be determined by Christian justice and Christian charity.

Income maintenance is tied to the future in the sense that it is a capital investment of society in the development of its children. Children cannot grow in poverty and destitution.[27] Certain conditions are less human and impair development; others are more human and aid it. Income maintenance has much to do with overcoming the former and fostering the latter.[28]

However, the underlying issue in all the discussions of income maintenance is really a more general one. "The world is sick. Its illness consists less in the unproductive monopolization of resources by a small number of men than in the lack of brotherhood among individuals and peoples." [29] "The exclusive pursuit of possessions thus becomes an obstacle to individual fulfillment and to man's true greatness. Both for nations and for individuals man's avarice is the most evident form of moral undevelopment." [30]

The solution is a sense of brotherhood that in Christian theology revolves around seeing Christ in our brothers [31] and the one mind and heart that enables goods to be used in common.[32] "The obligation of every man, the urgent obligation of the Christian man, is to reckon what is superfluous by the measure of the needs of others and to see to it that the administration and the distribution of created goods serve the common good." [33]

27 Pope Paul VI, "On the Development of Peoples," par. 6.
28 *Ibid.*, par. 20–21.   29 *Ibid.*, par. 66.   30 *Ibid.*, par. 19.
31 Matt. 25:31–45.   32 Acts 4:32.
33 Pope John XXIII, radio-television message, September 11, 1962, cited in Abbott, *op. cit.*, par. 69 footnote.

Decision-Makers in Social Policy

ALAN K. CAMPBELL

THE QUESTION, "Who makes social policy?" is but a specialized version of the broader question: Who governs? Political scientists have been investigating that question since at least the time of Plato and Aristotle. Plato, of course, asked the value-oriented version of the question: who ought to govern. Aristotle, however, began the stream of research pointed to the more empirical question: who, in fact, governs.

Since Aristotle, political scientists have approached this question both broadly and narrowly: from trying to determine who actually governs the nation to the much more restricted issue of "Who runs this town?" Within the American context the answers have been as far-ranging as the approaches. Those selected for power structure membership include a small social-economic elite, political party bosses, Congressional committee chairmen, ethnic group leaders, and "the effete Eastern intellectual establishment."

SOCIAL POLICY

Since there is little agreement on who in general governs, it is not likely that agreement will be found on the question of who makes social policy. The question, however, raises the issue whether those who make social policy are different from those who make other kinds of policy, such as foreign policy, agricultural policy, defense policy, urban policy. Or, relative to the total governmental system, are there differences in who makes national policy, state policy, and local policy?

Social policy does differ from other types of policy, and these differences are of a character that makes the discovery of who formulates it most difficult. Policies in agriculture, business regulation, and the like, are directed to specific, easily defined groups. Social policy is more like urban policy. The clients are diffuse, normally unorganized, and, even more significant, social policies are designed for people primarily in their consuming roles rather than their producing roles. Yet, society to the extent that it is organized into interest groups tends to organize around production rather than consumption roles.

Another general characteristic of policy, which applies with particular force to social policy, is that it is often a product of legislation passed to accomplish other purposes. For example, during the 1930s housing legislation was prompted more by the desire to increase employment in the construction industry than it was to meet the housing needs of the nation; certainly it was not designed to expedite the movement of people from city to suburbia, which proves to be one of its outcomes. The same kind of comment could be made about highways, health, agriculture, and most other domestic policies. The unintended consequences of legislation have perhaps had more to do with shaping social policy than programs designed specifically for that purpose.

Despite these difficulties in determining who makes social policy, there are interpretations of the American political process which at least provide some clues, while simultaneously indicating the likelihood that the American political process will produce policies relevant to genuine social need.

COALITION POLITICS

The most common description of the American political process is coalition-making. Groups with quite diverse interests have come together and by trading support for each other's programs put together, at least on a temporary basis, majority support for their disparate needs.

The great periods of economic reform in America were from 1870 to 1914 and the New Deal years. The politics of reform in these two periods were strikingly similar. The political base consisted of a strong coalition of farmers, small businessmen, and organized labor. The coalition was a national one with influence primarily on national public policy, but also to a less extent on state and local public policy.

As political parties and interest groups have struggled since the end of the Second World War to put together a new majority coalition, the result has been long periods of policy stalemate accompanied by an occasional short period of significant policy output. The most notable example is, of course, the time immediately following President Kennedy's assassination and the first year following President Johnson's election. The coalition of these years was short-lived.

Other partial explanations of American politics revolve around the power structure interpretation, the social-economic variables explanation, and "expert" policy-making. None of these explanations is entirely satisfactory, but each makes a contribution to our understanding of the nature of the political process.

ELITIST DOCTRINE

Since the Second World War, political scientists have placed considerable emphasis on determining who runs America's local communities. Out of this research has emerged an elitist doctrine which claims that policy-making is controlled by a small group of social and civic leaders. Not all studies have produced the same results, but this pattern has been the most common.

This research has undergone much criticism, and there are many who argue that it is the technique used in attempting to discover who possesses power that determines who will be found.

A sometimes acrimonious debate has grown out of the findings of these studies. The debate has been centered on the issue of whether community power is held by a single elite or by several overlapping elites. The anti-single elitists argue that the methodology used by the elitist make the findings of a single elite inevitable. This technique, usually called the "reputational" method, locates its governing elite by the use of many informants. As an individual's name appears on more and more lists, he is then interviewed and his role in community affairs investigated. Through this process a single elite is isolated and described.

Critics suggest that a better method is to examine specific policy areas or issues and to determine who does make the decisions in these areas. This approach permits the emergence of several governing groups, if, indeed, there are several.

It is true that the use of these two techniques has often resulted in finding different systems of power relations. It is quite possible that the results of individual studies accurately reflect community differences: some communities are elitist in their government and others pluralistic.

If such differences from community to community could be classified and translated into meaningful variables, it would then be possible to test the relevancy of such differences to the policy decisions, social and otherwise. Students of power structure tend to assume that the power arrangements which exist in a particular community are the inevitable result of the social-economic characteristics of that community. In other words, the system is assumed to be a product of its environment and one which will change only as the social-economic characteristics of the individual community change.

We do not know whether a community governed by a single elite is more likely to respond wisely to pressing social problems than one which is governed by overlapping elites. Nor do we know what difference it makes who composes the single elite, or what groups make up the pluralistic system. What difference does it make, for example, if there is a tendency to draw governing individuals from commercial rather than manufacturing interests? Or from labor leadership rather than from socially prominent individuals?

On the whole, these efforts to identify community leadership have not improved our understanding of the public policy-making process. It appears unlikely that differences in local leadership have much impact on over-all social policy-making. Rather, such responses tend to be more a product of the national social climate than of who possesses local political power, whether through formal office or informal influence.

THE "BLACK BOX" STUDIES

This negative conclusion is to some degree confirmed by a recent set of studies. These studies have attempted to determine the causation of different policy decisions in different kinds of communities by examining the differences in characteristics of these communities. It is also possible to analyze through appropriate statistical techniques the differences in policy outputs in each of the fifty states, particularly as measured by differences in fiscal levels of support for public programs.

There is a considerable body of literature which attempts to relate differences in basic social-economic characteristics and differences in the political process to various policy decisions as measured by levels of resource support. In these studies, the most important determinants have been found to be differences in the social-economic characteristics of the population of the policy-making unit, usually the state. One of the matters most disturbing to political scientists is the implication that what goes on in the little "black box" (the political process) is not significant. Variables which tested the impact of variations in party systems, in party control, in the characteristics of legislators, and in the relative role of legislatures and governors, have all tended to be overpowered by income levels, educational attainment, and other social characteristics of the population.

Such evidence is by no means conclusive, but it does suggest that the political process is very complex, and that it is difficult to measure its impact. Further, it illustrates what political scientists have known for a long time; many of those involved in politics are there for personal rewards, not because of any great interest in policy-making except as policy decisions can be used to support the personal reward system. In other words, success is dependent upon being able to interpret the public mood rather than upon providing policy leadership. If the "public mood" is a product of socioeconomic characteristics, then the reason for their importance in determining policy is clear.

THE NEW SOCIAL MANAGERS

Another interpretation is that the outputs of the American political process are more and more determined by the new managers of society. Armed with the techniques of computerized decision-making, they use these tools to make very precise decisions as to what is needed to solve social problems. The war on poverty is often offered as an example of this kind of policy-making. It is argued that the legislation which produced this program did not come about because of any great public demand; nor was it adopted because one, two, three or more major interest groups demanded it. The originators of the bill were essentially experts in the social field, some from within the bureaucracy and some from without. The war on poverty was the product of a rational analysis of the characteristics and problems of American society and, on the basis of that analysis, contained a series of programs designed to meet underlying causation.

Daniel P. Moynihan argues that the origin of the effort cannot be explained in deterministic terms. It was a rational rather than a political event. "The record is that of a set of ideas making their way from university lecture rooms and professional journals to the halls of Congress and the statute books of the national government." [1] This interpretation of the source of the war on poverty is in my judgment largely true, and perhaps explains why the program was so short-lived. To survive, any program needs strong political support. Without that support, other priorities will push it aside.

POLITICAL SUPPORT

If political support is necessary for making and continuing a particular social policy, the question becomes whether a coalition sufficiently strong to produce and support meaningful social policy can be created. It seems doubtful. Perhaps a stalemate has been reached in American politics. Perhaps the democratic system is simply not able to respond to a situation in which the

[1] Daniel P. Moynihan, *Maximum Feasible Misunderstanding* (New York: Free Press, 1969), p. 6.

majority is unwilling to take action which a minority insists is necessary. Democratic theory requires that minorities be allowed to make their wishes known through free speech, right of assembly and of petition, and a free press, but it does not require that policies be adopted to meet their demands.

What do minorities do in this situation? Joseph Featherstone suggests:

They have two perennial weapons of the underdog: the appeal to universal values—equality, justice—America says it lives by, and the threat of disruption. The first has produced some gains, but is not likely to carry them very much farther, and the second is wearing dangerously thin.[2]

THE COALITION ALTERNATIVE

Another alternative, the coalition, has worked to some extent in American politics in the past. Minorities have joined together, thus creating a majority with a sufficiently diversified program to meet at least some of the demands of each. Is such a coalition now possible? There is overwhelming evidence that it is unlikely. The various minority groups simply do not have enough in common to agree on a program. It is somehow difficult to imagine that a political coalition of civil rights groups, college students, clergymen, and the poor can replace the familiar triad of organized farmers, organized labor, and small businessmen.

Some have argued that strong and well-articulated political leadership could provide the necessary glue to put together a new coalition. It is suggested that if society could be made aware of the problems it faces, and their consequences, the voters would support the kind of action needed. However, no social scientist—be he sociologist, psychologist, or political scientist—has been able to predict or even provide the basis for understanding what produces such leadership and under what conditions it is effective. Nevertheless, it seems unlikely that such leadership could come from any source in the American political system other than "the bully good pulpit" which Theodore Roosevelt believed the President's office to be.

2 Joseph Featherstone, "Anti-City, a Crisis of Authority," *New Republic*, August 23 and 30, 1969, p. 22.

Leadership from the private sector is perhaps a meaningful alternative, and to some extent it is being tested by John Gardner and the Urban Coalition. Whether the Urban Coalition can do more than provide some legitimacy for the demands which are being made on the system is still not clear. There is little evidence to date, however, that it possesses the necessary political muscle to accomplish the changes it champions.

It has been suggested that a program is needed whose components are sufficiently diverse to attract a much wider range of support than do currently proposed social policies. James Reichley says that what is needed is a total program for the reconstruction of our entire society.

In this way, the interest as well as the moral sympathy of the suburban and out-state majority could be touched. Creation of such a program and development of political enthusiasm that would be needed to put it into effect are, of course, unlikely, but they are not impossible.[3]

However, the groups who might form the basis for such a coalition see their interests as competitive rather than complementary. The lower-middle-income person does not recognize a commonality of interests with those who need some form of income maintenance. The factory workers and the construction workers do not see that their interests would be served by opening up union membership to those who are now excluded.

THE REPUBLICAN STRATEGY

With these kinds of antagonism dominating the American political scene, it seems doubtful that a program capable of binding the groups together in common political action could be developed. No political party today has found the right formula. Further, if the strategy suggested for the Republican party by Kevin P. Phillips,[4] is followed, that party will not even try. Rather, Phillips' plan is for a coalition which will actually respond to most of the crucial social needs.

3 A. James Reichley, "The Political Containment of Cities," in Alan K. Campbell ed. *The States and the Urban Crisis* (Englewood Cliffs, N.J.: Prentice Hall, 1970), p. 195.
4 Kevin P. Phillips, *The Emerging Republican Majority* (New Rochelle, N.Y.: Arlington House, 1969).

It is possible that the recent emphasis on environment does offer an alternative approach. The deterioration of the environment contains dangers and problems for all citizens; not just for the poor but for cityite and suburbanite alike, and even for the farmer, who is dependent upon metropolitan areas for markets and services. With this substantial common interest it is, perhaps, possible that a program mix could be developed which would serve all.

The mix would include, at a minimum, education and health services, pollution control, adequate housing, and jobs for all. The problem would not be one of finding areas of common concern, but rather of finding solutions which would satisfy all concerned. All solutions require resources, however, and the allocation of such resources often produces political quarrels and deep societal division.

There is, for example, no easy way to convince the suburban homeowner that he should pay more taxes to improve education in city ghettos. Similarly, the middle-income taxpayer does not look with favor upon providing government-supported health insurance so that his low-income fellow citizens may obtain health services. Thus, finding areas of common interest is not sufficient. The present system, in which power resides with the majority, makes it highly unlikely that a permanent minority, if such exists, could ever acquire sufficient influence to overcome majority resistance to their demands.

SOCIAL SCIENCE

This rather dismal outlook for new directions in social policy must be modified by admitting the inability of the social scientist to predict with accuracy. The social scientist, like the politician, tends to argue that things are as they are because that is the way the underlying forces make them. The new scientific thrust of the social scientist has removed, particularly from political science, its reform orientation. The quality of social science research has improved as a result, but the findings take on an inevitability characteristic.

Since his tools are only precise enough at best to explain why things are as they are, the social scientist often misses important shifts or movements in these underlying forces. Thus, predictive ability is small indeed.

The social scientist's explanation of the current situation, however, does lead me to believe that the crucial need of social policy-making is not the issue of what ought to be done but rather the political question of how to get it done. In my judgment, Moynihan is quite wrong when he suggests that social scientists have little if anything to contribute to the making of social policy. They have much to contribute, and many of the programs they have designed along with their professional colleagues in education, welfare, mass transit, and housing are clearly pertinent to the problems they are intended to solve. The failure of the social scientist has not been in the development of policy but in the field of political persuasion. Many would argue that he does not belong there. Whether he does or not, thus far his contribution has been small.

To understand, therefore, who makes social policy it is not sufficient to examine the role of political influentials in Congress or the relative roles of causal factors. It is necessary to look to the environment of decision-making. That environment is a product of the views, prejudices, and ideas of the public at large and, in many instances, that public's views are not, as is so often assumed, consistent with those of so-called "opinion leaders." Although negative, the deep vein of disillusionment which Spiro Agnew and George Wallace have discovered in the American body politic is perhaps a more significant determinant of the kinds of social policy which legislators and executives are likely to promote than are the views of the editorial writers of the New York *Times* or the underlying emphases of network newscasters.

Thus, the issue becomes whether a major shift in public attitudes can be anticipated. No one knows the answer, but it would seem incumbent upon those of us who have some expertise in social policy, whether we are in academic institutions or in public or private agencies, to continue the kind of research and analysis necessary to the formulation of viable policies. Society is exceedingly complex, and no longer can programs emerge full-blown from the heads of politicians, legislators, or cabinet secretaries. Rather, there needs to be substantial background research, and this research needs to be more policy-oriented. Further, recommendations must be much more comprehensive than they have been. Both government and academic institutions tend to be organized in ways which produce fragmented policy recommendations—policies pointed specifically toward solving individual problems, be they in education, welfare, or transportation. There is a need for an over-all framework for social policy in order that the unintended consequences of specific policy thrusts can be minimized. No longer is it possible, for example, to decide where a highway should go, or whether a mass transit system should be adopted, by simply analyzing traffic. Instead, transportation policy, like policy in so many other areas, must be related to residential patterns, to the distribution of economic activities, to the relative needs of very different kinds of population.

Such attention to comprehensiveness is a particular obligation of those of us who are outside government. We are not locked into the bureaucratic system in the way that many of our government colleagues are, nor are we tied to the vested concerns of a particular functional area. If there has been any failure on the part of the student of social policy, it has been his failure to recognize the necessity to develop policy recommendations which cut across the functional divisions represented by government organizations, as well as those discipline divisions which have for too long regulated his own academic work.

Perhaps even more pressing is the need for broad-gauged extensive research about the political process. The examination of the minutiae of decision-making must be, if not abandoned, at least accompanied by more general approaches to the examination of that process.

Neither I nor any other academic person whose work I know can definitely answer the question of who makes social policy. That inability is illustrative of how social science, by its insistence on following an unachievable scientism, has failed to provide the policy leadership needed. Perhaps a great deal of the discontent and unhappiness on our campuses is a result of student recognition of this failure.

I do not know who makes social policy. I do know this: we are not doing it very well. I also know, from my own knowledge and values, that political support for the kind of social policies that is needed does not exist. If that message is too negative, then I can only plead that it is an honest effort to report reality as I see it.

Institutionalized Racism
in Social Welfare Agencies

DAN W. DODSON

WE ARE LIVING in a climate of white backlash and racial acrimony. The Republican party succeeded in forging a coalition between the institutionalized bigotry of the South and the conservative elements of the remainder of the country to win the election in 1968. The party of Lincoln now has the albatross of institutionalized Southern bigotry around its neck.

The unwillingness of the Justice Department to enforce school desegregation, the recommendations on "benign neglect," the alteration of the nature of the Supreme Court, all suggest the pressure on the Nixon Administration to pay its debt for Southern support. These actions also indicate the insight of the Kerner Commission when it dubbed the white society "racist." What that term implies is not alone that individuals are prejudiced, but that the entire society, including its institutions, is racist.

If social agencies, then, are to meet their obligation to the day and age in which they serve, they must examine their own structures to discover whether they too are infected with the virus of racism and, if possible, find ways of ridding themselves of this infection. If there is one challenge for the seventies, surely this is it.

Let us begin by admitting that practically all social welfare agencies are historically innovations of the power arrangement of society to deal with social welfare. To the extent to which these are voluntary associations working within the power arrangement to serve those in power, they are exemplary. It is quite thrilling to observe middle-class people come together in their communities to do things for themselves which public effort cannot or will not do. If one has any criticism, it would be that sometimes these efforts to provide service for one's own drain off the desire to provide service for all. For instance, it is nice for the PTA in a middle-class neighborhood to run benefits to raise money for movie projectors or curtains for the school stage. However, if their activity stops, leaving the children in low-income neighborhoods without this same equipment for their schools, the attendant unshared privilege becomes corrupting. Voluntary associations are all right when they make possible services within the system which are not otherwise provided.

The difficulty with voluntarism is that it becomes a panacea by means of which the powerful serve the powerless. Under these circumstances the powerless can receive services only under the rituals laid down by the powerful. It means that service is geared to the goals of the dominant society. The goal is either to "squirt enough welfare on the powerless" so that they will be willing to remain "content in Egypt rather than to seek the promised land"—as is sometimes the case—or else the most often professed, that of involving them with, and bringing them into membership in, the dominant group. This latter process might be thought of as socialization. The model is to get the powerless person involved, get him to participate, alienate him in his sympathies and sentiments from the group of which he is a part, and get him to subscribe to the mythology of the dominant group. There is no panacea for serving powerless people under this type of goal except to "wash" them through this process and transmute them into reasonable facsimiles of the dominant group members.

Since blacks tend to be powerless people, this means that those with the mythologies which are being copied become the Brahmins. Their standards are those against which the worth of the black is measured—almost always to his disadvantage—and they become, as a consequence, racist in nature. Not many agencies would know how to program their service in any manner other than to alienate the black from his group, make him ashamed of who he is, instill in him what is familiarly called "group self-hate," a depreciation of his race and an overidealization of the dominant group. (It should be noted that this has been characteristic of the second generation of every minority which has been served in America.) The goal is to make him a "black Anglo-Saxon." It is what some blacks call "cultural genocide" that is being practiced on their youth.

The private agency has been the chief broker for the power structure. It has been the instrumentality through which millions of minority persons in the past have become socialized into the ethos of the dominant society. It has provided sufficient service for the majority of the powerless groups to keep them tranquilized. At the same time, such agencies have provided some escalation for the few bright ones who were siphoned off, leaving the remainder to stew in their impotence. America was never forced to become truely democratic and to make adjustments to a genuinely pluralistic society. Its agencies helped the siphoned-off members of the minorities to escape detection, once they had acquired the manners, language, and dress of the dominant group. In other words, those who were siphoned off "passed," if one uses the terminology of the present minority, the black group. The agencies thus helped shield the power arrangement from confrontation, and from pressure to change.

In this respect, the black is in a different situation from that of other minorities in our history. His color prevents him from escaping his identity. Furthermore, the technological revolution has necessitated his leaving the rural sections and moving to the heart of our large cities. There is no influx of new populations to push him out to the suburbs, as has happened to minorities in past years. Hence, he is challenging the entire system in ways never before possible. He is demanding that the society be restructured so that it is more human, rather than that he be expected to succumb to the mythology of the dominant society. This is creating confrontation, conflict, and disruption of the process operated by the power group.

It is not enough to diagnose these problems. Where do we go from here? Let me suggest some possibilities.

LEGITIMATION

First, all institutional services must become legitimated in the lives of the persons served. Heretofore, those without power had to become "rice Christians," no matter how galling to selfhood, if they were to receive services. Yet, many of the poor preferred to do without services rather than accept them on these terms. Tomorrow, with the federal government putting a floor under income, the people in this segment of the population will no longer allow themselves to be used in the "tear-jerker appeals" that exploit their impotence for the aggrandizement of some social agency. In the future, the agencies will not be able to advertise how many they "save" by their services.

A democratic society presumes that those served as well as those who operate the agency work through the principle of "the consent of the governed." This means that consumers of services as well as those who provide them must participate in policy-making. No agency of the future can do things "for the blacks." The agency in its entirety, from board to consumer, must be conceived as a partnership. Otherwise, the black community is likely to interpret the service as "welfare colonialism," as one agency proposing services for Harlem, has already learned.

What can be done to legitimate the institutions?

1. *Nondiscrimination in services.* It seems almost too obvious to mention, but elimination of all discrimination in services must be the first step. The United Methodist Church found in a recent survey [1] that in the homes for the aged which it operates, 98.4 percent of the tenants were white. In their homes for children, 94 percent were white. Yet the church claims some 500,000 blacks as members, about 5 percent of the total membership.

Many agencies have become quasi-public, yet they insist on "creaming" the easy-to-serve clients, leaving the others to be served by public agencies if they are served at all. This is par-

1 Reported in the New York *Times,* April 23, 1970.

ticularly true in education, camping, and many aspects of health. This means that there is a built-in racism here, for in many communities the poor are the blacks.

Many discriminations are subtle and represent downright racist arrogance. Not long ago an obviously poor Puerto Rican was turned away from one of New York's best hospitals. He had come to have his "stitches taken out," but he was late for his appointment. He was told abruptly that he would have to make another appointment, that he could not be served when he was one hour late.

Another example of institutional arrogance is the selection of intake in the name of "training leadership." One youth-serving-agency bused in youths from outlying regions, neglecting the blacks on its doorstep, in the name of training the leadership. This is racism at its subtlest.

2. *Nondiscrimination in control.* The boards of most agencies are made up of status persons from the community. Too often, those who are black are not recognized as status persons. Again, the United Methodist Church study reported that only 14 of its 1,463 hospital board members were black. This amounts to 99 percent white—almost the standard that a famous soapmaker sets for purity.

Under these circumstances, it is hard to imagine such agencies being "of the people." By and large, they are *for* the people, under policies set by the dominant society. A courageous neighborhood house director resigned recently because his board, whose members lived outside the community served, insisted on making an award to the governor, who, in the eyes of the agency's clients, had been instrumental in cutting welfare services.

The mere fact that they are black does not necessarily mean that those who may be selected for policy-making roles will be representative of the people. In one city, after a riot, the power structure had to employ a militant off the street to "tell it to them like it is," for the blacks on whom they had traditionally relied were then as unacceptable as were the whites—they were "washed persons," black Anglo-Saxons. When such a situation exists, the tendency is for the powerless to withdraw in apathy.

3. *Nondiscrimination in employment.* In the name of employment standards, many agencies lose their legitimacy in the black community. Agencies frequently consider it better to have high standards than to serve people. Not the least of the problem is their demand that agency workers have social work degrees. The time has come to reexamine the credentials trap. It should not make any difference whether or not a person has such a degree, provided he has the competence.

Then there is the matter of the employment test. It is incongruous that the Civil Service type of test, which for years stood as the best measure of fairness in employment, should now be complemented with batteries of personality and aptitude tests, and that these *en toto* become a symbol of discrimination. We need continuously to ask whether the test is relevant to the job to be performed. In most instances it is not. It has become a means of screening out those who would not uphold the desired image of the agency. The image of the agency is not unlike that of the neighborhood school—when it becomes "too black" it tends to be thought of as "second-class." Less is expected of it; standards fall. It fulfills the prophecy that it would become "Jim Crow." This is racism at its worst. All of us wish to maintain racially balanced programs in our agencies. The fear of imbalance should not allow us to close doors of economic opportunity and leadership for the minority.

Closely related are differences in life style. We often do not want our agency to become contaminated by the language, manners, and dress of the minorities. We cringe when we think how it would look for our representatives to wear dashikis, Afro hairdos, and loud or eccentric dress. We often place image above competence, and in this we are racist.

SOCIAL ACTION

The second suggestion is a plea for social action. The agency must identify with the upthrust of the human spirit in these minority communities, and make common cause so that the society will be restructured. It is the arrogance of the power arrangement that makes it and its agencies willing to serve the needy, but unwilling to change the structure so that these same people will not be needy. Policy statements and protestations make little difference in dealing with racial attitudes. The Roper Data Service says that in all the polls it has taken in America, no statistical difference has been found between church people and nonchurch people on issues of social concern.

If preaching, teaching, praying, and pleading could have restructured society, it would have been done a long time ago.

The fact of the matter is that it is very difficult to teach morality. Morality emerges out of the quality of relationships which exist between people. If one wishes to change the structure of the society so that it will be more moral, one must engage in social action. Restructuring cannot be accomplished by teaching. William Heard Kilpatrick's famous dictum that "people learn what they live," not what they are taught, is to the point.

In this respect another aspect of the situation seems clear. James and Lange [2] in their theory of emotion contended that people are frightened because they run, not the other way around. May it not also be the same with prejudice? May it not be that people hate because they discriminate rather than discriminate because they hate? The major discrimination in America is practiced by people of good will who lead personal lives of piety—and of unshared privilege, living in housing which does not admit blacks, working in employment which excludes blacks, enjoying recreation which is restricted to their own kind. It becomes necessary, under these circumstances, for them to develop rationalizations as to why they are entitled to such advantages beyond those of the other race. These rationalizations become racist dogma. They are stereotypes which pervade every aspect of social life. The white society will be a racist society supported by appropriate mythologies [3] so long as the social structures remain as they are.

If the agencies wish to alter this situation, they must assist in altering the structures through which we relate to each other as

[2] William James, *Psychology* (New York: Henry Holt, 1890).
[3] I use "mythology" here in the sense of only partially true stories and legends of groups, which are usually accepted as historical.

races. This is a social action job, not a teaching job and not a service job. It is programming to make service less necessary. The black community has come to perceive the acid test of sincerity to be whether groups will make common cause with them through social action, when the chips are down. In the school boycotts in New York City the agencies' coalition fell apart when action was called for. This was the real test. Most needs for service represent dysfunctions of the system. It is racial arrogance which allows an agency to continue to provide service without also being concerned to change the system through social action.

REEXAMINATION OF THE MYTHOLOGY

We must reexamine the mythologies on which our programs rest. For the most part, the agencies have not been able to elicit creative participation from the black community. Aside from the fact that the agencies are not indigenous to them, they are surfeited with mythology which precludes effective work in such black neighborhoods. Largely, these rationalizations are efforts to keep attention focused on the limitations of the human potential, and away from the limitations of our agencies. One wades through such clichés as "low I.Q.," "low social class," "weak ego strength," "lack of father with whom to relate," "inability to forego immediate pleasures for long-range goals," "matriarchal domination," "cultural deprivation," and now "lack of preschool stimulation." Remember when the professionals said that the poor could not be induced to participate, and that it was impossible to get grass-roots participation from tar pavements? Then the community action programs came along. The poor participated with a vengeance; so much so, that it sent the politicians scurrying to get that money back under the control of city hall. Whatever else it did, the poverty money knocked into a cocked hat the myth that they could not participate. These clichés about "those people" are rationalizations developed by the powerful to explain why the faults are in the human potential and not in the establishment. If the agencies take these clichés seriously, it is a foregone conclusion that they will be limited in what they can accomplish, for they will be victims of racial arrogance.

REEXAMINATION OF METHODS OF WORKING

Those who are in the power arrangement try to work through integrative nonconflict processes. This means involvement, participation, earned leadership, and the use of such methods as will insure peace and tranquillity within the organization. If those who are powerless are served through such processes, they are on their way to being "washed." Most of the agencies point with pride to the way in which they have involved such persons, and point to how they have grown through participation. Usually "growth" means the extent to which they have become like the dominant leadership providing the service.

In the days ahead this way of working is going to be increasingly challenged. People are going to be increasingly sensitive about being "washed." They are going to demand that the establishment change also. They are going to present the agencies with the need to use new methods. These are likely to require skills in dealing with confrontation, disruption, conflict, arbitration, reconciliation, and honest compromise. Groups will come into confrontation rather than let the agency set the standards, involve the bright ones, and siphon them off from the group. The agency which is unwilling to meet these new constituencies as peers and join with them in free and open encounter will have revealed its racism openly.

The major way through which power is redistributed in a democracy is political process. (Most of the gains of the past two decades in race relations are due to the shift in political balance of power occasioned by blacks moving into cities outside the South.) If the issues cannot be settled through political process, the alternative is disruption. Now the major portion of the welfare establishment is not amenable to change through political process. Most of our agencies came out of an authoritarian tradition. They have been "sacred cows," exempt from fair employment and other regulatory laws. The black minorities do not consider them in such a hallowed light. Hence, there is likely to be disruption and conflict as the minorities bring these agencies to account. However, frustrating this may be to any social institution, it is necessary if racism is to be exorcised from its tradition. Few agencies or persons will give up without resistance time-honored practices which favor the dominant group. It will be the fortunate agency which can steer its way through this process with equanimity. What this probably means is that not many of us are going to do anything about institutionalized racism unless and until we are confronted by the black group, and forced to change both ideology and program. This sounds rough, but it comes near to being the fact of life.

We are entering a new era in welfare. As soon as the proposed federal Family Assistance Plan comes into operation, and the incomes of the poor are raised more than is now proposed, as they will be, a whole section of America is going to be sprung loose from the clutches of both the public and the private welfare establishment. The worth of a man will no longer be measured by whether he succeeds in the market place. He will no longer be thought of as dishabilitated if he is poor; hence no longer will he be vulnerable to those who would *re*habilitate him. His status will be in his citizenship.

Equally important, if and when the proposed federal welfare plan is effected, the blacks who now bear the brunt of the welfare system will experience a new emancipation. They will be sufficiently independent that they can demand services on their own terms. No longer will there be this denigration of selfhood in order to get bread; no longer this apathy which stems from fear of withdrawal of services; no longer this "washing" process. We may yet see maximum feasible participation of the poor on such a scale that it will startle the welfare establishment.

What is equally important is that the welfare organizations will be brought to new confrontations. They will be required to square their practices with their professed ideals. They will be obliged to root out the last vestiges of this damnable racism which pervades every aspect of their operation. They will be obliged to meet the consumers of their services—not their clients—in free and open encounter. If this happens, as we hope it will, it will have a cleansing effect on the whole society. Martin Luther King's memorable cry, "Freedom at last," will ring not only for the blacks but for the whites as well; for no man is free so long as he is burdened with prejudice toward his fellow man.

Social Change or Service Delivery? [1]

ROBERT R. MAYER

DURING THE PAST FIFTEEN YEARS, the field of social welfare has gone through a revolution in ideology. Things which we once thought were adequately explained suddenly appeared unexplained. First from the President's Committee on Juvenile Delinquency and then from the Office of Economic Opportunity came attacks on traditional social welfare methods. There went out a clarion call to change institutions, to change the system in order to meet the age old problems of poverty, illness, and despair. Problems which were thought to represent conditions of individuals, suddenly became redefined as conditions of systems in which people live.

Crime and delinquency, for example, were once thought to result from character deficiencies. Now it seems that they reflect a blocked opportunity structure. Poverty used to be simply a matter of the poor not getting enough money to live on. How it has become a function of the maldistribution of power in society. Even mental illness, the last bastion of individualism as an explanatory model, has given rise to the community mental health movement and social psychiatry. These new formulations of old problems fall under the rubric of social change. But what does all this talk about social change really mean? Does it amount to anything more than agitating? Is it not simply the old, familiar process of social action or social reform?

Social welfare has a long and venerable history of involvement in social reform. Social workers for generations have been concerned about the living conditions of the poor and the disadvantaged. For the most part, however, efforts at social reform

1 Based on a forthcoming book, *Social Planning and Social Change*, by Robert R. Mayer, by permission of Prentice-Hall, Inc., Englewood Cliffs, N. J. (copyright 1971).

have been based on conviction or intuition stemming from professional experience in working with individuals. They have not resulted from a systematic view of the world, from an understanding of the way in which society is put together. There has been no basis for development of a technology of social change or of a professional role as a social change agent.

The interest in social planning which emerged in the 1950s and which has been recast as social policy in the 1960s, has established new functions for social welfare which demand the formulation of such a technology or expertise. The traditional view of planning as social service delivery grew out of the experiences and roles familiar to social workers, the provision of services to individuals and families in stress. The predominant notion of social planning in the fifties was that of mobilizing community resources to meet community needs. This process resulted in a kind of count of specific conditions among a given population to be compared with a count of the available services directed toward alleviating those conditions.

As the 1960s wore on, this approach to social planning left many a thoughtful practitioner with the uneasy feeling that something important was being left out. There was constant reference to the neighborhood as having something to do with the nature and extent of social problems, but nobody could quite figure out what. And there was the business of social class highlighted by the dramatic findings of Hollingshead and Redlich.[2] But that concept was treated by sociologists as a kind of God-given phenomenon over which man had no control.

It was not until the recent emergence of social systems theory that an adequate conceptual handle was provided for a new definition of planning. Under a social systems approach, problems reflected in individual behavior are treated as a function of some aspect of the social system in which those individuals act. In this sense, then, social planning becomes a process of planned change of social systems. I shall elaborate a model of social planning which focuses on social systems as the object of

---

[2] August B. Hollingshead and Fredrick C. Redlich, *Social Class and Mental Illness* (New York: John Wiley & Sons, Inc., 1958).

practice and contrast it with the traditional social welfare view of planning as the provision of services to individuals. The central problem is to show how characteristics of social systems relate to the behavior of individuals, and to identify the opportunities for intervention on the part of the planner.

The purpose of this presentation, therefore, is to find answers to two questions:

How do problems get translated into social system terms?

What are the tools of intervention for changing social systems?

We will answer these questions by analyzing cases that involve planned social change. These cases articulate the given problem as well as its solution in terms of the system of social relationships in which that problem takes place. But first let us lay out the conceptual tools with which we will analyze these cases. What is a social system? What are its elements? How does it change?

In its simplest sense, a social system can be defined as patterned or structured social interaction. A social system exists when any two or more persons engage in continuing interaction which exhibits pattern or form.

There are basically three criteria for defining a social system:

1. It must consist of individuals who do in fact interact with one another. This factor distinguishes a system from an abstract aggregate of individuals who have some characteristic in common but may never interact, such as social workers, recipients of social security, black people, and so on.

2. Any social interaction which constitutes a system must have boundaries. There must be some way to determine when a person is part of that interaction and when he is not, to separate elements which are part of the system from those which are outside it.

3. The interaction must persist over time. Obviously, sporadic interaction, such as crowds or individual acts of violence, cannot develop structures or patterns which influence the behavior of the participants. Social systems exist only when there is the expectation of repeated and continued interaction among the persons involved.

What is a social system made of, what are its components?

Obviously if we are going to change social systems, we have to understand their nature. The description which I find most useful is the one developed by Merton, with modifications from Parsons and Linton.[3] A social system has essentially six parts:

1. It has boundaries which can be thought of as membership rules.

2. It has norms which can be thought of as rules governing behavior.

3. It has structure, that is, a certain arrangement among the members of the system.

4. It has institutions or prescribed activities which fulfill certain functions for the system.

5. It has processes which typify the way its members interact, such as cooperation or competition.

6. It has goals or outputs.

We shall concentrate on only two of these elements: the question of who gets included or excluded from systems, which is a reflection of boundaries; and the structure of systems, or how people are arranged once they become members. The cases which we shall analyze involve attempts to change either the membership composition or the structure of a given system. In this sense the model of social planning which I am presenting can be thought of as social structural change.

In sociology the term "social structure" has generally come to mean the peculiar combination of statuses and roles of a given system. For example, a classroom consists essentially of two roles, that of teacher and that of student. Teachers are expected to provide leadership and direction to the class, while students are expected to listen and learn. Each of these roles implies certain statuses. Teachers have the power to flunk students, but students have the right to raise embarrassing questions. Even though statuses and roles are intertwined, they do refer to different aspects of the arrangement among persons in a social system. Role refers to an expected pattern of behavior, while status refers to the particular rights and obligations ascribed to that role.

3 Robert K. Merton, *Social Theory and Social Structure* (New York: Free Press, 1968); Ralph Linton, *The Study of Man* (New York: Appleton-Century, 1936); Talcott Parsons, *The Social System* (Glencoe, Ill.: Free Press, 1951).

One more conceptual tool essential to this analysis is the matter of social change. What constitutes change in a system? In what ways can systems be changed?

This seemingly simple notion of change causes much confusion. There is much rhetoric today about social change meaning complete and total system change. In this sense, social change is equated with revolution. But as Parsons points out, change is a characteristic of social systems.[4] Some of it amounts to nothing more than adjustments to maintain an equilibrium. Sometimes internal adjustments will not suffice, and the system really does change in nature. How do we distinguish such "wheel spinning" from real change?

For our purposes the solution provided by Cancian will be used.[5] Cancian observes that change is meaningful only in relation to a specified state of a system. If a change takes place which results in the elimination of that state, then change *of* the system has occurred. If, on the other hand, a change is compensated for by another aspect of the system, resulting in maintenance of that state, then change *within* the system has taken place.

Social structural change, therefore, is a means of eliminating some undesirable state of a social system. What can be said, then, about the nature of social structural change? There are three distinct ways in which such change can occur: (1) by changing the membership or personnel occupying a given structure; (2) by changing the combination of roles characteristic of that structure; or (3) by redistributing the rights and obligations inherent in the statuses of that structure. We will elaborate each of these ways briefly.

Parsons notes that one of the critical issues for the maintenance of a social system is regulating the assignment of new people to the given roles of that system. "It is . . . essential to stability," Parsons says, "that this should not come all at once." [6] If we are interested in change, therefore, we can simply turn Mr. Parsons around to come up with our first method. That is, by changing

---

[4] Parsons, *op. cit.*, Chap. 11.

[5] Francesca Cancian, "Functional Analysis of Change," in Amitai Etzioni and Eva Etzioni, eds., *Social Change* (New York: Basic Books, Inc., 1964), pp. 112–25.

[6] Parsons, *op. cit.*, p. 117.

the set of people who get assigned to given roles in a system, we can change a state of that system. Thus the introduction of a large number of black students on previously all-white campuses has given birth to considerable change in certain states of those university systems.

The second method, that of changing the composition of roles can best be illustrated by the poverty program. When neighborhood service centers were set up as part of community action programs, a new role, that of the neighborhood aid, was introduced into the system of delivering social services. The neighborhood aid was neither client nor professional but somebody in between. His entrance on the scene changed the roles not only of the client but also of the clinician.

The third method has to do with upsetting another one of Parsons's prescriptions for maintaining stability in social systems. Parsons refers to a process whereby "the right people get into the right roles, and that people stay where they belong in terms of status." [7] By redistributing the rights and obligations ascribed to different roles in a social system, a change in the state of that system can take place. The most notable example of this process has been the change in the occupational structure of our labor market. Whereas years ago unskilled and service occupations drew large numbers of workers, today they are a small part of the labor force. Increased technology has resulted in giving more weight to technical occupations than to labor-intensive occupations.

CASE STUDIES IN STRUCTURAL CHANGE

Let us now examine some cases involving social structural change, with an eye to answering two questions: How are social problems conceptualized in social structural terms? What are the tools of intervention for changing such structures?

Changing the membership. Examples of the phenomenon of changing the membership of a given structure are easy to find. Particularly relevant to the social welfare field is the analysis by Irving Rosow of the social isolation of the aged.[8] This isola-

---

[7] *Ibid.,* p. 133.
[8] Irving Rosow, *Social Integration of the Aged* (New York: Free Press, 1967).

tion has been particularly severe in older industrial cities in the North and the East. Here persons of retirement age have spent their years of employment in industries with minimal or no retirement benefits and minimal coverage under the Social Security Act. Their economic plight is complicated by the out-migration of the younger generation to the Midwest and Far West where economic opportunity has been greater over the past twenty years, leaving elderly parents separated from family.

One problem facing the urban planner is how to overcome the social isolation of this dependent segment of the population. Rosow argues that two essential factors enter into the formation of friendships: friends are drawn primarily from peer groups; and with increasing age, elderly persons become more dependent on physical proximity for finding friends.

To test these hypotheses, Rosow studied the residential settings of elderly people in the city of Cleveland. He divided housing units into three groups: (1) those where 15 percent or less of the tenants were elderly, a distribution comparable to that in the population at large; (2) those units where 33 percent to 50 percent were elderly, a concentrated population; and (3) a group of densely populated units having more than 50 percent elderly residents. Social isolation was measured by questions in household interviews dealing with the number of friends, the type of activities engaged in, and the frequency of contact with friends.

Rosow found that as the concentration of elderly persons in residential settings increased, so did their integration into friendship groups. In such settings, elderly people reported more friends and more frequent contact with friends. Rosow went on to demonstrate that residential concentration produced more than an additive effect on friendships, that is the amount of increase in friendship activity was greater than simply the numerical availability of other elderly people in the same residential setting.

The Rosow example has to do with the neighborhood as a social system. The structure consists of the roles and statuses which exist among neighbors. It is an example of changing the membership of that structure rather than the structure itself. When the immediate neighbors of elderly persons are other elderly persons, the chances for social integration are greatly increased.

The opportunity for intervention in this particular case is provided by the housing policies which establish eligibility requirements for residence. Public housing authorities obviously control these requirements. Such control can be extended to the private market by means of public expenditure policy. Restrictions can be attached to public funds made available to the private builder to induce the establishment of housing projects which are conducive to the social integration of elderly people.

This social planning approach is distinctly different from a social service approach. For years it has been standard practice in social welfare to attempt to overcome the social isolation of elderly persons by organizing golden age clubs or friendly visiting services. However, as Rosow himself points out, in most American cities, golden age clubs reach no more than 5 percent of the elderly population. It would appear, therefore, that a more effective method of dealing with this problem would be to operate housing developments in which at least 50 percent of the units are occupied by elderly residents. This method utilizes the natural process of social integration fostered by the system of social relationships prevalent in the neighborhood.

Changing the role composition. We turn now to a case of change with respect to the composition of roles in a system of social relationships—the discussion by Jane Jacobs on the uses of sidewalks to achieve safety, contained in her much debated book.[9] I am particularly fond of this case because it awakened in me the recognition that something is missing in our traditional understanding of social planning as service delivery. Although Miss Jacobs has been much maligned by city planners whose traditional methods she has attacked, her critics for the most part have overlooked her real contribution, namely, the identification of the structure of social interaction as an important part of the urban scene.

The social problem with which Jacobs is concerned is the lack

[9] Jane Jacobs, *The Death and Life of Great American Cities* (New York: Random House, Inc., 1961).

of safety on the streets. There has been much talk of the increase of crime in cities—a rather heterogeneous and complicated set of phenomena. However, Jacobs is concerned with only one aspect, the seemingly random acts of larceny, vandalism, and personal assault which are reported so frequently in the daily newspapers. She is not dealing with organized crime or with acts of violence which are forms of social protest.

Jacobs's approach to the problem of crime on the streets is particularly important because it is based on a realistic assessment of the social structure of cities. She recognizes that large cities are not small communities; the informal methods of gossip and approval, effective in suburban villages and rural towns, will not work in urban centers. The city is inhabited by strangers, a fact which is both its source of strength and its source of weakness. The predominance of strangers provides a sense of public privacy which is one reason people seek to live in the city. However, this public privacy eliminates the usual means of social control that emanates from personal familiarity.

Jacobs asserts that the social context of the street can be a deterrent to crime. In essence, her argument is that busy streets are safe streets, because the constant activity is a natural attraction to watchers who provide "eyes on the street." It is this natural form of surveillance that is the most effective deterrent to crime.

The constant activity on the street is created by a variety of land uses which attract a steady movement of pedestrian traffic at different times throughout the day. In sociological terms, a busy street is one on which many roles are played: the resident sweeping his front steps; the shopper making his purchases; the worker going to and from his job, the pleasure seeker on his way to a place of diversion.

However, the mere fact that there is activity on the street is not enough to turn the watchers into enforcers of the peace. A sense of proprietorship, Jacobs points out, must abide in the mind which lies behind the "eyes on the street." Such a sense of proprietorship comes from repetitive, superficial contacts between different people in different roles on a given street; neighbors exchanging greetings while walking their dogs; the newsboy and his regular customers; those who frequent the neighborhood bar. These proprietors are in contrast to strangers who come into the neighborhood without getting involved in the web of public identity, who presumably play only a limited role on the street, they may only work in the neighborhood, or come there to catch a bus, or to avail themselves of some entertainment.

Thus, according to Jacobs, safety on the public streets is assured by a proper balance among its users, between strangers whose activity attracts eyes on the street and proprietors whose use of the street creates a web of public identity resulting in a sense of ownership and a desire to maintain the peace. Under such a balance, argues Jacobs, strangers are not only welcome, they are an asset, as long as they do not overwhelm in numbers the proprietors.

Jacobs has no objectively derived evidence to back up her proposition. Her argument remains essentially an untested hypothesis. She has convincing illustrations of her point. There is, for example, the sterile public housing project devoted to a single land use, whose open spaces and lack of activity during certain periods of the day create a natural vacuum for crime, contrasted with New York City's Greenwich Village, where varied land use creates constant activity almost twenty-four hours a day.

However, her real contribution is in demonstrating how to conceptualize a social problem such as street crime in social structural terms. She places individual acts in the context of the system of social relationships in which they occur. She has identified the various roles in that system, not just the perpetrators of the crime or their victims. She has analyzed the functions performed by those roles with respect to preventing crime.

Jacob's analysis is in marked contrast to a service-delivery approach to street crime which focuses efforts on individual actors in the situation. For example, group work services have been organized to redirect the interests and frustrations of delinquent youth into socially constructive channels. Such an approach may be necessary. However, in lieu of a social structure which prevents such acting-out behavior, directing efforts only at the criminals involved constitutes an interminable task.

The tool of intervention in this particular case is land-use controls, which have long been used by city planners to shape the face of cities. Such controls determine whether a given neighborhood shall be entirely residential or whether it will be a mixture of commercial, residential, and even manufacturing enterprises.

Changing the composition of statuses. It is very difficult to find cases which illustrate change generated by redistributing rights and obligations among the various statuses of a social system. At first I thought this resulted from my lack of familiarity with the literature. I have come to believe, however, that a real scarcity exists due to the fact that status changes are more radical in nature, and thus less frequent. Efforts to redistribute rights, whether these be economic resources or political power, inevitably encounter vested interests which resist such changes. It is interesting to note that the published cases approach the matter indirectly and are more complicated. Change is achieved by regrouping or reforming systems in order to alter statuses. New systems of social relationships are established in which this redistribution is feasible.

I shall use a straightforward though unpublished case. This one has to do with the provision of public assistance to able-bodied men who inhabit Skid Row as, reported by Carpenter.[10]

Able-bodied men under the age of sixty-five who are unemployed and not heads of families are eligible only for General Public Assistance (GPA) under the present welfare system. Such assistance is usually time-limited and dependent on the recipient's subjecting himself to rehabilitation. The assumption is that such persons should be employed, and government policy discourages providing them financial support.

However, the inhabitants of Skid Row are, for the most part,

10 Edward Carpenter, "Treatment at a Rehabilitation Center and the Subsequent Adjustment of Chronic Drunkenness Offenders" (unpublished D. S. W. dissertation, University of California, Berkeley, 1964), and private interviews held with the author in 1969.

unemployable in a social sense, even though they may be physically able-bodied. Therefore, they are chronic applicants for GPA. They are periodically sent to "farms" for "drying out" or detoxification, put through alcoholic clinics for therapy, and enrolled in job training for vocational rehabilitation.

As indicated by experience in most cities, these men are poor rehabilitation risks. They fail to sustain any involvement in treatment, and they make no effort to change their dress or appearance or to hold jobs found for them. Consequently, after a period of time they are dropped from the welfare rolls or leave the program voluntarily.

Carpenter undertook a follow-up study of a group of such men who were incorrigible in the eyes of the San Francisco Welfare Department. He found in a substantial number of instances that as the men reached sixty-five and became eligible for Old Age Assistance (OAA), their behavior changed markedly; they began to keep appointments with their caseworkers, dress more acceptably, manage their money, and they were less likely to be "floaters" or to come into conflict with the law. Under OAA, willingness to accept employment is no criterion for eligibility; in fact, retirement from the labor market is a norm in the eyes of society.

The point of this case is that the inherent characteristics of these men as social dependents did not change. Rather society changed their status by altering their rights and obligations. Upon reaching age sixty-five they had a right to OAA without employment, and they had a position of respectability rather than degradation. This status alteration involves a change in the law defining socially acceptable standards of behavior with respect to economic dependency.

A THEORY OF SOCIAL STRUCTURAL CHANGE

It should now be possible to arrive at some answers to our questions: How are problems conceptualized in terms of the structure of social systems? What tools of intervention are available to the planner for changing such structures?

Conceptualizing problems in structural terms. In each of our cases, there were four steps by which the given problem was conceptualized in terms of a social structure. In the first place, a social problem must be specified. This constitutes a pattern of behavior or condition among individuals which is unacceptable to some segments of society. This problematic condition becomes the undesirable state of a system of social relationships in which a change is desired. Each case had this requisite: loneliness among the aged; crime in the streets; social deviancy.

The second step is to identify the boundaries of the system of social relationships in which the problematic behavior takes place. This identification must conform to several criteria. It must refer to a group of actors, that is, people who interact with one another. It must include all participants involved in the interaction, not just those who exhibit the problematic behavior. It must refer to a sustained pattern of interaction, and not an *ad hoc* one. In our first case, this system consisted of the immediate neighbors in a housing development; in the case presented by Jacobs it was the users of a city street; and in the Carpenter case, the clients and workers of a welfare agency.

Having specified the state to be changed, and the system of relationships of which that state is a characteristic, the next step is to examine the various structural aspects of the system which may maintain the behavior in question. We have already said that three general aspects of structure can affect behavior in a system: the composition of the population occupying the structure; the composition of roles; and the composition of statuses in that structure. Lastly, having identified the structural feature which maintains the undesirable state, analysis is made of the alternative means of changing that feature.

It should be obvious that these four steps are not independent of each other, that there is a good deal of interaction among them. For example, the particular way in which the problem is formulated will have something to do with determining the system involved. Similarly, selecting the structural feature to be changed will depend in large part on the tools of intervention available to the planner. At this stage of development, I do not think we are able to be very prescriptive about these decision-making steps. We are left essentially with a judgmental process which will consider trade-offs among choices in these four situations.

Tools of intervention. Given social change as a way of analyzing social problems, what practical opportunities are available to the planner to effect structural changes?

When we look at the three cases analyzed, we find an array of such tools. In the Rosow case, the principal tool was housing policies, particularly those which dealt with eligibility requirements for residence in public projects. In addition, it suggested the use of restrictions on public expenditures to extend this control over the private housing market. In the Jacobs case, the principal tool is land use controls; familiar to city planners. In the Carpenter case, the principal tool was legislation which changed the eligibility requirements for public assistance.

These few cases do not provide a comprehensive listing of tools of intervention. They are more illustrative than informative. What is needed is an organizing principle with which to elaborate the tools of intervention for social change. In this regard the work by Lindblom is particularly useful.[11] Lindblom identifies four basic ways in which policy is formulated: (1) by administrative regulation; (2) by legislation; (3) by judicial review; and (4) by citizen pressure.

The tools of intervention employed in these cases fall under administrative regulation and legislation. For example, housing policies, public expenditures, and land-use controls are worked out in large part by governing boards or administrators within the broad guidelines established in law. However, legislation is also involved in establishing the framework for such regulations. That our cases fell primarily into these two categories is not unreasonable, given the context of traditional planning practice.

It is significant that judicial review was not present in any of our cases. A classic example of this means of achieving social change is the Supreme Court decision regarding school desegre-

11 Charles E. Lindblom, *The Policy-making Process* (Englewood Cliffs, N.J., Prentice-Hall, Inc., 1968).

gation. The Court's directives have led in some communities to a change in the membership of school systems based on racial balance. Judicial review is being increasingly relied upon as lawyers, welfare workers, housing authorities, and others seek to change the rights of poor people to receive benefits.

Lastly, Lindblom identifies the role of the citizen as voter, as a member of organized pressure groups, and as a participant in civil disobedience. In this connection the phenomenon of social movements is relevant. Such efforts are necessary when changes are sought which go against the interests of those in power, and when those who seek change do not grant legitimacy to those in power. The current interest in community organization, expressed through the civil rights movement, the welfare rights movement, and the peace movement, is an example of this tool of intervention in social structural change.

Earlier, we noted that the difficulty of finding cases that involved changes in statuses probably stemmed from the fact that such efforts are bound to encounter strong resistance. This kind of social structural change may depend most heavily on social movements as a tool of intervention. It is questionable whether the gentlemen of Skid Row will ever experience a change in welfare policies without engaging in something like the welfare rights movement.

Limitations. There are some obvious limitations to this theory. Like most theories, it is based partly on evidence and partly on conjecture. Some of the cases—the Jacobs analysis for instance—represent hypotheses of how social structures affect social problems. They need to be tested against more rigorous observation. One of my students attempted a replication of the Jacobs thesis, using crime data for the city of Durham, North Carolina. He found that in neighborhoods of considerable poverty, the crime rate was high despite mixed land-use patterns. This finding suggests that in the presence of real poverty no amount of social interaction on the street may obviate crime.

A second important limitation is that we have been talking essentially about micro-systems rather than macro-systems. As

Blau points out, micro-systems are comprised of individuals as the basic elements.[12] In this sense, our formulation of social structure is appropriate. In contrast, macro-systems are complex systems, the constituent elements being other social systems. Blau points out that the interaction processes of macro-systems are significantly different.

Thirdly, we have said nothing about the effect of the environment, or what may be called the more inclusive system, on attemps to change a given social system. For example, it may be possible to desegregate a public housing project in a Northern city where public attitudes support friendly relations among the races, but impossible to do so in communities in the South where the more inclusive system is hostile to such a state of affairs. We have ignored the effect of reactions in the environment on the ability to change micro-systems.

Lastly, it must be recognized that social structural change is not the answer to all social problems. Given the most desirable social structure. problems may remain which stem from individual disabilities, either psychological or physiological. There still will be a need for individualized treatment. What I am suggesting is that there is a variety of ways in which to conceptualize problems, one of which is in terms of the social system in which they occur. Such an approach may enable us to get at solutions which have certain advantages. It should not, however, be thought of as excluding other approaches.

Implications. At the outset it must be recognized that social structural change as a methodology for problem-solving is not the prerogative of any one of the socially oriented professions. Rather it is a methodology for each of the professions to use in dealing with the social problems with which it is particularly concerned. Within the field of social welfare the kind of analysis used by Rosow could be applied to residential treatment institutions. Synanon and Alcoholics Anonymous are obvious examples. The kind of analysis fostered by Carpenter has implications for

12 Peter M. Blau, "The Structure of Social Associations," in Walter L. Wallace, ed., *Sociological Theory* (Chicago: Aldine Publishing Co., 1969), pp. 187–200.

the treatment of social deviants. Status degradation is involved both in alcoholism and in mental illness.

Social structural change has obvious implications for education. The individual classroom becomes a social system in which learning or the lack thereof is a problem state. Educators are beginning to think about the composition of the classroom as well as the respective roles and statuses of students vis-à-vis teachers.

The applications in the field of city planning have already been indicated. City planners in their proposals for land use and capital expenditures have a direct impact on forming the systems of social interaction in which people are involved.

A less clear case is the field of health. Here I think the distinction must be made between health problems which have an exclusive physiological origin and health problems in which social interaction may be a heavy contributing factor. For example, alcoholism and mental illness are known to have an etiology stemming from social relationships. In this case, social structural change may have an important bearing on treatment itself. For other kinds of health problems, social structural change may only be relevant in terms of the organization of treatment facilities and their use by target populations.

Most professions use a technology or set of skills to which they claim exclusive competence. Our analysis of social change encompasses a variety of tools of intervention used by different professions. For example, housing policies and land use controls have been identified with city planning; community organization, is a method of social work and, to some extent, adult education and public health. Administrative regulation is characteristic of all professions. The formulation of legislation and the use of judicial processes have been the traditional domain of the legal profession. It is interesting to note that most of the socially oriented professions are beginning to introduce law courses into their curriculum. This tendency of social change to cut across the skill base of professions, suggests an alternative approach to professional education.

Social structural change as a model of planning makes possible interdisciplinary training. Since the integrating principle in this model is change of systems of social relationships rather than tools of intervention, it should be possible to develop training programs which bring together lawyers, social workers, public health officials, city planners, educators, and public administrators around a common interest in structural change. Each profession could contribute knowledge about techniques accumulated within its own field which has relevance for structural change as a method of problem-solving.

There is a tendency in formulating a new idea, or a new way of looking at old ideas, to oversell under the influence of the excitement of discovery. I make no such claims for social structural change as a model of social planning. However it appears to provide a different way of responding to some of the age-old problems with which social welfare workers have struggled. These new ways may increase our results by adding to our armamentarium.

Neighborhoods and Social Policy: Continuities and Discontinuities with the Past

DANIEL M. FOX

THE WORD "NEIGHBORHOOD" has long been used to define, defend, or promote ways in which people and their environment are or should be arranged. A variety of frames of reference, about the purposes and methods of neighborhood-community development, has considerable respectability and deep historical roots in social policy. These frames of reference are the product of professional education and experience, institutional loyalties, political and social values and aspirations, and none exists in pure form. Some people combine several into coherent programs; others, in order to gain access to funds or authority, give overt support to one in order to move covertly to another.

Both within and among these frames of reference there are unresolved, ambiguous issues. What, for example, are the appropriate roles of experts and citizens, of neighborhood residents and outsiders? How should the mandates and responsibilities of public and private agencies be coordinated? What are the desirable relationships between neighborhood communities and other neighborhoods, cities, metropolitan regions, state and national governments? What effects should particular services and activities have upon the lives of individuals, families, and larger groups? According to what criteria and with what methods ought change to be measured?

These issues are not susceptible to rational analysis and prescription. They raise questions of value, emotion, attitude; they are part of the struggle for power and influence in our society. But divergent frames of reference, competing in a context of ambiguity, condition the process of political bargaining. They will continue to complicate efforts to find orderly answers to questions about the role of neighborhoods in social policy.

The different neighborhoods in the minds of contemporary theorists and activists can be described as those of planners, therapists, administrators, social scientists, politicians, and citizens.

The planners' neighborhood. This neighborhood is a location for facilities and services which provide comfort, safety, convenience, and opportunity to families and institutions. Although there are many disagreements among planners, one is particularly noteworthy: a controversy, rooted in the early years of the century, between those who plan for neighborhoods in the context and the employ of public or private bodies that claim concern for the total city and those who see their constituency as particular neighborhoods or interest groups within a city or region. Most planners share, however, the assumption that "rational" deployment of resources and arrangement of the environment lead to desirable changes in the lives of people. In recent years, many planners have moved from environmental and physical determinism toward concern with institutions and institutional change, but this concern is more prominent in the academic world than among most planning commissions and departments.[1]

The therapists' neighborhood. This frame of reference, dating from the nineteenth century, defines a neighborhood as the most effective place to offer services which enable people to adjust to difficult situations, improve their health, and partici-

[1] A useful survey of assumptions and methods in Suzanne Keller, *The Urban Neighborhood; a Sociological Perspective* (New York: Random House, Inc., 1968). Two early justifications of advocacy or counterplanning are Benjamin C. Marsh, "Can Land Be Overloaded?" *Annals of the American Academy of Political and Social Science*, LI (1914), 53–70, and William H. Allen, "Interpreting Expert Government to the Citizen," in Edward A. Fitzpatrick, ed., *Experts in City Government* (New York: D. Appleton, 1919), pp. 165–85. A recent statement is Lisa Peattie, "Reflections on Advocacy Planning," *Journal of the American Institute of Planners*, XXXIV (1968), 80–88; see also Herbert J. Gans, "Regional and Urban Planning," *International Encyclopedia of the Social Sciences* (New York: Macmillan, 1968), xii, 129–37.

pate in activities which alleviate alienation, apathy, and anomie. Though often allied with planners, therapists generally regard individual and family change as leading to, rather than following from, environmental change. Originally identified with low-income neighborhoods, therapists have, in the past generation, applied their insights and skills to more affluent communities.[2]

The administrators' neighborhood. The neighborhood of public and private administrators is the manageable unit for delivering and coordinating various services. Unlike planners and therapists, who usually claim legitimacy on the basis of training and expertise, administrators are legitimized by satisfying public and private disbursers of funds. Administrators' neighborhoods are rarely those defined by the people living in particular areas. Planners and therapists frequently exercise or seek bureaucratic legitimacy, and administrators are often committed to particular plans and programs. But the administrative role demands primary concern with effectiveness, economy, and, most important, accountability to those who control resources.[3]

The social scientists' neighborhood. This is an area in which to investigate how and why people interact with each other, participate in various activities, define who and what is important and threatening to them, change and maintain particular styles of life. Sociologists (and more recently, anthropologists) have,

[2] The history of the community as a locus for therapeutic intervention is documented in Roy Lubove, *The Professional Altruist* (Cambridge, Mass.: Harvard University Press, 1965), and Gary A. Lloyd, "Charities and Settlements— Methods of Retail and Wholesale Reform, 1890–1915" (New Orleans: Tulane University School of Social Work, 1968; mimeograph). A more recent analysis is Richard Cloward and Irwin Epstein, "Private Social Welfare's Disengagement from the Poor," in George Brager and Francis P. Purcell, eds., *Community Action against Poverty* (New Haven, Conn.: College and University Press, 1968). A major critique of the assumptions of therapeutic intervention is Charles A. Valentine, *Culture and Poverty: Critique and Counterproposals* (Chicago: University of Chicago Press, 1968).

[3] A classic statement of the relationship between democratic values and planning for manageable units is David E. Lilienthal, *TVA; Democracy on the March* (New York: Harper & Bros., 1944). An illuminating study of the results of competition among frames of reference is Peter Marris and Martin Rein, *Dilemmas of Social Reform: Poverty and Community Action in the United States* (London: Routledge & Kegan Paul, 1967). Conflicting frames of reference in one city are described in Stephan Thernstrom, *Poverty, Planning, and Politics in the New Boston* (New York: Basic Books, 1969).

for seventy-five years, influenced the design and evaluation of policies and programs. Indeed, the concept of a neighborhood as an area in which to solve the problems of urban life originated, in large part, with sociologists, as has the critique of that notion. But social scientists are often frustrated by the boldness with which activists push beyond theory and data because of pressure to perform. On the other hand, social scientists frustrate performers by their desire to measure and analyze what the latter, under the constraints of organizational and political life, must justify. Moreover, there are numerous sociological neighborhoods, a bewildering variety of spatial and human relationships which are difficult to translate into policy, program, and procedure.[4]

The political neighborhood. This area is one in which people act to change or maintain the distribution of power, influence, and resources. It is the neighborhood of politicians, those who hope to benefit from political action, potential recruits for causes, and recipients of benefits. Constant conflict and bargaining occur: within and among groups and factions; between groups, coalitions, and larger units of public and private government. This neighborhood is a source of some support, but more often annoyance, to administrators, planners, and therapists. Its volatility and unpredictability interfere with their attempts at orderly analysis and planning.[5]

The citizens' neighborhood. This is the most difficult one to describe. Its elements—individuals and families with different experiences, desires, opinions, and problems—must be caricatured if sociologists are to generalize, politicians to claim representativeness, therapists to offer services, administrators to coordinate, and planners to arrange the environment. The central dilemma of social policy is the impossibility of taking into account the variety of citizens' attitudes and aspirations. Every

4 Keller, *op. cit.* An excellent summary is Scott Greer, "Neighborhood," in *International Encyclopedia of the Social Sciences*, XI, 121–25.

5 A useful analysis of issues and forces is Edward C. Banfield and James Q. Wilson, *At Politics* (Cambridge, Mass.: Harvard University Press, 1963). The ways in which the political neighborhood can deflect other goals is described by Earl Raab, "What War and Which Poverty?" *Public Interest*, No. 3 (1966), pp. 45–56.

policy, program, and project is more sensitive to the needs of some than of others. Any policy is a partial, disputed solution from the moment of its inception, more as a result of citizens' complexity than because of the venality, incompetence, or unimaginativeness of political and bureaucratic actors. Finally, most citizens, of every social class, regard themselves as coordinators of the services they consume and decision-makers about whom their "neighbors" are, where and how they desire to live.[6]

Contemporary analysts and promoters of neighborhood policy and action have much in common with those who preceded them, although assumptions, theories, and goals have changed. Yet there are assertions that the neighborhood concept, "unfashionable" for many years, is in the process of revival. Much polemical discourse is based on the assumption that from the 1930s to the mid-1960s public and private social policy submerged urban neighborhoods in larger units, and aggregated services so that quality and accessibility varied inversely with the affluence of those who needed them.[7]

Continuity with the past is easily demonstrated. Social scientists, though dubious about the concept of "natural areas," explore how class, ethnicity, and life-style determine relationships among people in particular census tracts. Reformers and the social welfare professions no longer idealize the healthy primary bonds of rural life, but they continue to aid and applaud local activities to improve the quality and cohesiveness of group life in urban and suburban areas. Planners, increasingly sensitive to the ways in which placement of services, housing, or transportation creates or perpetuates racial segregation and economic ex-

6 There is an extensive literature on the complexity of citizens' views. A helpful collection is Roland L. Warren, ed., *Perspectives on the American Community* (Chicago: Rand-McNally, 1966). Competing viewpoints and attitudes among black Americans are analyzed in Gary T. Marx, *Protest and Prejudice; a Study of Belief in the Black Community* (New York: Harper & Row, 1969). The historical case for citizens' lack of attachment to any particular urban space is argued in Stephan Thernstrom, "Working Class Social Mobility in Industrial America" (Boston: Massachusetts Institute of Technology–Harvard University Joint Center for Urban Studies, 1968; mimeographed).

7 Milton Kotler, *Neighborhood Government: the Local Foundations of Political Life* (Indianapolis: Bobbs-Merrill, 1969), is a closely reasoned argument for the neglect of neighborhoods in recent social policy.

ploitation, still design in reference to subunits of cities. Politicians have never ceased knowing that dispersed constituencies are useful but fragile supplements to a geographical area where, in exchange for services, facilities, and patronage, they receive overwhelming electoral support. Residents continue to define their neighborhoods as places to defend against outsiders, to engage in various activities and receive particular services, to improve or escape.

I suggest three causes for the contemporary polemicism about neighborhoods. Two are obvious: increased political consciousness and militancy of citizens previously excluded from the struggle to possess and rearrange power in the United States; and more funds than ever before to provide services and facilities to residents of segments of cities.

The third cause is more obscure. Defense of neighborhoods as viable political, economic, social, and cultural units has always been ambivalent. Advocates of neighborhood action, of devolution of resources and power from large to small units, have long recognized that neighborhoods are not isolated entities. They affect, and more often are affected by, regional, national, and international economic and political events. Ambivalence is painful, and present pain is usually more intense than remembered pain.

There is no need to recite the causes of rising aspirations and expectations among black and Spanish-speaking Americans. Nor is it necessary to demonstrate that their urban spaces (call them neighborhoods, or communities, or ghettos), have long been deprived of services taken for granted, as purchasable or obtainable through political influence, by citizens in other urban and suburban areas. Geographic concentration of these increasingly impatient and politically sophisticated citizens and their leaders—a result of deliberate exclusion and relative lack of income—has stimulated the mobilization of community power to prevent or encourage particular events.

Neighborhood organization and pressure in urban ghettos are often justified by political and historical analysis. Many leaders believe that their only reliable resources are ballots and bodies and, some add, bullets. A persuasive analogy between the plight of ghettos and colonialist exploitation separates the experience of darker skinned Americans from that of other immigrants and migrants and dissolves faith in both traditional social policy and the inevitability of upward mobility. Others, less convinced by the colonial analogy, read American history as a successful struggle for political and economic power by ethnic groups, mobilized politically and through voluntary associations and concentrated in particular areas. These arguments, whatever their validity, contribute to the intensity of debates about social policy and action.[8]

This intensity has led to the rejection by many citizens and their leaders of people long involved with, and committed to, the concept of neighborhood development. Many social scientists, social welfare professionals, planners, and politicians who seek to be brokers between ghetto neighborhoods and larger concentrations of power are regarded as enemies, impediments to an equitable transfer of power. Outsiders who offer help or service are often perceived as part of monolithic power structures. This rejection is the result of decades of accumulated resentment against describing immoral, pathological, or disorganized behavior which is often a necessary adjustment to the effects of exploitation; and of years of planning for, rather than with, residents of low-income communities. There is no point in lamenting the injustice which makes people who provide inferior services more visible targets than those who allocate inferior resources.[9]

[8] Robert Blauner, "Internal Colonialism and Ghetto Revolt," *Social Problems*, XVI (1969), 393–408; Nathan Glazer, "Negroes and Ethnic Groups," in Nathan Huggins, Martin L. Kilson, and Daniel M. Fox, eds., *Key Issues in the Afro-American Experience* (New York: Harcourt Brace & Jovanovich, forthcoming); Daniel M. Fox, "Community Power: Historical Revisionism without Historians," *Interplay*, III (1970), 56–59.

[9] Instances of rejection are described in Sherry Arnstein, "A Ladder of Citizen Participation," *Journal of the American Institute of Planners*, XXXV (1969), 216–24; James V. Cunningham, "Resident Participation," unpublished report to the Ford Foundation (1967; mimeographed); Shirley F. Barshay, *One Meaning of Citizen Participation* (Western Region, Office of Economic Opportunity, 1968). The critique of social welfare practice is ably presented in Valentine, *op. cit.*; Elliot Liebow, *Tally's Corner; a Study of Negro Street-Corner Men* (Boston: Little, Brown, 1968); Hylan Lewis, "The Culture of Poverty," in Anselm L.

The goals and strategies of neighborhood militancy vary widely. Goals include: influencing public and private decisions and obtaining increased political representation; improving social services, facilities, and housing; generating new sources of employment and income; establishing subunits of administration and government. Strategies range from increasing participation in traditional politics, to establishing new or competitive institutions, to confrontation and threatened or actual violence.[10]

These familiar goals and strategies are now being adopted by the misnamed "silent majority." Distrust of traditional political, religious, professional, and union leadership—and of neigborhood or group action based on that distrust—is mounting as working- and middle-class citizens grow uncomfortable with public and private decisions that seem beyond their control and that threaten their comfort, safety, and aspirations. It is oversimple to dismiss this discomfort as "veto group politics" in defense of the status quo. Negation is often a prelude to positive programs that reflect the demands of particular constituencies.[11]

Millions of citizens are "restless," in President Johnson's euphemism, and are expressing their concerns through local alliances and action. This is not a new phenomenon. But the crises of the past rarely hurt as much as the needs and grievances of the present. Those who urge "perspective," those who suggest, for instance, that localism has limits, that in the long run wounds are healed and heels wounded, that more democracy is not in-

---

Strauss, ed., *The American City* (Chicago: Aldine, 1968), pp. 175–78. See also Frederick S. Jaffe and Steven Polgar, "Family Planning and Public Policy: Is the 'Culture of Poverty' the New Cop-out?" *Journal of Marriage and the Family,* XXX (1968), 228–35.

10 Allan A. Altschuler, *Community Control* (New York: Pegasus Press, 1970), is an outstanding summary and analysis of goals and strategies.

11 The literature on this subject is impressionistic. An introduction is Eleanor P. Wolf and Charles N. Lebeaux, "Class and Race in the Changing City," in Leo F. Schnore, ed., *Social Science and the City: a Survey of Urban Research* (New York: Praeger, 1968), pp. 99–130. J. Clarence Davies, *Neighborhood Groups and Urban Renewal* (New York: Columbia University Press, 1966), describes tactics used by an upper-middle-class neighborhood which have more recently been adopted by other groups.

evitably the cure for the problems of democracy, may be right. But they do not communicate. Perspective seems to be a virtue derived from security and comfort.

Conceive an unreal world in which the constituency and logic that created the interstate highway system also existed in other areas of concern to Americans. We might then have national health insurance, in income policy that raised floors and lowered ceilings, a housing program unconstrained by governmental boundaries established at other times for different purposes.

Perhaps constituencies will be created to achieve these ends. Until then, we must accept or tinker with governmental and philanthropic policies in which the words "general welfare" are a euphemism for subsidies directed at particular groups and places. Put it another way: relatively homogeneous neighborhoods, contrary to myth, have been reinforced, strengthened, or created by legislation and administration on all levels of government and by private action.

The currently much abused New Deal did not, for practical and ideological reasons, destroy local sovereignty and choice in favor of centralization in the national interest. The idea that the eclipse of the community was assisted by public and private policy from 1932 until, in our time, the virtues of neighborhood and community bonds were rediscovered is a polemical balloon ripe for puncturing.

Foreshortened historical memory has led to neglect or out-of-context criticism of New Deal localism, such as: encouragement of local experimentation in social insurance; TVA efforts to involve citizens in planning; farmers' involvement in agricultural regulation; subsidized construction of new towns on the neighborhood unit model; loans and grants from relief funds to locally organized self-help groups; and a mortgage subsidy policy which deliberately sought to stabilize or create economically and racially homogeneous neighborhoods. It is easy to describe the flaws in these policies, particularly to criticize them for neglecting the poorest citizens. But it is distortion to describe the concern of many New Dealers with the viability of working- and middle-class neighborhoods as stupidity, cynicism, or disregard for the poor.[12]

Similarly, philanthropic social policy was probably more concerned with community affairs after political changes stimulated by the great depression made relief a public responsibility. Settlement houses became neighborhood information, referral, recreation, and service-delivery centers. The first program to attack juvenile delinquency through neighborhood organization was begun in the 1930s. Saul Alinsky's initial efforts to create neighborhood coalitions for abrasive social action were subsidized at the end of that decade.[13]

During the Second World War, as during the First, unprecedented international involvement and domestic geographic mobility were combined with public and private subsidy of neighborhood organizations for morale building, food production, and civil defense. Moreover, efforts were made to maintain war-related organized neighborliness as a means to revitalize democracy. Toward the end of the war the phrase "citizen participation" entered the language with several meanings, all of them expressing a conviction that the nation could not be governed effectively and sensitively through traditional political and administrative means. (It should be noted in passing that the ideal of democratic neighborliness reached the height of naïveté and moral ambiguity when federal guidelines required relocated

[12] The literature on the New Deal includes: Sidney Baldwin, *Poverty and Politics* (Chapel Hill, N.C.: University of North Carolina Press, 1968); Clark Kerr, "Productive Enterprises of the Unemployed, 1931–1938" (unpublished dissertation, University of California, Berkeley, 1939); Edward C. Banfield, *Government Project* (Glencoe, Ill.: Free Press, 1951); Paul Conkin, *Tomorrow a New World* (Ithaca, N.Y.: Cornell University Press, 1959); Richard Kirkendall, *Social Scientists and Farm Politics in the Age of Roosevelt* (Columbia, Mo.: University of Missouri Press, 1966); John D. Lewis, "Democratic Planning in Agriculture," *American Political Science Review*, XXXV (1941), 232–49, 454–69; Philip Selznick, *TVA and the Grass Roots* (Berkeley, Calif.: 1949).

[13] Sidney Dillick, *Community Organization for Neighborhood Development: Past and Present* (New York: 1953) is a useful survey. On delinquency prevention see Clifford R. Shaw and Henry D. McKay, eds., *Juvenile Delinquency and Urban Areas* (Chicago: University of Chicago Press, 1942); Solomon Kobrin, "The Chicago Area Project: a Twenty-five-Year Assessment," *Annals of the American Academy of Political and Social Science*, CCCXXII (1959), 19–29. Saul D. Alinsky, "Community Analysis and Organization," *American Journal of Sociology*, XLVI (1941), 797–808.

Japanese-Americans to elect representatives to advise the keepers of their camps.[14])

Between the end of the war and the early 1960s there were few substantial changes in public and private social policy affecting neighborhoods. The New Deal community experiments disintegrated or, like the TVA and the new towns, took few initiatives and were more imitated abroad than at home. Federal housing and redevelopment policy conferred the greatest benefits on citizens and neighborhoods with the most resources and political power, despite increased incentives for metropolitan and regional planning. Voluntary agencies, whether following their constituencies to the suburbs or remaining in rapidly changing central cities, continued to define their service areas and refine their techniques in neighborhood and community terms.[15]

Throughout these years, as in the more turbulent decade of the 1960s, reformers debated the merits of national or regional versus neighborhood-community answers to social problems. Except among a handful of extremists, the debate has never been concerned with either/or but rather with what combination. However, the struggle for scarce public and philanthropic funds, and the need for organizations to define their goals and strategies, created strife among people who agreed that the free play of market forces was not the most just or efficient way to improve the quality of American life.[16]

[14] Dillick, *op. cit.*, pp. 125ff; Office of Civilian Defense, *The Community Council* (Washington, D.C.: 1945). For early use of phrase "citizen participation," see *Conference on the Citizen's Participation in Public Affairs*, New York University, 1947 (New York: the University, 1948), pp. 26–31, for wartime learning. Strikingly similar phenomena in the First World War are described in Amos G. Warner, Stuart Queen, Ernest B. Harper, *American Charities and Social Work* (New York: Macmillan, 1930), pp. 462–70. Alexander Leighton, *The Governing of Men* (Princeton, N.J.: Princeton University Press, 1945).

[15] See Conkin, *op. cit.*, pp. 307–23, on the fate of New Deal community experiments; Selznick, *op. cit.*, pp. 262-66 on TVA; Alan A. Altschuler, *The City Planning Process: a Political Analysis* (Ithaca: Cornell University Press, 1965), on housing and redevelopment. See case studies in Jeanne R. Lowe, *Cities in a Race with Time* (New York: Random House, Inc., 1967). On voluntary agencies, see Cloward and Epstein, *op. cit.;* Dillick *op. cit.*, pp. 139ff. Nathan E. Cohen, ed., *The Citizen Volunteer* (New York: 1960).

[16] A trenchant defense of the localist-voluntary point of view is Alfred De Grazia, ed., *Grass Roots Private Welfare* (New York: New York University Press, 1957). More typical, however, are the essays in Cohen, *op. cit.* see also Fox, *op. cit.*, p. 56.

In the 1960s, the neighborhood-community approach dominated programs designed to meet the needs of the "rediscovered" (an interesting epistemological problem) poor. The growing militancy of black and Spanish-speaking citizens and their sense of confinement in territory they had not chosen and did not control provide only a partial explanation for the concentration of public and private subsidy.

Other factors help to account for the unprecedented amount of funds devoted to changes in segments of cities. Innovative professionals in health, mental health, social work, education, law, and city planning were convinced that their services must be made more accessible, responsive, and cheaper to consumers. They were supported by experts in public administration who urged the coordination of agencies and services. Fragmented bureaucracies, growing ever larger and more inert, dealing with segments of individual and family problems, seemed ineffective and dehumanizing; at worst destructive, at best impediments to equality and upward mobility. The neighborhood-community appeared to many to be the most appropriate area for service delivery, and the only manageable unit for coordination.[17]

The eloquence of these innovators and the eagerness of many federal, foundation, and church leaders for new approaches to social problems were important factors influencing the funds flowing to grey areas, juvenile delinquency, community action, legal services, and model cities programs, neighborhood health, mental health, and multiservice centers, demonstration schools, minority business development, and thousands of community organization, political, and social action projects.

These programs had roots in the past. But more important was the discontinuity created because there were more of them, spending more funds, allegedly reaching more citizens, receiving more publicity, than at any time in the past. Another factor was the public image of these programs. For the first time in a cen-

17 Marris and Rein, *op. cit.;* Richard Blumenthal, "Antipoverty and the Community Action Program," in Allan P. Sindler, ed., *American Political Institutions and Public Policy* (Boston: Little, Brown, 1969). John C. Donovan, *The Politics of Poverty* (New York: Pegasus Press 1968), and Raymond Vernon, *Metropolis 1985* (Cambridge, Mass.: Harvard University Press, 1960), are representative of works of the 1960s.

tury, attention was focused on the issue of public responsibility for redressing the wrongs done to, and opening opportunities for, people with darker skins than those of the majority of Americans. It was indeed a second Reconstruction; unlike the first, it was conducted in every region of the country.

Attacks on the viability of the spatially defined neighborhood community as a place to live, to engage in social, economic, and political relationships, and receive particular services have a venerable history among social theorists and activists. Every advocate of policy or action based on the neighborhood community has had to confront cogent arguments that, for example; the technology and division of labor of modern industry make local loyalties obsolete; focus on neighborhood activity reinforces racial and economic segregation, impedes class struggle, or shifts blame for exploitation from perpetrators to victims; or that neighborhood-based policies seek to revive a make-believe world of rural community in which whatever primary bonds exist often constrict. Other critics, more detached, have urged the historical inevitability of a (losing) conflict between the claims of smaller and larger communities.[18]

These arguments stem from uncomfortable facts which underlie the ambivalence among those for whom the neighborhood-community retains some value. Every politician and social reformer recognizes the value of coalitions based on shared interests or on grievances rather than space. It is not news that some economic and governmental activities require decisions and subsidies from larger units. Citizens need no special competence to know that neighborhood institutions cannot supply many of the rights, associations, goods, and services they desire.

It is, however, easier to resolve ambivalence intellectually than

18 The classic analyses of the limits of neighborhood strategies include: N. Dennis, "The Popularity of the Neighborhood Community Idea," *Sociological Review*, New Series, VI (1958), 191–206; Richard Dewey, "The Neighborhood, Urban Ecology, and City Planners," *American Sociological Review*, XV (1950), 502–7; Reginald Isaacs, "The Neighborhood Theory," *Journal of the American Institute of Planners*, XV (1948), 15–23; C. Wright Mills, "The Professional Ideology of Social Pathologists," *American Journal of Sociology*, XLIX (1943), 165–80; Harold A. Stone, Don K. Price and Kathryn H. Stone, *City Manager Government in the United States* (Chicago: Public Administrative Clearing House, 1940).

emotionally. Planners, social workers, militant reformers, advocates of community control and new governmental institutions, have had little trouble harmonizing—on paper—the relationship between neighborhoods and larger units. But logic has never managed to overcome ambivalence.[19]

For ambivalence about the neighborhood-community is part of our feeling and thinking lives. Most of us want better housing, facilities, and services at lower cost and with a minimum of dislocation. We are torn between loyalty to place and friends, the security of the familiar, and the desire for economic, social, and geographic mobility. Most Americans, whatever their class or race, have mixed feelings about where they came from, are, and are headed; about those who offer themselves as leaders or propose changes in accustomed, if sometimes painful, patterns of living. Moreover, most of us have been part of several communities—residential, economic, educational, military—in the course of our lives.

If a neighborhood is occasionally a refuge, it is also where one contemplates powerlessness to stop wars, inflation, and environmental pollution. If it is a place to be changed or escaped, it is also a source of pain when jobs are not available and laws are not equitably enforced. If it is a real or potential source of racial, ethnic, or class association and pride, it is likely to stimulate anxiety: the "wrong" group may be moving in; the most stable and upwardly mobile group may be moving out. Neighborhoods are always in transition.

The intensity of struggles for power and influence—competition among groups with different goals, frames of reference, interpretations of past and present events—makes it difficult to evaluate whether particular policies and strategies reduce poverty, provide better education, health, and housing, improve the quality of life—or whatever their advocates claim they can do. After almost a decade of unprecedented interest in, and

19 For example, see Kotler, *op. cit.*; Altschuler, *Community Control*, Chaps. 4 and 5; Saul Alinsky with Marion K. Sanders, "The Professional Radical, 1970," *Harper's Magazine*, January, 1970, pp. 35–42; *Reshaping Government in Metropolitan Areas* (New York, Committee on Economic Development, 1970). Probably the most extensive effort to harmonize the relationship between neighborhoods and larger units are the guidelines for the model cities program (called C.D.A. letters) issued by the Department of Housing and Urban Development.

spending on behalf of, neighborhood communities, considerable energy is still devoted to establishing preconditions for substantive change: powers, processes, procedures, plans, and personnel.

This situation is a result of the ways in which our political and administrative machinery operates to create and sustain what are often criticized as structural fantasies. Many people exhaust their energies in the apparent belief that rearrangement of governing systems, reorganization of bureaucracies, will change the attitudes and behavior of providers and recipients of particular services. This is not to deny that institutions influence attitudes, but the relationship is not clear. It may take as long to change beliefs as it did to create them. Structure may more often result from than create attitudes.

In the absence of proved and morally acceptable tools for human engineering, however, structural innovation is the only weapon available to activists who seek changes in the human condition. The alternatives are a source of impatience and anger to those who feel deeply about present injustice, inequity, and inadequacy: waiting for incremental changes in social and economic conditions and values to create new structures; or developing policies which in time might lead to changes in attitudes and beliefs. Working for structural change provide a sense of action, movement, purpose, whether the goals are revolution, changing the control or increasing the supply of services, or preventing children from being bussed to school.

Structural innovation, as practiced in our society, is recognition of the reality that competition among goals, interests, and values precludes broad agreement about what needs to be done about particular issues. Consensus, in practice, is a euphemism for a façade of agreement covering bitter struggle, the silence or exclusion of dissident voices, the temporary exhaustion or thwarting of opposition. Proponents of structural rearrangement generally accept existing values and interests as unchangeable in the short run: new institutions, or modifications in existing ones, are urged in order to change them in the long run.

Thus structuralism is not a fantasy even though it appears to oversimplify the problems of changing behavior, or to deal with parts of a problem (a neighborhood, an ethnic or racial group, particular services). Rather, it is the only credible tool for change; faith, exhortation, education, currency manipulation, to name a few others, having been consigned to the graveyard of reform strategies in the course of American history.

Almost a decade has been spent rearranging the structural preconditions for improving the status and standard of living of Americans with the lowest incomes, fewest opportunities, most threatening environment. It is tempting to accept the argument that more enlightened national income, health, housing, and employment policies would have dealt with many problems more effectively than emphasis on neighborhood-communities. It is debatable, however, whether there were or are strong enough constituencies to support such policies. Moreover, it seems impossible to gain consent to definitions of the public interest which prevent struggles over the adequacy, representativeness, and justice of institutional arrangements. No policy, short of repression, can ignore citizens' strong opinions and feelings about the space they occupy, the places and people they choose to call neighborhoods and neighbors.[20]

The illusion that we have been struggling about what ought to be done is more comfortable than the reality that individuals and groups have been in conflict about who does what to whom. This illusion has led to displacement of the messiness of political bargaining onto concepts: the relationship between coalition and adversary mechanisms in the planning process; the roles of institutions as arbiters and advocates; the appropriate methods to coordinate the delivery of particular services; the responsibility of experts and consumers in policy and administration. These concepts mirror issues, but at a tangent that obscures what has been happening.

[20] Emphasis on structural preconditions is reported in Ralph M. Kramer, *Participation of the Poor* (Englewood, N.J.: Prentice-Hall, Inc., 1969); *Citizen Participation in Model Cities,* Technical Assistance Bulletin No. 3, Department of Housing and Urban Development, 1968; Organization for Social and Technical Innovation, "Decentralization Training Paper" and "Case Studies of Seven Neighborhood Corporations" (reports to the Office of Economic Opportunity, 1969). The case for national policies, in the context of the failure of neighborhood-community policies, has been argued most dramatically by Daniel P. Moynihan, *Maximum Feasible Misunderstanding* (New York: Free Press, 1969).

Probably the best examples of displacement are the bitter controversies over "top-down" versus "bottom-up" planning among those who agree that the neighborhood is an appropriate unit for the delivery of particular services. Passionate arguments about maximum feasible, widespread, or whatever participation, who is representing whom, coordination and linkage, neighborhood control, and governmental responsibility have become part of the discourse of our time.

These debates mask conflicts about the sharing of scarce resources—money, power, influence. The abstractions also mask the differences of values and interests in every neighborhood, agency, governing body, and professional guild. It remains to be convincingly demonstrated that citizen or government or guild domination of the delivery of particular services necessarily means a higher or lower quality of output, a "package" more or less responsive to needs. About the only generalization on which there is agreement is that, following a decision to subsidize a particular purpose, more services are provided and more jobs created.[21]

This situation derives from more than the difficulty of determining what constitutes better quality and how different perceptions should be weighed. Doctors, lawyers, planners, social workers, bureaucrats, and politicians are no more monolithic than any other groups. Avarice, ambition, and self-righteousness are not a monopoly of any social class, profession, or ethnic group. Wisdom and sensitivity appear to be randomly distributed; as is the tendency for decisions, whoever makes them, to follow the path of least resistance and highest immediate gain.

Two common and contradictory explanations for the lag between promise and performance are the inappropriateness of the neighborhood as a focus for social policy and the disaffection created by externally imposed policy. Both arguments are suspect.

A neighborhood focus often appears to deflect attention from

21 The limited learning from existing evaluative research is analyzed in Martin Rein and Robert S. Weiss, "The Evaluation of Broad-Aim Programs: a Cautionary Case and Moral," *Annals of the American Academy of Political and Social Science,* CCCLXXXV (1969), 133–42.

issues of scale, aggregation, relationship between problems and solutions, economic, social, and political forces which transcend local areas. But it is questionable whether, in a large, relatively open society, there is a "rational" model for discussing and resolving these issues outside the heads of theorists. Neighborhood solutions are not panaceas. There is, however, little reason to believe that the neighborhood focus prevents the solution of problems beyond the reach of neighborhood action. It is more plausible to assert that neighborhood-community strategies are a result, not a cause, of the near impossibility of building constituencies and commitment at a level of generality that transcends territorial and group loyalties and the conflicting interests and goals they represent.

That level of general agreement, the history of the past century suggests, is only possible when there is widespread fear of an external enemy. When we have not been engaged in shooting wars, politicians and activists have sought to create them metaphorically. Americans have been urged to attack and defend against depression, inflation, monopoly, poverty, pollution, and communism—to name just a few causes—in the twentieth century. For better or for worse, a majority of citizens have not heeded every call to arms.[22]

At the opposite pole is the argument that external imposition of policies and rules stifles the urge to self-determination that is a necessary precondition for creative social action. This argument is compelling but more as a tactic than a principle. It rests on the assumption that democratic virtue derives from proximity, size, and relative homogeneity. But appropriate proximity, size, and homogeneity are defined differently each time the argument is used. States rights are trammeled by an insensitive federal establishment. States and feds interfere with county and municipal government. Both impose on and seek to manipulate the residents of particular neighborhoods. If only subsidies had no strings, outsiders did not set goals and standards, all would be well. It is painful to be accountable in a society with competing

22 A suggestive analysis of the use of the imagery of war is William E. Leuchtenburg, "The New Deal and the Analogue of War," in John Braeman, Robert H. Bremner, and Everett Walters, eds., *Continuity and Change in Twentieth Century America* (Columbus, Ohio: Ohio University Press, 1964), pp. 274–303.

interests; and more painful to account to somebody who has different values and goals.

External imposition is both limited and encouraged by the continuous struggle to share power and influence. There is an ongoing bargaining process involving institutions and citizens. This process inevitably creates conflict, tension, compromise, and bitterness. It also produces more external imposition as groups with relatively less local bargaining power escalate issues and decisions to levels of government or public opinion where their goals and grievances have more weight. The strains of this process inevitably modify—for better or worse is a matter of opinion—the goals and effects of any policy or cause.[23]

I would like to assign to the neighborhood concept a definition and frame of reference, an historical legacy, and a future role that a majority of citizens could or should accept. I long for the power to persuade people that it is misleading to define issues in terms of centralization versus decentralization when the problem is to seek leverage for change in the context of values, interests, goals.

I even indulge several fantasies about social policy. Instead of disputes about neighborhood policy there is dedication to such problems as how to make services more humane and accessible on the basis of need rather than ability to pay. Citizen participation and neighborhood organization are never mentioned; instead, all discussions emphasize building constituencies, redressing grievances, opening opportunities. It is generally recognized that most Americans identify with several communities. Moreover, it is agreed that services for the poor have traditionally been poor services; a sophisticated way of saying that those who have get.

None of these fantasies will be realized. The neighborhood-

[23] The classic statement and justification of this process are found in David B. Truman, *The Governmental Process: Political Interests and Public Opinions* (New York: Alfred A. Knopf, 1951). Grant McConnell, *Private Power and American Democracy* (New York: Knopf, 1966), and Henry S. Kariel, *The Decline of American Pluralism* (Stanford, Calif.: Stanford University Press, 1961), are less sanguine about its effectiveness and equity without more potent federal intervention. Theodore Lowi, *The End of Liberalism: Ideology, Policy, and the Crisis of Public Authority* (New York: W. W. Norton, 1969), finds the intellectual and administrative apparatus of "interest group liberalism" bankrupt.

community concept, rooted in the past, modified by events, inevitably ambivalent, reflecting diverse goals and interests, weighted with euphemisms which deflect the pain of, and make manageable the hope for, change, will continue to be a resource for those Americans who, bored with imagining total solutions to problems, take some comfort in doing one thing at a time.

Social Welfare Priorities— a Minority View

A SUMMARY OF THE OPENING GENERAL SESSION

T. GEORGE SILCOTT

In THE 1969 EDITION of *The Social Welfare Forum*, Mr. John Kidneigh writes that the National Conference on Social Welfare "is a loosely held together group of individuals who work in the [social welfare] field . . . a Forum for exchange of ideas," and as such "has little power over the field." [1] Historically, this role has been satisfactory for a large majority of those who participate in it. Over the years, however, a growing number of people have found this role gravely inadequate. Blacks, Puerto Ricans, La Raza, Indians, the National Welfare Rights Organization (NWRO), and others who petitioned the Conference to change were formerly labeled dissidents but have come to be known as the "emerging groups." Mr. Kidneigh describes these individuals as "members of the Conference for less than two years or . . . not members at all." [2] By characterizing them in this way, is Mr. Kidneigh questioning the legitimacy of the groups and ascribing an aura of novelty to the demands they make?

Actually, the demand that NCSW become action-oriented is far from novel. On the contrary, dissidents have been making that request for years, and every year new groups join the ranks.

Howard E. Prunty, of the National Association of Black Social Workers, reminds us that:

[1] John C. Kidneigh, "The New York Conference Story," in *The Social Welfare Forum, 1969* (New York: Columbia University Press, 1969), p. 183.
[2] *Ibid.*, p. 179.

In San Francisco, in 1968, severe criticism was leveled at the Annual Forum of the National Conference on Social Welfare as being irrelevant to the needs and problems of the day. . . . The inability of the Forum to move beyond a narrow definition of its role as a convening body created pessimism and prompted three organizations, the National Association of Black Social Workers (NABSW), the National Welfare Rights Organization (NWRO), and the National Federation of Student Social Workers (NFSSW), to attempt to radicalize the Conference and to call forth confrontations to move the Conference into a broader sphere of activity. . . . One organization, the NABSW, walked out of the Forum and set up its own separate conference.[3]

In regard to last year's Annual Forum (1969), Mr. Kidneigh tells us that:

Unscheduled speakers, through platform take-over or by speeches from the floor, released a torrent of emotional eloquence condemning the field for not moving fast enough toward particular social goals. . . . Often these impassioned speeches were attacks . . . upon NCSW itself and its leaders in the strangely misguided notion that social ills are somehow caused by the very agencies and persons who live to serve the needs of mankind.[4]

Is that a misguided notion? Who else but those who live to serve the needs of mankind can be held accountable when those needs go unmet? And certainly those needs are going unmet. We have only to look at the recent history of the 1970 Annual Forum, where again the people who need, came to confront those who live to serve. Names and faces change, but the requests remain strikingly, even shockingly, similar: people are angry; people are sick; people are unemployed—and humiliated by the lives they lead. What will the National Conference on Social Welfare do to help? The answer is also shockingly repetitive—"talk," or as Wilbur Cohen puts it, ". . . voice our convictions and explain our programs for making the United States of America a more perfect union." [5]

One might well question why groups continue to hope that

3 Howard E. Prunty, "The New York Story—A Participant's Viewpoint," *ibid.,* p. 184.

4 Kidneigh, "The New York Conference Story," *ibid.,* p. 179.

5 Wilbur J. Cohen, "Social Welfare Priorities for the 1970s," in *The Social Welfare Forum, 1970* (New York: Columbia University Press), pp. 3–10.

NCSW will change—why, in the face of all the past history, new groups emerge to take up the banner. But in fact they do.

This year we saw another attempt to make the National Conference on Social Welfare relevant. In the opening session of the Annual Forum, members of emerging groups were asked to react to Wilbur Cohen's presidential address: Some of the reactors chose to use this opportunity to read into the record statements of their particular grievances and request specific kinds of aid.

Russell P. Means, Executive Director of United Native Americans, the first reactor, came from Cleveland. He opened his remarks by saying, "I am here to tell you people of social concern that we are people too." He made it clear that American Indians are "no longer going to take the back seat to anyone," and that they insist on "an end to the war being perpetrated on them." Mr. Means said that it was necessary for him to "lay down some facts" because all that the educational institutions in this country tell about the American Indian is that "he beats a tom-tom and rows a canoe." Mr. Means presented some shocking statistics. The life expectancy of the American Indian, according to the Bureau of Indian Affairs, is forty-four years; the suicide rate among Indian teenagers is ten times the national average; the national average unemployment rate for Indians is 40 percent; their infant mortality rate is two and a half times the national average. Their median income is $1,500 per year; their educational level is at grade 5.5, as opposed to the national average which is 11.2, and their drop-out rate is four and a half times the national average.

Mr. Means reminded the Conference that because Indians comprise only one half of one percent of the total population they are likely to be overlooked. While the Indian has the "same needs, concerns, and wants as everyone else," apparently he does not have the same rights as everyone else. For example, Mr. Means noted that on the reservation any Indian can be declared incompetent without a hearing, and he has no legal recourse.

Saying that he represented native Americans in Chicago, Cleveland, Minneapolis, and all over the country, Mr. Means "demanded that the 97th Annual Forum on Social Welfare immediately stop its continued appraisal of its role in society and commit itself to the native Americans' need for self-determination."

He said that he talks to many groups, Kiwanis clubs, schools, churches, and so forth, and they all ask what can they do. His answer is: "This is an election year; your Congressmen and Senators are going to be responsive to you. . . . We would like you to express your concern about the war perpetrated on the American Indians by the Bureau of Indians Affairs."

Dr. George Wiley, Executive Director of NWRO, who was to be the second reactor, chose not to speak, but instead introduced Mrs. Johnnie Tillmon, the Chairman of NWRO. Mrs. Tillmon began her remarks by saying, "I will not say that it is a pleasure to be here." She made it clear that she did not believe in the good intentions of delegates to the Annual Forum of NCSW. "Your attitudes," she said, "are the same as they were in 1935." She accused social workers of being "coffee drinkers," and told the assemblage, "We are going to keep asking you for money because we do your job voluntarily." She recounted that "the telephone rings all the time for welfare rights workers, who have to beg to get the money needed to pay the telephone bill." But it rings all the time with people asking for social services. She remarked, "Imagine me doing social work with an eleventh-grade education."

"You can call me a revolutionist," she continued, "or a radical —or a subversive if you want to—you can call our organization Communist-inspired—but if it had not been for you people who administer social services we would have no organization. We organized because we were tired of being beat around by the social workers." She went on to say, "So if we are Communist-inspired, then you are the Communists, because you inspired us to organize." Mrs. Tillmon told all those who make such accusations: "You are just copping out because you don't want to do your jobs."

To those who "are content to stay where they are and let me stay where I am," she said: "We want change. We have become sophisticated. We teach our people to vote. We take people to the polls. . . . We've got some bills coming up in the legislature in California which we intend for some legislators to pass—if I have to be a legislator myself . . . . we are going to get $5,500 a year for a family of four on a guaranteed annual income, and all of you need to support that because it makes your check bigger."

"The heat is on," she warned. "Black folks and poor white folks are not fighting any more. You can't make one believe that he's better than the other. Dr. Cohen made some very good points but he's been making them for a long time. He's had many articles and books published, and yet the system stays the same . . . . we want change and we will get it because we are not divided—we are together."

In a show of solidarity, Mrs. Charles Brimingham, a white woman from Kansas City, Kansas, Mrs. Angie Matos, a Spanish-speaking woman from Brooklyn, and Mrs. Mary Cornelius, an Indian woman from North Dakota—all members of NWRO—spoke freely.

In summation, Dr. Wiley said that since the National Conference on Social Welfare has not provided sufficient money to support "the self-determination of poor people," the National Welfare Rights Organization was requesting that the agencies which make up the Conference "put at least 10 percent of their resources at the disposal of the self-determined organization of poor people." He concluded by saying, "Up the Nixon Plan—fifty-five hundred or fight!"

Another reactor, J. Julian Rivera, President of the Association of Puerto Rican Social Service Workers, described his presence at the Forum as a "last effort to make the social service establishment understand our needs and to find answers together before it is too late." He noted that "along with the blacks, the Chicanos, and the American Indians, the Puerto Ricans have decided to use this Forum to voice our concerns, frustrations . . . goals and aspirations hoping there are still avenues open." He identified their agenda for NCSW as being the establishment of a coalition between Puerto Ricans and Chicanos who, due to similar background and language, have also been kept out of the mainstream of American life.

Mr. Rivera accused "condescending whites" of "throwing crumbs in piecemeal fashion to keep us quiet and content." He accused "poverty and ghetto politicians of intending to divide Puerto Ricans and keep them fighting by allowing them to taste small pieces of the pie."

Mr. Rivera came to the Forum with messages for many groups. To politicians he said, "We will not support anything short of a genuine commitment to the solution of our problems and the fulfillment of our needs."

To policy-makers in the social welfare field he said. "We want participation on the policy-making boards, as well as in the administration and implementation of services to our people. We want community control of services." "If we are not successful," he added, "we will find a way to create our own institutions."

To schools of social work as well as other institutions of higher learning, he expressed "solidarity with their struggle of concerns," and to the people in Puerto Rico he expressed "solidarity in their fight for national liberation."

To the black community Mr. Rivera said, "We support their struggle—and we are ready to fight for the liberation of all peoples. Particular cultural differences and needs might direct our interest at different times, but ultimately we advocate the development of a unified front of blacks, Puerto Ricans, Chicanos, and American Indians."

In conclusion, Mr. Rivera encouraged the participants at the Forum "to unite in our struggle." He asked that they "not plan for us or show us your sympathy, but genuinely listen to what we have to say" in the hopes that "we can find solutions together."

Those who chose to respond directly to Dr. Cohen's address focused their response on the need for action, pointing up the lack of such an approach in Dr. Cohen's speech.

Pablo Sanchez, Director of the Graduate School of Social Work, San Jose State College, San Jose, California, reacted directly to Dr. Cohen's speech by taking several of the points he made and showing how they were irrelevant to the needs of La Raza. "Dr. Cohen," he began, "talked about great crisis in this country. For La Raza the crisis is the social service system which has done little for Chicanos except be paternalistic, inadequate, and harmful." Mr. Sanchez accused the leadership of NCSW as well as state-wide and local-level leadership of being "irrelevant."

He quoted Dr. Cohen as saying,, "Our political leaders must not hide behind constitutional niceties but must take the moral leadership to help eradicate the cancer of discrimination and racism from the body politic." "Excellent," answered Mr. Sanchez:

Rightly said. But what about the cancer in this body tonight? What about eradicating the cancer at home? In your agencies? In your actions? In your daily lives?"

Dr. Cohen says, "Poverty is the blight of our nation." He is no doubt right. I remember, though, that poverty was a top priority set at a national conference like this in Hamden, New Jersey, several years ago. I believe the people in this room and in this society have the leadership to eradicate poverty, but such strength is, in fact, geared to a materialistic system and power conditions that benefit only the white population and not all of us.

Dr. Cohen's faith in change through the ballot box, through the courts, through the development of adequate services, through jobs, through financial assistance, and through health insurance coverage, ignores our experience. Ever since we were conquered in 1840 each act of faith from the Chicano has been betrayed . . .

We see clearly the need for change, Dr. Cohen [Mr. Sanchez concluded]. Some of you indicate that change should start with the convention . . . . but La Raza will overcome, if we need to do it alone.

T. George Silcott, Executive Director of the Wiltwyck School for Boys, New York City, began his reaction to Dr. Cohen's speech by saying, "I'm not sure that I ought to be on this program. I don't think the people selected me." Mr. Silcott expressed ambivalence about his participation in the Forum since it was he who led the walkout of black social workers from the San Francisco Annual Forum in 1968. He noted that at that time blacks walked out because they found the Conference to be "irrelevant," and that "it really hasn't changed at all." He recalled an earlier speaker, Mrs. Tillmon, of NWRO, and allied his feelings with hers when he said, "She's back, but she doesn't want you to feel that she has enjoyed it," and wondered why he was there too.

Mr. Silcott was quite blunt when he said, "I tried very hard to find a polite way of responding to Dr. Cohen." He admitted that he was "terribly enraged" by the speech, which he called "cleverly phrased and eloquently delivered but void of suggestions as to potential solutions for the problems it raised." He continued:

I agree with Dr. Cohen that racism, discrimination, and poverty should be eliminated. . . . I agree that the right to vote is inalienable and should be protected. . . . I also agree with Dr. Cohen when he says that we need a broader and more comprehensive supplemental program than the one now pending in the Senate. . . . I agree with him that unemployment is too high and that hunger and malnutrition should be eliminated. In addition, I am against sin and for motherhood—and so is everybody here; expressing these sentiments is perhaps laudable, but it's certainly not helpful.

Mr. Silcott reminded the Conference that it was Dr. Cohen who said, "There is often rhetoric when it is least helpful," and then proceeded to add to the "growing body of useless rhetoric."

"We need an action program," he insisted. "Folks have been saying that since '68, but it's still a talk conference and probably always will be. Black history in this Conference goes way back—we know what a talk conference is, and I'm afraid the Indians are about to learn that frustrating lesson." He recalled:

it wasn't long ago that the story of a black man being burned alive at the stake was read into the records at one of these conferences. We are still reading stories of atrocities into the record and doing nothing about them. I don't know whether the Indians will succeed in helping this Conference focus on consistent action programs, but if their experience is like ours, twenty years from now they are likely to be back, asking about the promises made at this year's Forum and the rhetoric regurgitated during the ensuing years.

Mr. Silcott then accused the Conference leadership of having not been responsible. "Somewhere in the democratic process," he said, "there is a place for enlightened autocracy, a place for responsible direction, a place for accountability—and sometimes that's called leadership." He called upon the leadership "to challenge the membership—to push the seemingly reluctant membership into taking action."

Mr. Silcott confided that he believed his reaction to Dr. Cohen's speech was affected by the fact of his own blackness. "I couldn't give a speech like that," he said. "The black community wouldn't tolerate it." The fact that Dr. Cohen did, raises the question as to whether blacks have a place in the Conference.

"The tone of this Annual Forum is uneven," he concluded. "The melody I first heard was 'business as usual'; now I hear some folks saying, 'That's not good enough.' I'm hoping that this may produce some action, so that in 1971 when we assemble in Dallas, some of us will feel that our lives have been affected by what happens here and will see some new directions."

In his introduction, Leo Bohanon, Chairman of the Opening General Session, told the following story:

There was once a forum held by some medieval scholars. They had been debating, talking, and conferring the greater part of the day and night on the subject of the number of teeth in a horse's mouth. They had discussed it pro and con. They had looked it up in Plato, Aristotle, and Socrates—but they made no mention of the number of teeth in the head of a horse. Finally a "nontechnician," an unlettered man, hearing them discuss this portentous subject, stuck his head through the window and said, "Why in the hell don't you get a horse, look in his mouth, and count his teeth?"

Mr. Bohanon commented, "We are somewhat in the same position here in our Forum, year in and year out. This evening we have with us the reactors [to Wilbur Cohen's speech] who are going to do the 'counting'—who are going to get realistic in terms of seeing issues as they affect people."

Irwin Bahl, President of the National Federation of Student Social Workers, who is preparing to go into the social welfare field and deal with some of the problems raised by the reactors, like Mr. Bohanon understood the importance of hearing from the people but was so emotionally affected that he was nearly speechless. His reaction to Dr. Cohen's speech is printed here in its entirety:

Before this meeting, we were asked upstairs what we would want to say—if, in fact, we wanted to say anything. Dammit, I had nothing to say then and I have a hell of a lot less to say now. If you people haven't heard what went on, I've got a few questions for you. Why did you invite us here? Was it to let us know, like the Nixon Administration, that we are now so short of minority groups—the oppressed?

Was it to let us know somehow that we fit on the end of this program? To let us know that we are really clients? To let us really know that the people we could learn from are sitting right here? Was it to let us know that the schools of social work had failed? Continue to fail, and remain irrelevant? Was it to let us know finally who really is saying the truth? Who really knows it? Who really lives it? We've heard it and we know it, and now you want us to say something in response to Dr. Cohen.

Do you want to talk about oppression and campus killings? I have a question for you: What are you going to do for the people? There are people here. How do you intend to get the people—minority people—to positions which will affect policy, which will give them community control of the system? When are you going to recognize that they are human beings?

In his introduction, Mr. Bohanon stressed the importance of "going to the horse's mouth." But now, like Mohammed, we have been "to the mountain," we know the placement of every cavity, we have exposed every decaying tooth. We have heard from the people—again; we have heard from some of their leadership—again; we have heard from one who aspires to be a social worker; and we might properly ask: is the National Conference on Social Welfare able, in its present form, to play an effective role in solving these problems?

Where Are Solutions?

A SUMMARY OF THE CLOSING
GENERAL SESSION

VIRGINIA R. DOSCHER

IN A QUIET BUT FIRM VOICE the young man said, "The only solution is revolution."

This was the final comment from the four panelists who presented four quite different viewpoints on how social welfare needs to change in the decade of the seventies at the closing General Session of the 1970 Forum of the National Conference on Social Welfare. The speaker was Cha Cha Jiminez, national chairman of the Young Lords Organization, a group of young Puerto Ricans. The thrust of his message was that it is beyond the ability of social welfare to bring about solution of the problems of the poor—it is the economic system which must change.

Pointing out that laws that have been put on the books to help people have very often ended up having "exactly the opposite effect," David Friedman, of the conservative Young Americans for Freedom, advocated change through elimination of legislation and of regulations. "Increases in the power of government are not always a help to the poor," said the young University of Chicago graduate student in theoretical physics. "I think that decreasing it might be." Under the present system, discretionary power which is used for political ends is given to political bodies, he stated. (Mr. Jiminez commented that Mr. Friedman's approach was still a paternalistic one, with those who are "haves" making decisions for those who are "have-nots.")

For the blacks, what is required is that they reshape and rework the institutions of society to provide alternatives to the way that society now is moving, in the opinion of Dr. J. Archie Hargraves, chairman of the Black Strategy Center for Community Development and a member of the faculty of Chicago Theological Seminary.

Revising and refocusing social welfare programs through the legislative process was the solution offered by Representative Roman Pucinski, of the Eleventh U.S. Congressional District. Among other reforms, he proposed a six-hour workday for mothers. He also expressed belief that in the long run it will be demonstrated that Americans have made a greater effort toward elimination of racial discrimination than any other country in the world. But he did admit that the democratic process is slow.

A slow process will not do, Dr. Hargraves replied. It is necessary to have massive, comprehensive, and fast change. "The 'new nigger,'" he said, "is the black man who is about the job of bringing himself together, not surfacing until he has done his basic thinking, unifying himself to build and create those institutions that will be alternatives to the way society is now moving . . . . developing the confidences and skills and leadership that will make a new way possible . . . . [working at] development of a new congeries of social arrangements for their liberation, empowerment, and development." The object is to bring about a new kind of society that is developed and transformed, that will be interjected into the mainstream of society from the standpoint of a black perspective in order to make society over and give it a new transformation and a new kind of force.

Dr. Hargraves predicted that the seventies will see an escalation of the protest of the politics of disruption but advised his listeners to understand that it is the making of a new kind of skill. "By the year 2000 a new kind of society will come as a result of these sacrifices," he predicted.

"We're not fighting America," said Cha Cha Jiminez. "We're not fighting the mountains and trees. We're fighting the system of capitalism which is like a crap game where somebody wins and somebody always has to go home without his shirt and his shoes. And that's what the problem is." The reason our efforts to combat poverty have failed, he feels, is because we are trying to evade the real problem.

What of social workers in the seventies? Dr. Hargraves talked about how the day of the old game of helping blacks to adjust and accommodate was gone; the name of the new game is how to remove powerlessness and get power. He said he was leaving the question open as to whether social workers will be relevant to this new game.

David Friedman thinks that if the poor are given the money that is now being spent on them by others it will be their decision as to whether they want to hire social workers to assist them. And Cha Cha Jiminez said that it makes the poor people "uptight" when social workers come into their communities because social workers don't understand the poor, the junkies, the prostitutes—and these people don't understand social workers.

Judging by the response of members of the audience, they sometimes agreed and sometimes disagreed with the panelists. But possibly all agreed with the moderator, Studs Terkel, author of *"Hard Times: an Oral History of the Great Depression."* The aim of the session, he said, was to "pique us, to jab us" into continuing to think, after the Conference was over and everyone had returned home, about the unsolved problems of our society and about what social welfare can offer toward their solution.

Chicago Scene I: Conference Report

WERNER W. BOEHM

THE EVENTS OF THE 1970 CONFERENCE can best be reported by looking at some events which preceded it, reviewing the Conference itself, and then examining the meaning of these events.

THE EVENTS BEFORE THE EVENT

The decisions which were made at the 1969 Annual Forum in New York influenced the deliberations of the National Board of the Conference, membership referenda, and meetings of associate groups, which took place in the course of the year before the Chicago Annual Forum and cast their shadow on the Conference. Two issues stand out: One might be called the "$35,000 misunderstanding," and the other is the pressure to transform NCSW into a social action body. Despite efforts to clarify, explain, and call attention to official decisions in which the National Welfare Rights Association (NWRO) had participated, NWRO continued to contend that the Annual Meeting of members had voted in New York in 1969 to increase agency dues in order to be able to give NWRO $35,000, and that NCSW had broken this promise. Repeatedly, NCSW pointed out that although NWRO had demanded $35,000, the National Board announced publicly: (*a*) that it could not meet the request; (*b*) that it would submit any resolution on dues change passed at the Annual Meeting of Members to a referendum; and (*c*) that it had appointed an *ad hoc* committee to work with NWRO to try to secure funds (no amount stipulated). In March, 1969, the Executive Committee of NCSW had its first opportunity to review the financial status of the Conference after the January billings. The accounts showed a decrease in receipts from agency dues and, in addition, a $10,000 deficit on income from exhibits. The Executive Committee confirmed the Board's projection of $40,000 as what the Conference hoped to realize from the dues increase. It set the following priorities: (1) $18,000 to cover the deficit due to rising costs; (2) an allocation of $8,000 to enable the participation of emerging social welfare interests, including NWRO; (3) the remainder for the Division Program and special projects, including the Social Issues Forum and other activities, including the constitutional revision, which were mandated by the Annual Meeting of Members.

The $8,000 allocation could not be increased, therefore, but would enable forty to fifty representatives of the emerging social welfare interests (ESWI) to be participants. One half of this amount was earmarked for NWRO. The Board did not and could not accept the accusation that NCSW had acted in bad faith. The Board in New York in 1969 had disagreed with some of the NWRO requests, and there was no secrecy about its action. NWRO was represented on the National Board in 1969–70, although Dr. George Wiley, who accepted that position, did not attend a single meeting. Furthermore, NWRO has a policy not to raise funds for other organizations.

This issue continued to cause contention and recrimination both prior to and during the Annual Forum although repeated explanations of the facts were made. Since the Board at different times communicated with different representatives of the ESWI, it was difficult to know whether clarification had been achieved or whether this issue was kept alive in order to maintain militancy and credibility among the rank and file.

The other issue followed in the wake of the invasion of Cambodia and the killings at Kent State University. Efforts which had been made throughout the year to cancel the Chicago meeting and to engage in social and political action instead became stronger as a result of these events. The groups that urged NCSW to cancel the Chicago meeting were informed that as a result of the events in New York, the program format of Chicago had been changed. NCSW has to be, as its constitution stipulates, "a voluntary association of individual and organizational members, which includes those providing and using welfare services. It is an educational forum for the critical examination of basic welfare problems and solutions. Through its annual forums and its related activities, the Conference will provide opportunities for articulating issues, clarifying positions, and may take appropriate implementing measures."

THE CONFERENCE

The forum purpose of the Conference was frequently questioned, despite the fact that the following changes in the format and content had been made: Every opportunity was used to stress action strategies and the participation of the emerging social welfare interests in the program. Racism and poverty were stressed for these sessions. A number of social problems were highlighted, such as, income maintenance, human rights, drugs, delinquency, crime, aging, unemployment, hunger and malnutrition, community-police conflicts, and the like. Several general sessions and a number of major meetings were planned with reactors from the emerging social welfare interests. The Wednesday night General Session was planned by representatives of the ESWI. A series of social action workshops was scheduled, and students were included in most of these sessions. Caucuses were planned by groups concerned with welfare rights, hunger, peace, racism, dissent, and repression. The Sunday night General Session was arranged to provide ample opportunity to introduce current issues, and five reactors to Wilbur Cohen's presidential address were scheduled. These reactors had been named by the EWSI and were to represent blacks, browns, NWRO, and students. Former NCSW president Wayne Vasey, representing a coalition of students and faculty, was scheduled to announce an *ad hoc* meeting of all attenders to remain at the conclusion of the opening General Session for the purpose of discussing current concerns relating to the war and the relationship of the United States involvement in it to dealing with social and human problems at home and abroad. In addition, the Social Issues Forum was held on Tuesday evening, June 2. At that time various groups presented resolutions and action proposals on various issues and concerns for debate by the attenders. Several organizations geared to social action made proposals which they intended to follow up after the meeting.

The major thrust of representatives of the ESWI, both in National Board meetings and in Annual Forum sessions, was to question the relevance of the Conference proceedings, to criticize the Conference for its lack of concern with social action issues. It was not easy to convey that even if NCSW had the power, the membership referendum to the contrary notwithstanding, to become a social action body, another forum organization would undoubtedly emerge. These critics also did not realize that NCSW is not an organization of professional social workers but is much more broadly constituted, including also volunteers, nonprofessionals, lay persons, and agencies. In a number of meetings, broadside attacks were made on social work's goals and methods, and at times one could gain the impression that the fire department was being blamed for the fire. Nevertheless, on the whole, the Annual Forum was productive and carried on its activities in an orderly fashion, despite some minor and major incidents to the contrary. Many of the problems were ironed out by dint of much effort, good will, and forebearance on the part of Conference staff, NWRO organizers, and others. In fact, the underpublicized decision by NWRO not to disrupt the Annual Forum enabled it to present to its membership and the public a picture of militancy coupled with sagacity.

THE MEANING OF THE CONFERENCE

Probably it is more important to examine what underlies the events than to report the events themselves. For this writer, three conclusions emerge:

1. A strong conviction felt and held not only by the ESWI but also by other members of the Conference and the National Board, that social action geared to social change through both volunteer and professional activities is critically urgent.

2. NWRO has emerged as the leading organization of welfare consumers and as such renders an important service to American society. This is true despite the questions one may raise about

some of its tactics. It is true even despite the doubts it casts upon itself by the ambiguous position it assumes by, on the one hand, trying to maintain the militancy through attacks on the social work establishment while, on the other hand, making deals with "establishment" organizations such as the National Conference, from which it accepts funds badly needed for the conduct of its operations. NWRO must be considered a valid force in American society because it has succeeded in improving the welfare situation by mobilizing social welfare consumers.

3. NCSW has an obligation to exercise leadership toward the creation in social welfare of social action programs.

At the National Board meeting on May 3, the Board agreed that the NCSW has a social action responsibility and resolved to "direct the Executive Committee on a continuing basis to follow up on methods of initiating and pursuing the possibilities through mergers, coalitions, and other joint ventures for social action and to report to the National Board at its November [1970] meeting and periodically thereafter." This writer, speaking personally, would underline the urgency of this step. He also reaffirms the need for an educational forum. Even if the educational function of the National Conference on Social Welfare could be or were abandoned, another organization would sooner or later spring up to engage in educational and forum activities now carried forward by NCSW. Nevertheless, it may be important for the Conference to give additional thought to possible links between forum and social action activities. There may be wisdom and advantage in linking the identification of issues, which is a key function of the Annual Forum, to the identification of solutions in the form of social welfare programs and the execution of such programs through appropriate action, civic, legislative, and professional. Has the time come to clarify what the words of the constitution, "take appropriate implementing measures," really should mean? Would it be premature and inappropriate to explore again with the National Association of Social Workers, the National Assembly for Social Policy and Development, NWRO, and other organizations, the possibility of doing what the constitution and the national Board's resolution of May 3 make possible? If we can look at what lies underneath the rhetoric of the emerging social welfare interests, we may find that our goals are similar to theirs and we may want to decide that coalition can take the place of contention.

Chicago Scene II:
Report from a Participant

HOWARD E. PRUNTY

When Sinatra sings "Chi-ca-go, Chi-ca-go that wonderful town," the song and phase evoke different images for different people—Mrs. O'Leary's cow and the great Chicago fire; Hugh Hefner and the Playboy Club and bunnies; Mayor Daley and the Democratic Convention charade; Judge Hoffman and the Chicago Eight; District Attorney Stamos and the Black Panther subjugation, and so on. One might ask how all this relates to the National Conference on Social Welfare. The answer: Far more than one might at first believe. The "reputation" of Chicago certainly influenced an individual's decision regarding his attendance at the NCSW's 97th Annual Forum.

Some individuals refused to attend in order to express their opposition to holding the Conference in Chicago. Others decided to attend, looking forward to a repeat of the drama, excitement, and fascination of the New York City Conference. Still others, possibly the majority, came reluctantly, fearful of experiencing a repeat of the New York unfoldings, but they came anyway, apparently out of a timeworn tradition and a votive duty. Nearly all Conference attendants came with expectations tempered by New York and the infamous "reputation" of Chicago. However, all were destined for a week of disappointment and ennui.

There was a small group that went to Chicago with a sense of mission, a determination to make the Conference relevant to current issues—racism and poverty—and to make possible a collective sharing of information for purposes of social activism. This group was comprised of individuals and representatives of emerging groups who had since New York labored on varied program planning committees to assure that the viewpoints of minority groups were appropriately represented. Their other large goal was to help white social workers become far more conscious of the widespread existence of racism in all its forms and of the immense costs that racism imposes on minority groups and the poor.

Some few program participants were also members of this small group. All held the belief that meaningful change in the behavior of whites and the structure of institutions will come about when everybody understands the necessity for the change. They came with an eagerness, an outside hope, and an expectation that the planned sessions, workshops, and general sessions would provide the key that would open the door to a more realistic and humanistic level of communication between whites and members of minority groups.

There was the glimmer of hope that cutting through the dialogue blocks would enable both groups to cross the racial river Styx to an open field of honest and humane communication, affording removal of discriminating barriers and equal access to opportunities. If nothing else, it was hoped that the white participants would come to an awareness that cooperative alliances with minority groups were in their own best self-interests. This was not to be at this Conference. They learned that white Americans have little or no disposition to "sacrifice" their personal and psychological prosperity and that their attitudes cannot be transformed by new information, exhortation, or appeals. The ranks of the disheartened swelled.

In fact, it became clear, following the opening General Session, that the Conference week was to be one of resistance to a responsible dialogue. From that point on the Conference developed an air of dullness and spiritlessness. The white participants very early adopted an attitude of hostile resignation. It was conveyed that they would attend sessions, participate in workshops, but would not permit themselves to achieve a level of understanding that would irrevocably compel them to enlist in the struggle, with others, to achieve true social justice and promote the ideals and concepts of an operative pluralistic society where members of different groups can live, work, and act together. They would be spectators but not participants.

Very early during the week the emerging social welfare groups, particularly the National Welfare Rights Organization (NWRO), the Social Welfare Workers Movement (SWWM), and two American Indian organizations (the Native American Committee of Chicago and the Cleveland American Indian Center) became subconsciously aware of the settling indifference of the whites in attendance. (Later during the week this subconsicious awareness was confirmed.) They then began to employ various strategies to achieve their goals of forcing the NCSW to become more politically and social action-oriented. Their aim also was to establish a social action wing of NCSW that would be actively involved in the eventual eradication of racism, social injustice, political repression, and poverty in the country.

Some of the strategies used were:

Direct confrontation. On Sunday at the opening sessions, on Monday night at the General Session, and again on Friday at the NCSW national Board breakfast, NWRO utilized this method to radicalize, to inform, and to assure that the concerns of, and information from, minorities and the poor received sufficient exposure and consideration.

SWWM issued its own forms and badges, stamped "People's Delegate," and encouraged its members to attend sessions, thereby forcing a counteraction from the Conference.

Disruption. The activities of the SWWM people's delegates were also utilized to disrupt planned sessions. They "seized" some programs to dramatize their concerns and to discourage registrations for the Annual Forum.

Conference-wide participation. NWRO assigned one member to each and every planned session. The aim was to inform the attenders of the goals of NWRO—for example, a minimum income of $5500 for a family of four—in efforts to elicit individual and financial support.

Quiet diplomacy. Again, NWRO members and other minority representatives participated in meetings and sessions where policy decisions were made. In addition, they articulated their program to individual members and to groups.

Unfortunately, none of the strategies achieved the desired goals or even remotely touched or influenced those individuals who, in the final analysis, made the decisions—NCSW's membership. So, at the annual meeting of members the membership for the third year voted to have the NCSW remain as it has for the past ninety-seven years—an educational forum. "Business as usual" was the order of the day. The old order doesn't changeth.

Occasionally, there were times when individual participants were really striving to understand, to reach beyond the barriers of their ingrained and ingrown prejudices. A very few succeeded.

As one wandered about, into sessions, through the corridors, and in the exhibition halls, one began to become aware of a new group of people at the Conference. They had an air of excitement, were enthusiastic, and attended as many sessions as they could—sometimes as many as four or five in one day. They purchased and collected as much material as they could. Interestingly, and strictly speaking, they were not recognized social workers nor were they from traditional social work agencies. They were paraprofessionals from day care programs primarily, but also from model city programs, neighborhood programs for the single mother and her child, and the like. They represented a new breed of "social worker." Although small in number this year, they will be a group to reckon with in the future. The participation and expectations of this new group will have an influence and an impact upon NCSW far beyond their numbers. Will NCSW react to this new challenge as it has in its past relationships with the "emerging groups," such as NWRO and SWWM, or will it wisely utilize their unique talents in making efforts to change and improve its own operations in relation to the responsibility of dealing socially and politically with the formidable social issues of today? Placing more minority group representatives on the national Board, on program-planning committees, and so forth is not enough. Opening up opportunities for program participation is also insufficient. Nothing short of being a catalyst for constructive social change will do.

There were during the week, moments of fun and even moments of high comedy. Those who failed to catch the NWRO dance and George Wiley's rendition of "Casey at the Bat" missed a treat.

There were also moments of high drama. I refer here to the vital and vivid emergence of the "true American" on the social welfare scene. This militant assertion of their just claims and of their sense of identity is a forecast of their future activities.

The "liberation" of the Bureau of Indian Affairs booth is an indication of their rejection of continued federal paternalism and oppression; an assertion of their rights to run their own schools and welfare programs and a warning that their re-entry into American life will be on their own terms. Their presence will be felt, no matter what the opinion or reaction of the Conference and the social welfare system turns out to be. Like the blacks, the Chicanos, and the Puerto Ricans the American Indian has traveled the same historical path in the struggle to achieve social justice and racial equality. Others will soon follow: the Appalachian whites and the isolated urban dwellers.

For the past three years NCSW has related passively to the incessant demands for change and to the increasing polarization between whites and minority groups. The time for a decision to change is long overdue. Prolonging the decision serves no useful purpose. It tends only to alienate and erode the support of both groups, those fighting for social justice and those content with business as usual. NCSW needs; I believe, both groups if it is to continue as a viable organization. It is essential, then, that NCSW not lose this opportunity—perhaps the last opportunity—to lead in building coalitions that will hasten the abolishment of poverty, racism, and economic exploration. Failure to seize this opportunity "would be as fatal as it is cowardly." [1]

---

[1] John Tyndall, "Science and Man," in *Essays on the Floating Matter of the Air in Relation to Putrefaction and Infection* (New York: Johnson Reprint Corp., 1967), p. 131.

National Conference on Social Welfare: a Report to the Membership

NEW YORK TO CHICAGO: CONFERENCE REPORT

In accepting the gavel in New York, President Wilbur Cohen stated his position and that of the Conference: "We shall make every earnest effort to involve more representative groups in the planning of the next Forum and its program. I hope that when you come to next year's conference you will come with a spirit of idealism and compassion, of dedication and of participation—full participation for the minority and the majority."

Many of the groups most active in San Francisco failed to appear at the New York Forum. Others—the National Welfare Rights Organization (NWRO) and the National Association of Black Social Workers (NABSW)—had grown stronger. The National Federation of Student Social Workers (NFSSW) was active, but portions of its membership appeared to have joined with other groups to form the new Social Welfare Workers' Movement (SWWM). La Raza, a coalition of Spanish-speaking Americans, and numbers of smaller groups spoke for the first time.

The unprecedented confrontations at the New York Annual Forum raised many questions. These were reported in the Summer issue (1969) of the Conference *Bulletin,* as were the decisions made by the National Board in its seven meetings held in New York and a special meeting held on July 18–19, 1969. Basically, the questions raised in New York may be summarized under two general issues:

1. Increased participation of "emerging social welfare interests" (ESWI)

2. Increased "social action" involvement by existing social welfare organizations, including the Conference

With regard to the latter, the Conference membership has expressed itself clearly by referendum vote, first on revision of the Preamble to the Constitution and recently by a second referendum on revision of the Constitution. In both instances, the membership has rejected the social action function for the Conference in favor of its educational function.

The "earnest effort(s) of the Conference to involve more representative groups" during the past year are listed below:

1. During the 1969 Annual Forum, six proposals, including a "Revision of the NCSW Constitution" and a "Revision of Membership Dues," were submitted to the Annual Meeting of Members and fourteen to the Social Action Forum.

2. The NCSW National Board in seven meetings held in New York examined each proposal to determine future action by the Conference.

3. The NCSW Editorial Committee authorized the commissioning of two papers recounting the New York confrontations, to be published in *The Social Welfare Forum, 1969:* one by NCSW Vice President John C. Kidneigh, from the Conference point of view; the second by Howard Prunty, from a participant's point of view.

4. The National Board at a special meeting on July 18–19 authorized two membership referenda:

   a) The first, on membership dues, to be sent as amended and approved by the Annual Meeting of Members accompanied by a Board statement recommending defeat and substitution of its own proposal, to be mailed in September

   b) The second, on revision of the NCSW Constitution, to be mailed in January, 1970

The Program Committee was instructed to focus on racism and poverty at the 1970 Annual Forum.

A full report of major actions was published in the Summer (1969) Conference *Bulletin*.

5. NWRO, NABSW, and NFSSW were invited to nominate representatives to serve on the NCSW National Board, the 1969–70 term of the Program Committee, and the U.S. Committee of the International Council on Social Welfare.

6. A five-member NCSW committee with Leo Bohanon as chairman was appointed to work with a similar committee from NABSW in implementing the NCSW-NABSW "Statement of Understanding" formulated at the New York Annual Forum. (The committee was terminated and the planned meeting canceled on July 22, 1969, when NABSW "nullified" the agreement.)

7. An *ad hoc* committee with Bob Shea as chairman was appointed to "assist La Raza to secure funds for a joint meeting with NCSW." (The meeting was canceled when a Foundation grant could not be obtained.)

8. A special meeting of executives of Associate Groups was held in New York, July 25, to review the New York experience.

9. A check for $1,025 in "voluntary contributions" made during the Opening General Session was mailed to NWRO.

10. The membership dues referendum was mailed to members on September 15.

11. A second meeting of executives of Associate Groups was held in New York, September 18.

12. Representatives of ESWI were invited to a luncheon meeting to formulate plans for a general session on "Emerging Groups."

13. The NCSW Tellers' Committee met to tabulate votes on the membership dues referendum. (The National Board's proposal was adopted by 54.4 percent of the 3,884 voting members.)

14. Major actions taken at the NCSW National Board meeting in Columbus, November 20–21, 1969, were:

   a) The sum of $8,000 was designated to be set aside for expenses of program participants from the ESWI at the 1970 Annual Forum, to be reviewed by the Executive Committee at the March meeting to determine whether additional funds might be available for such participation.

b) The Social Action Forum was renamed the "Social Issues Forum." Funds were allocated for this and other special activities.

c) The NCSW Constitution was revised, with primary consideration to insure ESWI representation on the National Board Nominations and Program committees.

d) Exhibit space for organizations representing ESWI was approved.

15. A luncheon meeting with ESWI representatives was held on December 5 to plan a general session.

16. The referendum on NCSW constitutional revision was mailed to members; closing date for return, May 4, 1970.

17. ESWI groups were invited to name reactors to Annual Forum sessions.

18. The NCSW Executive Committee meeting was held on March 19:

a) Approved assignment of meeting rooms, caucus rooms, exhibit space, and final program listing for ESWI groups at NCSW expense

b) Reaffirmed the National Board's allocation of funds for ESWI program participation

c) Reaffirmed the National Board's decision "that NCSW would take no responsibility for fund-raising for other organizations"

d) Approved discontinuance of *ad hoc* committee for voluntary collection of NWRO contributions

e) Authorized NCSW to pay EWSI program participants' expenses at economy air fare rates and $23 per diem, with complimentary Registration for two days

19. ESWI groups were invited to submit nominations for Annual Forum registration of "low-income users."

20. The third meeting of executives of Associate Groups was held on April 23.

21. A second invitation to Associate Group status in NCSW was issued to NWRO on April 20.

The National Board feels that we have made progress. Events in Chicago will determine whether the membership agrees.

NEW YORK TO CHICAGO:
AN OBSERVER'S COMMENT

FLORENCE HORCHOW

Mindful of Robert Burns's belief in the value of seeing ourselves as others see us, the National Conference on Social Welfare asked an observer with many years of experience on boards
and committees of local and national social agencies to take a
look at what had happened to the Conference between the 1969
and the 1970 Annual Forum.

As ONE WHO TAKES A JOURNEY inevitably looks back
and questions whether the route followed was the best one, so
to understand the activities of the National Conference on Social
Welfare today one must look back, briefly, over the journey from
the Pacific to the Atlantic and now to the middle of the country.
In San Francisco in 1968, for the first time in more than 90 years
NCSW experienced a forceful take-over of program in the Annual Forum, and 400 black social workers walked out of the hall.
"Emerging social welfare groups" became an integral part of
our vocabulary, and the Forum moved toward "issues" rather
than "methods" as its focus of purpose.

The road from San Francisco to New York has been told in
detail in the Conference *Bulletin,* but for the sake of newcomers
a few milestones might be recalled.

A revision of the Preamble to the NCSW Constitution made
possible consideration of courses of social action which have been
discussed in joint meetings with allied organizations. Three
"emerging groups," the National Welfare Rights Organization
(NWRO), the National Association of Black Social Workers
(NABSW), and the National Federation of Student Social Workers (NFSSW), were invited to Associate Group status. The Conference offered "support" to NWRO in approaching foundations
for funds to pay expenses of fifty "users of service" at the 1969
Annual Forum.

The rumblings in San Francisco exploded in New York with the take-over of registration and the General Session on opening day. The Summer issue (1969) of the Conference *Bulletin* relates in detail the events during and immediately following the New York Forum. Many of the issues involved are still present.

This observer, looking down the road from New York to Chicago, is impressed by the heavy traffic as the National Board, the Executive Committee, Associate Groups, and the NCSW staff sought to reach understanding with emerging groups and, where possible, to accede to their requests.

Two subjects stand out as areas of greatest concern: money and participation in policy-making.

The National Board at a special meeting in July 1969, agreed to accept as members-at-large three nominees designated by NABSW, NFSSW, and NWRO. Soon thereafter, NABSW nullified its agreement with the Conference and terminated all relationships.

NWRO was highy critical of NCSW when its 1970 appeal for funds failed to bring expected results and was unimpressed with the explanation that potential contributors found the tactics employed in New York had created an "unfavorable climate" for funding.

La Raza, a coalition of Spanish-speaking Americans, blamed NCSW for its failure to provide funds and assume full responsibility for "joint" meetings although the NCSW National Board had authorized appointment of an *ad hoc* committee only to "assist" La Raza in securing funds and planning meetings.

In October, 1969, representatives of NWRO, NFSSW, and La Raza were invited to a luncheon meeting on December 5 to plan a General Session for "emerging groups" at the 1970 Forum. Because of poor attendance this was rescheduled for December 29.

In November, the National Board, in recognition of their financial need, set aside the sum of $8,000 to pay expenses for participation of "emerging social welfare interests" at the 1970 Annual Forum. The Social Action Forum was renamed the "Social Issues Forum," and a referendum on revision of the NCSW

Constitution was approved to insure representation of emerging social welfare interests on the National Board and on the Nominating and Program committees of the Conference.

Throughout the early months of 1970, NCSW worked tirelessly, and not too successfully, in trying to secure names of program participants from "emerging groups" and to fill requests for exhibit space and caucus rooms. Changes in personnel within the various organizations accounted for some of the difficulty in getting needed program information. As the Forum hour grew closer misunderstandings arose over NWRO and La Raza pressure for increases in the number of participants to be paid for by NCSW.

Budget limitations forced the NCSW to be firm but other requests were granted. Notices of NWRO and La Raza meetings were carried in the final program without charge, and complimentary registrations for 500 "low-income users of service" were provided. Emerging interest groups were asked to submit names of persons from their organizations.

In March, after 1970 program plans had been completed and speakers invited, the Social Workers Radical Caucus (SWRC), formerly the Social Fund for the Conspiracy, asked for a general session and several small discussion sessions devoted to the trial of the "seven conspirators." The Executive Committee at its March Meeting approved an SWRC meeting for Thursday, June 4, to avoid conflict with other major meetings already planned. This was unsatisfactory, and the group planned a meeting for Tuesday morning, June 2.

In two meetings of executives of Associate Groups, NCSW officers were charged with responsibility for "taking all necessary measures to insure the rights of participants in 1970 to assemble and speak in safety, without coercion or intimidation, and to insure the participation of emerging groups in orderly deliberation and policy-making." In viewing the activities of NCSW officers and staff it seems to this observer that these recommendations have been carried out.

Appendix A: Program

THE MAJOR FUNCTION of the National Conference on Social Welfare (NCSW) is to provide a dynamic educational forum and the critical examination of basic welfare problems and issues.

Programs of the Annual Forums are divided into two parts: (1) the General Sessions and the meetings of the section and division committees, all of which are arranged by the NCSW Program Committee and the National Board; and (2) meetings which are arranged by the associate and special groups affiliated with the NCSW.

In addition to arranging these meetings, associate and special groups participate in the over-all planning of the Annual Forum programs.

In order that the NCSW may continue to provide a democratic forum in which all points of view are represented, it is prohibited by its Constitution from taking positions on social issues. Individuals who appear on Annual Forum programs speak for themselves and have no authority to use the name of the NCSW in any way which would imply that the organization has participated in or endorsed their statements or positions.

Theme: Social Policies for the 1970s: Prospects and Strategies

SUNDAY, MAY 31

2:00 P.M.—3:15 P.M.

ORIENTATION SESSION
Presiding and speaker: John H. McMahon, Director of Public Relations, State Communities Aid Association, New York; Chairman, Public Relations and Development Committee, NCSW
Speaker: Sara Lee Berkman, Associate Executive Secretary, NCSW, New York
Sponsor: NCSW

2:00 P.M.—4:30 P.M.

SECOND REGIONAL MEETING FOR NORTH AMERICA, INTERNATIONAL COUNCIL ON SOCIAL WELFARE
Presiding: Reuben C. Baetz, Vice President, ICSW; Executive Director, Canadian Welfare Council, Ottawa
Report on ICSW and Its XVth International Conference, Manila
Speaker: Mrs. Kate Katzki, Secretary-General, ICSW, New York
Summary of National Report: International Federation of Social Workers
Speaker: Nelson C. Jackson, Secretary-General, International Federation of Social Workers, New York

Summary of National Report: International Association of Schools of Social Work
> *Speaker:* Kurt Reichert, Director, Division of Educational Standards and Accreditation, Council of Social Work Education, New York

Summary of National Report: U.S. Committee, ICSW
> *Speaker:* Norman V. Lourie, Executive Deputy Secretary, Pennsylvania Department of Public Welfare, Harrisburg

Summary of National Report: Canada
> *Speaker:* Charles E. Hendry, Consultant, Department of Social and Family Services, Toronto, Canada

What One Should Know about Manila
> *Speaker:* Cayetano Santiago, Project Director, Illinois Migrant Council, Chicago

Sponsor: Regional Meeting, U.S. and Canadian Committees, ICSW.

2:00 P.M.—5:00 P.M.

IN-BASKET FOR VOLUNTEER BUREAUS:
SIMULATION EXERCISES IN RESPONDING TO
PRESSURES AND PRIORITIES
> *Presiding:* Mrs. Frederic Harwood, Director, Volunteer Service Bureau of the Greater Dayton Area, Dayton, Ohio
> *Speakers:* Rhoda M. Andersen, Executive Director, Volunteer Bureau, Los Angeles Region, Los Angeles
> Marilyn Jensen, Associate Professor, College of Applied Science and Arts, California State College, Los Angeles

Sponsor: United Community Funds and Councils of America–Association of Volunteer Bureaus

7:30 P.M.—10:00 P.M.

OPENING GENERAL SESSION
> A Program of Priorities for the 1970s; the Presidential Address
> *Invocation:* Dr. D. E. King, Monumental Baptist Church, Chicago
> *Introduction:* M. Leo Bohanon, Midwest Regional Director, National Urban League, St. Louis; Chairman, Advisory Committee on Program Scope, Content, and Participation, NCSW
> *Speaker:* Wilbur J. Cohen, Dean, School of Education, University of Michigan, Ann Arbor; President, NCSW

Black Point of View
> *Reactor:* T. George Silcott, Executive Director, Wiltwyck School for Boys, New York

La Raza-Chicano Point of View
> *Reactor:* Pablo R. Sanchez, Director, Graduate Department of Social Work, San Jose State College, San Jose, Calif.

La Raza-Puerto Rican Point of View
> *Reactor:* Julian Rivera, President, Association of Puerto Rican Social Workers, New York

National Welfare Rights' Point of View
> *Reactors:* Jennette Washington, Henry Johnson, Koro Roosen-Runge, Carol J. Irons, Mrs. Rosa Jimenez

10:00 P.M.

CONFERENCE RECEPTION

Monday, June 1

9:00 A.M.—10:45 A.M.

GENERAL SESSION
The Administration's Proposals
> *Presiding:* Wilbur J. Cohen, Dean, School of Education, University of Michigan, Ann Arbor; President, NCSW
> *Speaker:* John D. Twiname, Administrator, Social and Rehabilitation Service, Department of Health, Education, and Welfare, Washington

11:00 A.M.

FILM THEATER
> Film: The Battered Child
> *Discussant:* Shelton Key, Director, Social Services, Children's Memorial Hospital, Chicago
Sponsor: NCSW Audio-Visual Committee

11:00 A.M.—10:00 P.M.

CAUCUS
Sponsor: La Raza

CAUCUS
Sponsor: National Welfare Rights Organization

11:15 A.M.—12:45 P.M.

SOCIAL POLICIES FOR THE 1970s:
PROSPECTS AND STRATEGIES
> *Presiding:* James R. Dumpson, Dean of Social Service, Fordham University, New York
> *Panelists:* Bert Jay De Leeuw, National Welfare Rights Organization, Washington
> Michael J. Austin, Student, University of Pittsburgh, Pittsburgh
> Thomas C. Moan, social worker, Child Welfare Department, Oregon Department of Public Welfare, Eugene

YOUTH AND DRUGS
> *Speakers:* Col. Hassan Jeru-Ahmed, Director, Blackman's Development Center, Washington

Charles "Sonny" Long, Vocational Rehabilitation Specialist, Community Addiction Treatment Center, Washington
Sponsor: Section I (Casework), Group Meeting 1

PRIORITIES IN IMPROVING THE DELIVERY OF
SERVICES IN OUR CITIES

Presiding: Peter G. Gaupp, Chairman, Community Practice Sequence, Graduate School of Social Work, University of Texas, Arlington
Panelists: Franklin D. Yoder, M.D., Director, Illinois Department of Public Health, Springfield
Edmund M. Burke, Chairman, Community Organization and Social Planning, Boston College Graduate School of Social Work, Chestnut Hill, Mass.
Jack Meltzer, Director, Center for Urban Studies, University of Chicago, Chicago
The Rev. Carl D. Nighswonger, Chaplain, University of Chicago Hospitals and Clinics, Chicago
Sponsor: Section I (Casework), Group Meeting 2

A VOLUNTARY AGENCY SHARES CONTROL:
AN INTERIM REPORT

Presiding: James Mitchell, Social Work Assistant, Child and Family Services, Chicago
Speakers: Leon W. Chestang, Director, Casework Service, Child and Family Services, Chicago
Joe M. Jenkins, Executive Director, Child and Family Services, Chicago
Mrs. Manja Davis, Director, Homemaker Service, Child and Family Services, Chicago
Mrs. Pearlie Robinson, member, Advisory Board, Lawndale Homemaker Service, Chicago
Sponsor: Section I (Casework), Group Meeting 3

CLIENT ADVOCACY IN SOCIAL WORK PRACTICE

Presiding: Wayne Vasey, Professor, School of Social Work, University of Michigan, Ann Arbor; Past President, NCSW
Panelists: Mrs. Mary Ellyn Cain, client, Ann Arbor, Mich.
Mrs. Dojelo Russell, faculty member, Richmond School of Social Work, Commonwealth University of Virginia, Richmond
Halloway C. Sells, Jr., Executive Director, Seven Hills Neighborhood Houses, Cincinnati
Louis E. Weissman, Training Specialist and Acting Group Chief, Community Services Administration, Social and Rehabilitation Service, Department of Health, Education, and Welfare, Washington
Cosponsors:
Section II (Group Work), Group Meeting 1
Section I (Casework), Group Meeting 4

THE GROUP AND SOCIAL CHANGE: PERTINENT
THEORY AND PRACTICE KNOWLEDGE—
Presiding: Henry Johnson, Director, Group Care and Counseling, W. J. Maxey Boys Training School, Whitmore Lake, Mich.
Speaker: Elizabeth Lewis, Lecturer, School of Applied Social Sciences, Case Western Reserve University, Cleveland
Discussant: Maeda Galinsky, Associate Professor, School of Social Work, University of North Carolina, Chapel Hill
Cosponsors:
Section II (Group Work), Group Meeting 2
Section III (Community Organization and Methods of Social Action), Group Meeting 1

THE CONTRIBUTION OF PHASE THEORY OF GROUP
DEVELOPMENT TO PRACTICE
Presiding: Sallie Churchill, School of Social Work, University of Michigan, Ann Arbor
Speaker: Margaret E. Hartford, Professor, School of Applied Social Sciences, Case Western Reserve University, Cleveland
Discussant: Mary Louise Somers, Professor, School of Social Service Administration, University of Chicago, Chicago
Cosponsors:
Section II (Group Work), Group Meeting 3
Section III (Community Organization and Methods of Social Action), Group Meeting 2

PROFESSIONAL IMPACT ON THE AGENCY SYSTEM
Presiding: James White, Social Work Program Specialist, Social and Rehabilitation Service, Department of Health, Education, and Welfare, Chicago
Speakers: Lawrence Shulman, Assistant Professor, School of Social Work, McGill University, Montreal, Canada
Archie J. Hanlan, Associate Professor and Chairman, Social Policy and Practice Department, Washington University, St. Louis
Cosponsors:
Section II (Group Work), Group Meeting 4
Section V (Administration), Group Meeting 1

THE REVOLUTION IN SOCIAL WELFARE
(Lindeman Memorial Lecture)
Presiding: Hobart A. Burch, Division of Health and Welfare, United Church Board of Homeland Ministries, New York
Discussants: Sherman Merle, Interim Professor, School of Social Work, Catholic University of America, Washington
Hyman Weiner, Associate Professor, School of Social Work, Columbia University, New York
Michael Tabor, Center for Community Planning, Department of Health, Education, and Welfare, Washington

Cosponsors:
Section I (Casework), Group Meeting 5
Section II (Group Work), Group Meeting 5
Section III (Community Organization and Methods of Social Action), Group
Meeting 3

ATTITUDES OF TODAY'S YOUTH
Presiding: Catherine S. Chilman, Dean of Academic Affairs and Professor of Psychology, Hood College, Frederick, Md.; Chairman, Section IV, NCSW
Speaker: Elizabeth Herzog, Chief, Child Life Studies, Office of Child Development, Department of Health, Education, and Welfare, Washington
Discussants: M. Brewster Smith, Department of Psychology, University of Chicago, Chicago
Sponsor: Section IV (Social Research), Group Meeting 1

ANALYSIS OF RACIAL DISORDERS IN CAMBRIDGE, MARYLAND
Presiding and discussant: Ernest Kahn, Assistant Professor of Social Work, University of Maryland, College Park
Speaker: Gilbert Ware, Research Associate, Institute for Urban Studies, Washington
Discussant: Lee Satterfield, attorney-at-law, Chesapeake and Potomac Telephone Co., Washington
Sponsor: Section IV (Social Research), Group Meeting 2

PROS AND CONS OF A SYSTEMS APPROACH IN
HUMAN WELFARE
Presiding: John G. Geist, Associate Executive Director, Health and Welfare Council of the Baltimore Area, Baltimore
A New Approach to Measuring the Effectiveness of Welfare Services
Speaker: Robert Elkin, Research Associate, Peat, Marwick, Mitchell and Co., Washington
The Pros and Cons of Systematic Evaluation of Social Welfare Programs
Speaker: Eugene Litwak, Professor, School of Social Work, University of Michigan, Ann Arbor
Discussant: Saul Kaplan, Research Director, Jewish Welfare Federation, Chicago
Cosponsors:
Section I (Casework), Group Meeting 6
Section IV (Social Research), Group Meeting 3

SOCIAL WORK ESTABLISHMENT: LIBERATOR OR TRAP?
Presiding: Warner Saunders, Executive Director, Better Boys' Foundation, Chicago
Speaker: Edwin C. Berry, Executive Director, Chicago Urban League, Chicago
Sponsor: Section V (Administration), Group Meeting 2

THE MISUNDERSTOOD MINORITIES
>*Presiding:* John H. McMahon, Director of Public Relations, State Communities Aid Association, New York; Chairman, Public Relations and Development Committee, NCSW
>*Speaker:* The Rev. Andrew M. Greeley, Program Director, National Opinion Research Center, University of Chicago, Chicago
>
>*Sponsor:* NCSW Public Relations and Development Committee

12:45 P.M.

FILM THEATER
>Film: Making Ends Meet
>*Sponsor:* NCSW Audio-Visual Committee

1:00 P.M.

FILM THEATER
>Film: A Piece of the Cake
>*Sponsor:* NCSW Audio-Visual Committee

1:58 P.M.

FILM THEATER
>Film: Not Sick Enough
>*Sponsor:* NCSW Audio-Visual Committee

2:00 P.M.—3:30 P.M.

WHO MAKES SOCIAL POLICY?
>*Presiding:* Henry Weber, Director, Washington Office, United Community Funds and Councils of America, Washington
>*Speaker:* Alan K. Campbell, Dean, Maxwell School of Citizenship and Public Affairs, Syracuse University, Syracuse, N.Y.
>*Discussants:* Mrs. Cernoria D. Johnson, Director, Washington Bureau, National Urban League, Washington
>William G. Reidy, Director, Washington Office, National Assembly for Social Policy and Development, Washington
>
>*Sponsor:* Division

PRIORITIES IN IMPROVING THE DELIVERY OF
SERVICES IN OUR CITIES
>*Presiding:* Peter G. Gaupp, Chairman, Community Practice Sequence, Graduate School of Social Work, University of Texas, Arlington
>*Panelists:* Franklin D. Yoder, M.D., Director, Illinois Department of Public Health, Springfield
>Edmund M. Burke, Chairman, Community Organization and Social Planning, Boston College Graduate School of Social Work, Chestnut Hill, Mass.
>Jack Meltzer, Director, Center for Urban Studies, University of Chicago, Chicago

The Rev. Carl D. Nighswonger, Chaplain, University of Chicago Hospitals and Clinics, Chicago
Sponsor: Section I (Casework), Group Meeting 1

PROGRAMS FOR DEVELOPMENT AND CARE OF CHILDREN LIVING IN THEIR OWN HOMES

Presiding: Bernice E. Kennedy, Specialist in Community Programs for Children, Office of Child Development, Region VI, Department of Health, Education, and Welfare, Kansas City, Mo.

The Social Worker's Contribution to the Nursery Teacher and Family Worker in the Head Start Program
Speaker: Marian Barnes, Case Consultant, Child Psychiatry Clinic, University Hospital of Cleveland, Cleveland

Services to Children and Families in Their Own Homes to Avoid Foster Placement
Speaker: Mrs. Harriet Goldstein, Assistant Director, Association for Jewish Children of Philadelphia, Philadelphia
Discussant: Helen Pinkus, Acting Dean, School of Social Work, Smith College, Northampton, Mass.
Sponsor: Section I (Casework), Group Meeting 3

PEOPLE IN FLIGHT: THE IMPLICATIONS OF UNPLANNED MIGRATION FOR SOCIAL WORK AND PSYCHIATRIC SERVICES

Presiding: Mrs. Catherine C. Hiatt, Executive Director, Travelers Aid Society, Washington

People in Flight: a Comparative Study of Migrants without Plans
Speaker: Leonard U. Blumberg, Project Consultant and Professor of Sociology, Temple University, Philadelphia

Psychological and Psychiatric Findings on People in Flight
Speaker: Alan DeWolfe, Psychology Research Laboratory, Veterans Administration, Downey, Ill.

Casework Profiles of Clients in Flight
Speaker: Grace Yocom, Director, Casework Services, Travelers Aid Society of Philadelphia, Philadelphia

An Experimental Casework Program with People in Flight
Speaker: Catherine Kerner, Executive Director, Travelers Aid Society of Philadelphia, Philadelphia
Sponsor: Section I (Casework), Group Meeting 4

INTERPERSONAL PRACTICE IN SOCIAL WORK

Presiding: Allen Pincus, Professor, School of Social Work, University of Wisconsin, Madison
Speakers: Charles Garvin, Professor, School of Social Work, University of Michigan, Ann Arbor
Paul H. Glasser, Professor, School of Social Work, University of Michigan, Ann Arbor
Discussants: Bernece K. Simon, Professor, School of Social Service Administration, University of Chicago, Chicago
Mrs. Kate Emerson, client, Ann Arbor, Mich.

Helen Northen, Professor, School of Social Work, University of Southern California, Los Angeles

Julian Rivera, Coordinator of Information Services, Office of Admissions, City College of New York, New York

Sponsor: Section II (Group Work), Group Meeting 1

THE GROUP WORKER IN CORRECTIONS

Presiding: Paul Isenstadt, Director of Social Work, Center for Forensic Psychiatry, Ann Arbor, Mich.

Speaker: Charles Wolfson, Associate Professor, School of Social Work, University of Michigan, Ann Arbor

Discussant: Arthur Blum, Professor of Social Work, School of Applied Social Sciences, Case Western Reserve University, Cleveland

Cosponsors:

Section II (Group Work), Group Meeting 2

Section III (Community Organization and Methods of Social Action), Group Meeting 1

A YOUTH-SERVING AGENCY MODEL FOR MAXIMIZING AGENCY AND COMMUNITY RESOURCES FOR AN EDUCATIONAL EXPERIENCE FOR LOW-INCOME GIRLS

Presiding: Catherine V. Richards, Youth Activities Division, Children's Bureau, Office of Child Development, Department of Health, Education, and Welfare, Washington

Speaker: Dagmar Edith McGill, Urban Program Consultant, Girl Scouts of Metropolitan Detroit, Detroit

Discussant: Mrs. Mamie Blakely, Recording Secretary, National Welfare Rights Organization, Detroit

Cosponsors:

Section II (Group Work), Group Meeting 3

Section III (Community Organization and Methods of Social Action), Group Meeting 2

HOW SHOULD SOCIAL SERVICES BE DELIVERED TO MINORITIES? A BLACK PERSPECTIVE

Presiding: Leon L. Haley, Assistant Professor of Social Sciences, Point Park College, Pittsburgh

Speaker: Donald J. Roberts, Assistant Director, Neighborhood Service Organization, Detroit

Panelists: Walter R. Tarpley, Executive Director, United Community Council, Columbus, Ohio

Maria Canino, Fellow, Metropolitan Applied Research Center, New York

Mrs. Annie Smart, Southern Regional Representative, National Welfare Rights Organization, Baton Rouge, La.

Sponsor: Section III (Community Action and Methods of Social Action), Group Meeting 3

POLARIZATION OF THE COMMUNITY
  Presiding: Melvin H. King, Executive Director, Urban League of
  Greater Boston, Roxbury, Mass.
  Speakers: Marion MacChlenay, Chairman, People's Elected Urban Re-
  newal Committee, Boston
  Theodore Parrish, Community Organizer, Self End Tenants Council,
  Boston
Sponsor: Section III (Community Organization and Methods of Social Ac-
tion), Group Meeting 4

DECISION-MAKING
  Presiding: Kiernan F. Stenson, Administrative Assistant for Planning,
  Catholic Diocese of Pittsburgh, Pittsburgh
Can the Walls Come Tumbling Down?
  Speaker: The Hon. Gerald Kaufman, Pennsylvania House of Repre-
  sentatives, 23d District of Allegheny County, Harrisburg
  Discussants: William H. Schoen, Director, Urban and Community Af-
  fairs Department, Ford Motor Co., Dearborn, Mich.
  John A. Conley, Esq., Associate Professor, Graduate School of Social
  Work, University of Pittsburgh, Pittsburgh
  Mrs. Beulah Sanders, First Vice Chairman, National Welfare Rights
  Organization, New York
Sponsor: Section III (Community Organization and Methods of Social Ac-
tion), Group Meeting 5

EMERGING CHALLENGES IN COMMUNITY PLANNING AND
ACTION: AN AGENDA FOR THE 1970s
  Presiding: Harold Johnson, Professor and Head of Community Practice
  Sequence, School of Social Work, University of Michigan, Ann Arbor
  Speaker: Bertram W. Gross, Director, Center for Urban Studies, Wayne
  State University, Detroit
  Discussants: Olga Madar, member, International Union Executive
  Board, United Automobile Workers, Detroit
  Edward M. Levin, Jr., Special Assistant to Regional Administrator, De-
  partment of Housing and Urban Development, Chicago
Sponsor: Section III (Community Organization and Methods of Social Ac-
tion), Group Meeting 6

ISSUES IN THE TRAINING AND EMPLOYMENT
OF AFDC RECIPIENTS
  Presiding: Mrs. Geraldine Aronin, Assistant Acting Director for Com-
  munity Relations, Baltimore Department of Social Services, Baltimore
Employment of Mothers as a Means of Family Support
  Speaker: Irene Cox, Social Science Analyst, Office of Research, Demon-
  strations, and Training, Social and Rehabilitation Service, Department
  of Health, Education, and Welfare, Washington
An Analysis of the Effectiveness of Work and Training Projects for AFDC
Recipients
  Speaker: Abraham Levine, Acting Director, Office of Research, Dem-

onstrations, and Training, Social and Rehabilitation Service, Department of Health, Education and Welfare, Washington
Sponsor: Section IV (Social Research), Group Meeting 1

RESEARCH USING HUMAN SUBJECTS
Speakers: Carol H. Weiss, Research Associate, Bureau of Applied Social Research, Columbia University, New York
Sidney Hollander, Vice President, Sidney Hollander Association, Baltimore
Sponsor: Section IV (Social Research), Group Meeting 2

STUDIES OF MEXICAN-AMERICAN STUDENTS AND WORKERS
College Students and Ethnic Differences in Respect to Attitudes toward the Law
Speakers: Lyle Shannon, Professor, Department of Sociology, State University of Iowa, Iowa City
Jerry Borup, Professor, Department of Sociology and Social Work, Weber State College, Ogden, Utah
Raymond Clark, Professor, Department of Sociology, Weber State College, Ogden, Utah
Sponsor: Section IV (Social Research), Group Meeting 3

ROMANCE OF COMPUTERS AND SYSTEMS CHANGE IN RELEVANT ADMINISTRATION OF SOCIAL WELFARE
Presiding: Chauncey A. Alexander, Executive Director, National Association of Social Workers, New York
Obstacles to the Development of Computerized Health and Social Welfare Information Systems: a Critical Appraisal
Speaker: John H. Noble, Project Director, Information Systems Development, the Medical Foundation, Boston
Action or Reaction: a Plan toward Systems Change
Speaker: Eunice Shatz, University Research Corporation, Washington
Speaker: Sheldon S. Steinberg, University Research Corporation, Washington
Sponsor: Section V (Administration)

2:08 P.M.

FILM THEATER
Film: Pull the House Down
Sponsor: NCSW Audio-Visual Committee

2:46 P.M.

FILM THEATER
Film: Chump's Change
Sponsor: NCSW Audio-Visual Committee

2:54 P.M.

FILM THEATER
Film: Tomorrow Never Comes
Sponsor: NCSW Audio-Visual Committee

3:03 P.M.

FILM THEATER
Film: Jenny is a Good Thing
Sponsor: NCSW Audio-Visual Committee

3:21 P.M.

FILM THEATER
Film: Lonnie's Day
Sponsor: NCSW Audio-Visual Committee

3:35 P.M.

FILM THEATER
Film: A Case of Suicide
Sponsor: NCSW Audio-Visual Committee

4:00 P.M.—5:30 P.M.

THE HUMAN RIGHTS REVOLUTION AND SOCIAL POLICY
Presiding: Sanford Solender, Executive Vice President, Federation of
Jewish Philanthropies of New York City; formerly Executive Vice
President, National Jewish Welfare Board; Past President, NCSW
Speaker: Kenneth B. Clark, President, Metropolitan Applied Research
Center, New York
Sponsor: Division

PRIORITIES IN IMPROVING THE DELIVERY OF
SERVICES IN OUR CITIES
Presiding: Peter G. Gaupp, Chairman, Community Practice Sequence,
Graduate School of Social Work, University of Texas, Arlington
Panelists: Franklin D. Yoder, M.D., Director, Illinois Department of
Public Health, Springfield
Edmund M. Burke, Chairman, Community Organization and Social
Planning, Boston College Graduate School of Social Work, Chestnut
Hill, Mass.
Jack Meltzer, Director, Center for Urban Studies, University of Chicago,
Chicago
The Rev. Carl D. Nighswonger, Chaplain, University of Chicago Hos-
pitals and Clinics, Chicago
Sponsor: Section I (Casework), Group Meeting 1

ASPECTS OF MOTIVATION, EMPLOYMENT, AND
TRAINING OF PARAPROFESSIONALS
Presiding: Virginia L. Tannar, Director, Children's Bureau, Social and

Rehabilitation Service, Department of Health, Education, and Welfare, Washington

Paraprofessionals, Anomie, Militancy, and Activism

Speakers: Frederick L. Ahern, Jr., Assistant Professor, Boston College Graduate School of Social Work, Chestnut Hill, Mass.

Eulene Hawkins, Regional Training and Manpower Specialist, Social and Rehabilitation Service, Department of Health, Education, and Welfare, Washington

Sponsor: Section I (Casework), Group Meeting 2

FANTASY AND REALITY INTEGRATED THROUGH EXPRESSIVE ARTS AND SOCIAL GROUP WORK

Presiding and coauthor: Esther Marine, Chief of Psychiatric Social Work, Pittsburgh Child Guidance Center, Pittsburgh

Speaker: Mrs. Mattie B. Addis, Supervisor, Group Work Services, Pittsburgh Child Guidance Center, Pittsburgh

Discussants: Eleanor Irwin, Expressive Arts Therapist, Pittsburgh Child Guidance Center, Pittsburgh; Lecturer in Speech, Carlow College, Pittsburgh

Mary Ann Lacy, Ann Arbor, Mich.

Sponsor: Section II (Group Work), Group Meeting 1

INTERPERSONAL PRACTICE IN SOCIAL WORK

Presiding: Allen Pincus, Professor, School of Social Work, University of Wisconsin, Madison

Speakers: Charles Garvin, Professor, School of Social Work, University of Michigan, Ann Arbor

Paul H. Glasser, Professor, School of Social Work, University of Michigan, Ann Arbor

Discussants: Bernece K. Simon, Professor, School of Social Service Administration, University of Chicago, Chicago

Mrs. Kate Emerson, client, Ann Arbor, Mich.

Julian Rivera, Coordinator of Information Services, Office of Admissions, City College of New York, New York

Sponsor: Section II (Group Work), Group Meeting 2

FAMILY MILIEU THERAPY: THE USE OF MULTIPLE THERAPEUTIC INTERVENTIONS FOR FAMILY TREATMENT

Presiding: Janice Schaub, Mental Health Outpatient Clinic, Veterans Administration Hospital, Minneapolis

Speaker: Mrs. Carole S. Noreen, Chairman, Field Work Sequence, School of Social Work, University of California, Los Angeles

Discussants: Louise P. Shoemaker, School of Social Work, University of Pennsylvania, Philadelphia

Loraine Cook, Professor, School of Social Work, University of Michigan, Ann Arbor

Cosponsors:

Section I (Casework), Group Meeting 3

Section II (Group Work), Group Meeting 3

MUTUAL CARE HOME FOR MOTHER AND CHILD
  Presiding: Robert W. Roberts, Assistant Professor, School of Social
  Service Administration, University of Chicago, Chicago
  Speakers: Sue Henry, Special Services Director, Young Women's Chris-
  tian Association, Denver
  Delores M. Schmidt, Department of Public Welfare, Denver
  Discussant: Mrs. Joan S. Wallace, Assistant Professor, Jane Addams
  Graduate School of Social Work, University of Illinois, Wilmette
Cosponsors:
Section II (Group Work), Group Meeting 4
Section III (Community Organization and Methods of Social Action), Group
Meeting 1
Section V (Administration), Group Meeting 1

STRATEGIES FOR CHANGE
  Speaker: Edward P. Dutton, Associate Professor, School of Social Work,
  Fresno State College, Fresno, Calif.
  Discussant: Mrs. Sylvia Herrerra de Fox, Executive Director, ASPIRA
  of Illinois, Chicago
  Mrs. Geraldine Smith, Financial Secretary, National Welfare Rights
  Organization, Los Angeles
Sponsor: Section III (Community Organization and Methods of Social Ac-
tion), Group Meeting 2

COMMUNICATION GAPS BETWEEN WELFARE WORKERS AND
CLIENTS AND INVESTMENT IN HUMAN RESOURCES
  Presiding: Jack Wiener, Assistant Chief, Center for Studies of Mental
  Health and Social Problems, Department of Health, Education, and
  Welfare, Chevy Chase, Md.
  Speaker: Virgil B. Smith, Associate Professor, Department of Sociology,
  Youngstown State University, Youngstown, Ohio
Sponsor: Section IV (Social Research), Group Meeting 1

PARENT EDUCATION AND PARENT PARTICIPATION:
IMPLICATIONS FOR PROGRAM AND POLICY WITH
EMPHASIS ON LOW-INCOME FAMILIES
  Speaker: Catherine S. Chilman, Dean of Academic Affairs, Hood Col-
  lege, Frederick, Md., Chairman, Section IV, NCSW
Sponsor: Section IV (Social Research), Group Meeting 2

THE 1970 WHITE HOUSE CONFERENCE ON CHILDREN AND
YOUTH: SOME ISSUES AND CONSTRAINTS IN
PROGRAM DEVELOPMENT
  Speakers: Ralph Susman, Washington; former Acting Director, 1970
  White House Conference
  Israel Gerver, Professor, John Jay College of Criminal Justice, New
  York
Sponsor: Section IV (Social Research), Group Meeting 3

SOCIAL POLICY ANALYSIS: THE USE OF SOCIAL INDICATORS
Presiding: Charles X. Sampson, Associate Executive Director, United Community Funds and Councils of America, New York
Speakers: Howard A. Palley, Associate Professor, School of Social Work, Adelphi University, Garden City, N.Y.
Mrs. Marian L. Palley, Political Science Department, Rutgers—the State University, New Brunswick, N.J.
Sponsor: Section V (Administration), Group Meeting 2

6:30 P.M.—8:30 P.M.

BLACK CAUCUS
Sponsor: National Association of Black Social Workers

8:30 P.M.—10:30 P.M.

GENERAL SESSION
The Elimination of Hunger and Malnutrition
Presiding: Wilbur J. Cohen, Dean, School of Education, University of Michigan, Ann Arbor; President, NCSW
Speakers: The Hon. George McGovern, U.S. Senator, State of South Dakota, Washington
The Rev. Jesse L. Jackson, Director, Operation Breadbasket, Southern Christian Leadership Conference, Chicago
Jean Mayer, Professor of Nutrition, Harvard University, Cambridge, Mass.
Presentation of NCSW fifty and seventy-five-Year Plaques

Tuesday, June 2

9:00 A.M—10:45 A.M.

WHERE DO WE GO FROM HERE?
Presiding: David Jeffreys, Director, National Affairs, American Association of Retired Persons–National Retired Teachers Association, Washington; Vice Chairman, Combined Associate Groups, NCSW
Speaker: Dan W. Dodson, Professor of Education; Chairman, Department of Educational Sociology and Anthropology, and Director, Center for Human Relations and Community Studies, New York University, New York
Discussants: William H. Robinson, Director, State of Illinois Department of Registration and Education, Chicago; Chairman, Section V, NCSW
Edith M. Lerrigo, Executive Director, National Board, YWCA, New York
Mitchell I. Ginsberg, Administrator, Human Resources Administration, New York
Sponsor: Combined Associate Groups

11:00 A.M.

FILM THEATER
Film: A Demand to Be Heard
Sponsor: NCSW Audio-Visual Committee

11:00 A.M.—10:00 P.M.

CAUCUS
Sponsor: La Raza

CAUCUS
Sponsor: National Welfare Rights Organization

11:15 A.M.—12:45 P.M.

THE CHURCH TAKES A NEW LOOK AT AGING
Presiding: Esther C. Stamats, Consultant to Religious Organizations,
American Association of Retired Persons—National Retired Teachers
Association, Washington
Speakers: The Rev. Harold W. Reisch, Board of Social Ministry,
Lutheran Church of America, New York
Abraham Kostick, Director, Levindale Hebrew Home and Infirmary,
Baltimore
The Rev. Charles J. Fahey, Chairman, Commission on Aging, Na-
tional Conference of Catholic Charities, Syracuse, N.Y.
Discussant: Willis W. Atwell, Deputy Commissioner, Administration on
Aging, Department of Health, Education, and Welfare, Washington
Cosponsors:
American Association of Homes for the Aging
American Association of Retired Persons, Group Meeting 1
Executive Council of the Episcopal Church
National Council of Churches of Christ in the U.S.A., Committee on Social
Welfare, Group Meeting 1
National Retired Teachers Association, Group Meeting 1
United Presbyterian Health, Education, and Welfare Association
The Volunteers of America, Group Meeting 1

NEW STRATEGIES FOR SHAPING SAFER CITIES: REDUCING
POLICE-COMMUNITY CONFLICTS—A PROGRAM TO
WIN SECURITY WITHOUT REPRESSION
Presiding: Harry Fleischman, Race Relations Coordinator, American
Jewish Committee, New York
Speaker: Lloyd N. Cutler, Executive Director, National Commission
on the Causes and Prevention of Violence, Washington
Cosponsors:
American Jewish Committee
American Social Health Association
National Assembly for Social Policy and Development
National Council on Crime and Delinquency

STUDIES OF MILITARY FAMILY LIFE:
IMPLICATIONS FOR PRACTICE
> *Presiding:* Lt. Col. Frank F. Montalvo, Social Work Consultant, Army Community Service, Department of the Army, Washington

A Comparative Study of Military and Civilian Family Life
> *Speaker:* Patricia M. Jermon, Director, Service to Military Families, Prince Georges County Chapter, American Red Cross, Hyattsville, Md.

Surveying Life Styles in the Military Community
> *Speaker:* Capt. Willis K. Bright, Jr., Army Community Service Officer, U. S. Army, Fort Belvoir, Va.
>
> *Discussant:* Maj. Joseph J. Bevilacqua, Social Work Research, Computer Support in Military Psychiatry, Walter Reed General Hospital, Washington

Cosponsors:
American National Red Cross
Army Community Service

CULTURAL DISHARMONY BETWEEN THE SYSTEM AND
THE PEOPLE
> *Presiding:* Kenneth Watson, Director, Foster Care and Adoption, Chicago Child Care Society, Chicago
>
> *Speaker:* Charles G. Hurst, Jr., President, Malcolm X. College, Chicago

Cosponsors:
Child Welfare League of America, Group Meeting 1
Florence Crittenton Association of America, Group Meeting 1

COMMUNITY INVOLVEMENT IN THE ESTABLISHMENT
OF DAY CARE
> *Presiding:* Edward Weaver, Director, Department of Children and Family Services, Springfield, Ill.
>
> *Speakers:* Jack D. Sparks, Group Vice President, Whirlpool Corp., Benton Harbor, Mich.
>
> Harry Hiltner, Community Planning Specialist, Michigan Department of Social Services, Lansing
>
> Mrs. Joyce Miller, Administrative Assistant to the Manager, Amalgamated Clothing Workers of America, Chicago

Cosponsors:
Child Welfare League of America, Group Meeting 2
Florence Crittenton Association of America, Group Meeting 2

ESTABLISHMENT MONEY AND COMMUNITY CONTROL
> *Presiding:* Richard J. Bond, Director, Division of Child Welfare, Department of Children and Family Services, Springfield, Ill.
>
> *Speakers:* Mrs. Henry Steeger, board member, Spence-Chapin Adoption Service, New York
>
> Mrs. Jane Edwards, Executive Director, Spence-Chapin Adoption Service, New York
>
> Joseph H. Smith, Executive Director, Harlem-Dowling Center, New York

Mrs. Thomas W. Matthew, member, Advisory Council, Harlem-Dowling Center, New York

Cosponsors:
Child Welfare League of America, Group Meeting 3
Florence Crittenton Association of America, Group Meeting 3
National Council on Illegitimacy, Group Meeting 1

INCOME MAINTENANCE: MORAL AND ETHICAL ISSUES

Presiding: The Very Rev. Msgr. Lawrence J. Corcoran, Secretary, National Conference of Catholic Charities, Washington

Speaker: Victor Obenhaus, Professor of Christian Ethics, Chicago Theological Seminary, Chicago

Discussants: Sol Koenigsberg, Executive Director, Kansas City Jewish Federation and Council, Kansas City, Mo.

The Rev. Robert P. Kennedy, Director, Social Action Division, Catholic Charities of Brooklyn, New York

Cosponsors:
Council of Jewish Federations and Welfare Funds
National Conference of Catholic Charities
National Council of Churches of Christ in the U.S.A., Committee on Social Welfare, Group Meeting 2

THE NEW CURRICULUM POLICY FOR GRADUATE
SCHOOLS OF SOCIAL WORK

Presiding: Werner W. Boehm, Dean, Graduate School of Social Work, Rutgers—the State University, New Brunswick, N.J.

Speaker: Lilian Ripple, Associate Executive Director, Council on Social Work Education, New York

Sponsor: Council on Social Work Education, Group Meeting 1

INFANT DEVELOPMENT AND EARLY LEARNING:
ITS IMPLICATIONS FOR SOCIAL WORK

Presiding: Mrs. Richard M. Lansburgh, President, Day Care and Child Development Council of America, Washington

Current Research in Infant Development

Speaker: Michael Lewis, Director, Infant Laboratory, Educational Testing Service, Princeton, N.J.

Implications for Program Development

Speaker: E. Robert LaCrosse, Jr., President, Pacific Oaks College, Pasadena, Calif.

Sponsor: Day Care and Child Development Council of America

WHOSE IS THE PROBLEM?

Presiding: R. Edward Lee, Social Work Director, Community Church of New York, New York

Timely Response to Present Pain

Speaker: Mrs. Geraldine M. Ellington, Director, Emergency Counseling Service, Family Service of Metropolitan Detroit, Detroit

Advocacy Seeks Results for People Hurting the Most in Our Society

Speaker: Mrs. Frances Brisbane, Consultant, Family Advocacy, Family Service Association of America, New York

How to Become Part of the Solution

Speaker: Benjamin F. Finley, Jr., Director, Inner City Office, United Charities of Chicago, Family Service Bureau, Chicago

Sponsor: Family Service Association of America, Group Meeting 1

STATE CITIZEN ORGANIZATIONS

Presiding: Cecil S. Feldman, Executive Director, Community Services of Pennsylvania, Harrisburg

Sponsor: National Association for Statewide Health and Welfare

SOCIAL ACTIVISM IN OR THROUGH THE CHURCH

Presiding: Merwin R. Crow, Executive Director, Orchard Place, Des Moines, Iowa; President, National Association of Christians in Social Work

Speaker: The Rev. William Leslie, Elm and LaSalle Bible Church, Chicago

Cosponsors:

National Association of Christians in Social Work

The Salvation Army, Group Meeting 1

NASW PROFESSIONAL ACTION FOR THE 1970s

Presiding: Leroy H. Jones, Director, Project on Utilization of Time and Cost Data (Local Community), Welfare Council of Metropolitan Chicago; President, Chicago Chapter, National Association of Social Workers

Social Strategies for Social Workers

Speaker: Whitney M. Young, Jr., Executive Director, National Urban League, New York; President, National Association of Social Workers; Past President, NCSW

Social Progress through Professional Action

Speaker: Chauncey A. Alexander, Executive Director, National Association of Social Workers, New York

Sponsor: National Association of Social Workers

FUNDING OF HOMEMAKER-HOME HEALTH AIDE

SERVICES. INCLUDING AN ANALYSIS OF THE

LEGISLATIVE BASE FOR TAX-SUPPORTED SERVICES

Presiding: Eugene H. Freedheim, Attorney, Haln, Loeser, Freedheim, Dean and Wellman, Attorneys-at-Law, Cleveland

Speaker: John H. Moore, Executive Director, National Study Service, New York

Discussants: Maybelle Berg, Field Representative, State Department of Social Welfare, St. Paul, Minn.

Joe Jenkins, Executive Director, Child and Family Services, Chicago
John F. Larberg, Senior Staff Consultant, National Assembly for Social Policy and Development, New York

Cosponsors:
American Association of Retired Persons, Group Meeting 2
Child Welfare League of America, Group Meeting 4
Family Service Association of America, Group Meeting 2
National Council for Homemaker Services
National Health Council
National Retired Teachers Association, Group Meeting 2

"AND STILL THEY COME"—AN IMMIGRATION
CONFRONTATION
> *Presiding:* Ben Winitt, Director, Service for Foreign Born, New York
> Section, National Council of Jewish Women, New York
> *Speaker:* John W. Weiner, Executive Director, Hebrew Immigrants Aid
> Society, Travelers Aid Society, Chicago
> *Discussants:* Daniel Koden, attorney, Legal Aid Immigrants Service,
> Travelers Aid Society, Chicago
> Mrs. Mola Cadet, social worker, Southwest Neighborhood Service to
> Latin Immigrants, Chicago

Cosponsors:
American Council for Nationalities Service
Family Service Association of America, Group Meeting 3
International Social Service, American Branch
National Council of Jewish Women, New York
Section, Service for Foreign Born
Travelers Aid Association of America

DEPOLARIZATION OF AGE GROUPS: THE UTILITY
OF AGE-YOUTH DYADS
> *Presiding:* Jack Weinberg, Clinical Director, Illinois State Psychiatric
> Institute, Chicago

The Social-psychological Consequences of Age Polarization
> *Speaker:* Ruth Boyer, School of Social Work, University of Arkansas,
> Fayetteville

Young and Old Serving One Another
> *Speaker:* Sholom Bloom, Executive Secretary, Department on Aging,
> Hartford, Conn.

Sponsor: National Council on the Aging

DRUG ABUSE AND PREGNANCY: IMPLICATIONS FOR SERVICES
FOR THE UNMARRIED MOTHER AND HER CHILD
> *Presiding:* John M. Hayes, Assistant Secretary, National Conference of
> Catholic Charities, Washington

Drug Abuse as It Affects Pregnancy and Planning for the Out-of-Wedlock
Child
> *Speaker:* Joseph H. Skom, M.D., Assistant Professor of Medicine,
> Northwestern University Medical School, Chicago
> *Discussant:* Mrs. Evelyn Crump, Assistant Director, Family Planning
> Center, Metropolitan Hospital, New York

Cosponsors:
Child Welfare League of America, Group Meeting 5
Family Service Association of America, Group Meeting 4
Florence Crittenton Association of America, Group Meeting 4
National Council on Illegitimacy, Group Meeting 2
National Urban League
The Salvation Army, Group Meeting 2
The Volunteers of America, Group Meeting 2

SETTLEMENTS' GOAL: COMMUNITY CHANGE
> *Presiding:* Paul A. Unger, President, Unger Co., Cleveland; board member, National Federation of Settlements and Neighborhood Centers
> *Speakers:* George Harris, Acting Director, Southside Settlement House, Columbus, Ohio
> James H. Sills, Jr., Executive Director, Association of Greater Wilmington Neighborhood Centers, Wilmington, Del.

Training Programs in Urban Exposure: a Model for Change Involving the Total City
> *Speaker:* Carroll Brown, Executive Director, Southwest Denver Community Center, Denver
Sponsor: National Federation of Settlements and Neighborhood Centers

11:27 A.M.

FILM THEATER
> Films: *A Demand to Be Heard* and *The Gap*
> *Discussant:* Daniel O'Connor, Radio-TV Film Officer, Social and Rehabilitation Service Department of Health, Education, and Welfare, Washington
Sponsor: NCSW Audio-visual Committee

1:00 P.M.

FILM THEATER
Film: *Man/Woman on Q Street*
Sponsor: NCSW Audio-visual Committee

1:15 P.M.—3:30 P.M.

THE CHANGING ROLE OF THE STATE
> *Presiding:* A Rowland Todd, Executive Director, Wisconsin Welfare Council, Madison
> *Speaker:* Allen Jensen, National Governors' Conference, Washington
Sponsor: National Association for Statewide Health and Welfare

1:22 P.M.

FILM THEATER
> Film: *A Case History of a Public Assistance Client Group*
Sponsor: NCSW Audio-visual Committee

2:00 P.M.—3:30 P.M.

CAMPING: NEW FRONTIER FOR OLDER AMERICANS

Presiding: Mrs. Lora G. Buckingham, Program Specialist, American Association of Retired Persons–National Retired Teachers Association, Washington

Speakers: Virginia Stafford, Director of Ministries to the Aging, United Methodist Church, Nashville, Tenn.

Martha M. Glascock, Assistant Professor Recreation Leadership Program, University of Iowa, Iowa City

Mrs. Carnella J. Barnes, Supervising Coordinator, Los Angeles County Department of Senior Citizens' Affairs, Los Angeles

Cosponsors:

American Association of Homes for the Aging
American Association of Retired Persons, Group Meeting 1
Executive Council of the Episcopal Church, Group Meeting 1
National Retired Teachers Association, Group Meeting 1
The Salvation Army, Group Meeting 1
The Volunteers of America, Group Meeting 1

AN INTERDISCIPLINARY APPROACH TO THE PROBLEM
OF CHILD ABUSE

Presiding: G. Lewis Penner, Executive Director, Juvenile Protective Association, Chicago

Panelists: Norman Paget, Executive Director, Children's Aid and Society for the Prevention of Cruelty to Children of Erie County, Buffalo, N.Y.

Theodore Putnam, M.D., Children's Hospital, Buffalo, N.Y.

Morris Mesch, attorney, Buffalo, N.Y.

Ellen Thomson, Project Director, Child Abuse Project, Children's Aid and Society for the Prevention of Cruelty to Children of Erie County, Buffalo, N.Y.

Mrs. Doris Bates, Social Worker, Children's Aid and Society for the Prevention of Cruelty to Children of Erie County, Buffalo, N.Y.

Cosponsors:

American Humane Association, Children's Division
American Legion, Child Welfare Division
American Public Welfare Association, Group Meeting 1
Child Welfare League of America, Group Meeting 1
National Council on Crime and Delinquency

YOUTH WANTS IN. NOW!

Presiding: Richard J. Bargans, Secretary for Personnel, National Federation of Settlements and Neighborhood Centers, New York

Speakers: Robert L. Andre, Executive Director, East Side Neighborhood Service, Minneapolis

Thomas Walz, Director, Living and Learning Center, University of Minnesota, Minneapolis

Youth Representative, East Side Neighborhood Service, Minneapolis

Discussion moderator: Thomas R. Bennett, Director of Graduate Studies, George Williams College, Downers Grove, Ill.
Cosponsors:
American National Red Cross
American Public Welfare Association, Group Meeting 2
Association of the Junior Leagues of America
Big Brothers of America
Executive Council of the Episcopal Church, Group Meeting 2
National Assembly for Social Policy and Development
National Association of Social Workers, Group Meeting 1
National Council of the Churches of Christ in the U.S.A., Committee on Social Welfare
National Council, YMCAs
National Federation of Settlements and Neighborhood Centers
The Salvation Army, Group Meeting 2
United Community Funds and Councils of America, Association of Volunteer Bureaus
The Volunteers of America, Group Meeting 2
YWCA of the U.S.A.

DESIGNING SOCIAL SERVICE SYSTEMS

Presiding: Guy R. Justis, Director, American Public Welfare Association, Chicago
Moderator: J. M. Wedemeyer, Lecturer on Social Policy, School of Social Work, Sacramento State College, Sacramento, Calif.; Consultant, American Public Welfare Association
Panelists: Jack C. Bloedorn, Consultant in Management Systems Engineering and Management Science, Glenview, Ill.; Director, American Public Welfare Association Maine Technical Assistance Project
William Friedlander, Consultant in Community Work, Evanston, Ill.; Supervisor, American Public Welfare Association Pennsylvania and Maine Technical Assistance Programs
John R. Gage, Business Manager, Douglas County Social Services Department, Omaha; Technical Consultant, American Public Welfare Association
Joseph B. Murphy, Welfare Analyst, American Rehabilitation Foundation, Minneapolis
Sponsor: American Public Welfare Association, Group Meeting 3

PLANNING FOR SERVICES TO THE AGED AND HANDICAPPED IN THE 1970s

Presiding: Bernard E. Nash, Executive Director, American Association of Retired Persons–National Retired Teachers Association
Speaker: James J. Burr, Acting Director, Division of Services to Aged and Handicapped, Community Services Administration, Social and Rehabilitation Service, Department of Health, Education, and Welfare, Washington
Discussants: Henry L. McCarthy, Chief, Division of Community Services, Illinois Department of Public Aid, Springfield

Robert E. Jornlin, Director, Contra Costa County Social Service Department, Martinez, Calif.

Mrs. Elizabeth B. MacLatchie, Consultant on Public Welfare, Mill Valley, Calif.

Sponsor: American Public Welfare Association, Section on Administration of Programs for Older Adults, Division on Administration

CONVERSATION ON SERVICES TO ABUSED CHILDREN AND THEIR FAMILIES

Speaker: Leontine R. Young, Executive Director, Child Service Association, Newark, N.J.

Sponsor: Child Welfare League of America, Group Meeting 2

SERVICES TO CHILDREN AND FAMILIES: IMPACT OF FEDERAL INITIATIVE

Speaker: Stephen P. Simonds, Commissioner, Community Services Administration, Social and Rehabilitation Service, Department of Health, Education, and Welfare, Washington

Sponsor: Child Welfare League of America, Group Meeting 3

CONVERSATION ON EMOTIONAL ASPECTS OF LEARNING IN THE INNER-CITY SCHOOL

Speaker: Ner Littner, *M.D.*, Institute for Psychoanaylsis, Chicago

Sponsor: Child Welfare League of America, Group Meeting 4

THE INDIAN LOOKS AT THE FUTURE OF SOCIAL WELFARE IN AMERICA

Presiding: Ruth Muskrat Bronson, Field Representative, Save the Children Federation, Community Development Foundation, Tucson, Ariz.

Panelists: Josiah Moore, Education Coordinator, Papago Indian Reservation, Sells, Ariz.

Abbott Sekaquaptewa, Director, Community Action Program, Oraibi, Ariz.

Mrs. Leah Manning, Owyhee, Nev.

Sponsor: Community Development Foundation—Save the Children Federation

RECRUITMENT AND INDUCTION OF MINORITY FACULTY IN SOCIAL WORK EDUCATION

Presiding and speaker: James R. Dumpson, Dean, School of Social Service, Fordham University, New York; Chairman, Council on Social Work Education Special Committee on Minority Groups

The Routes to Becoming a Social Work Educator

Discussant: Walter L. Walker, Vice President for Planning, University of Chicago, Chicago

The Supports that Facilitate the Induction of New Faculty

Discussant: Rita Ortiz, Assistant Professor, Columbia University School of Social Work, New York

Sponsor: Council on Social Work Education

CHILD DEVELOPMENT, EARLY LEARNING, AND MENTAL HEALTH

Presiding: Mrs. Louis Binstock, Chicago

Evaluation of Current Child Development Research

Speaker: Irving Gottesman, University of Minnesota, St. Paul

Implications for Social Work Practice

Speaker: Norman V. Lourie, Executive Deputy Secretary, Pennsylvania Department of Public Welfare, Harrisburg

Sponsor: Day Care and Child Development Council of America

A CENTER OF CHANGE

Presiding: Robert F. Nelson, Executive Director, United Charities of Chicago, Family Service Bureau, Chicago

Redirection of a Family and Child Service Agency Focus

Speaker: Ron Yoder, Program Director, Family and Child Service of Omaha, Omaha

A Center of Change

Speaker: Virgil Carr, Director, Logan-Fontenelle Multi-service Center, Family and Child Service of Omaha, Omaha

Discussant: Joseph McDonald, Executive Director, Family Service of the Cincinnati Area, Cincinnati

Sponsor: Family Service Association of America, Group Meeting 1

SINGLE PREGNANT GIRL BECOMES BACHELOR MOTHER

Presiding: Nic Knoph, President, Board of Directors, Florence Crittenton Association of America, Knoxville, Tenn.

Panel moderator: Mrs. Ruth E. Sharpe, Social Work Supervisor, Crittenton Comprehensive Care Center, Chicago

Panelists: A panel of bachelor mothers, introduced from the platform

Cosponsors:

Child Welfare League of America, Group Meeting 6

Florence Crittenton Association of America, Group Meeting 2

National Council on Illegitimacy, Group Meeting 1

National Urban League, Group Meeting 1

NASW RESPONSIBILITY FOR PROFESSIONAL LEADERSHIP IN SOCIAL WELFARE

Presiding: Whitney M. Young, Jr., Executive Director, National Urban League, New York; President, National Association of Social Workers; Past President, NCSW

The Role of Chapter Leadership in Meeting Priorities Set by the 1969 Delegate Assembly

Speakers: Hubert E. Jones, President, Eastern Massachusetts Chapter, National Association of Social Workers, Boston

Mrs. Virginia R. Jones, Assistant Director, Community Service Council of Jefferson County, Birmingham, Ala.

Sponsor: National Association of Social Workers, Group Meeting 2

HOMEMAKER SERVICE AS A TOOL IN ENABLING FAMILIES AND
INDIVIDUALS TO ACHIEVE A MORE SATISFYING
QUALITY OF LIVING

>*Presiding:* Ellen Winston, board member, National Council for Home-
>maker Services, Raleigh, N.C.; Past President, NCSW
>
>*Speakers:* Mildred Cruickshank, Type C Consultant for the Mentally
>Handicapped, Highland Park School District, Highland Park, Mich.;
>former Director, Homemaker Services for Highland Park Schools
>
>Mrs. Sandra Jones, Director, Peoria Area Homemaker Service, Illinois
>Department of Public Aid, Peoria
>
>Mrs. Phyllis Johnson, Homemaker, Peoria Area Homemaker Service,
>Illinois Department of Public Aid, Peoria

Cosponsors:
American Association of Retired Persons, Group Meeting 2
American Home Economics Association
Child Welfare League of America, Group Meeting 7
Family Service Association of America, Group Meeting 2
National Council for Homemaker Services
National Health Council
National Retired Teachers Association, Group Meeting 2

A PROPOSED BILL OF LEGAL RIGHTS FOR UNMARRIED
PARENTS AND OUT-OF-WEDLOCK CHILDREN

>*Presiding:* Anna Mae Steingraeber, Coordinator, Unwed Parents Ser-
>vice, Catholic Social Services of the Archdiocese of Milwaukee
>
>*Panel Moderator:* Karl Zukerman, Esq., legal counsel to New York
>City Department of Social Services, New York
>
>*Panelists:* Richard N. Hey, President, National Council on Family
>Relations, Minneapolis
>
>Alexander J. Allen, Jr., Director, Eastern Region, National Urban
>League, New York

Cosponsors:
Child Welfare League of America, Group Meeting 8
Family Service Association of America, Group Meeting 3
Florence Crittenton Association of America, Group Meeting 3
National Association of Christians in Social Work
National Council on Illegitimacy, Group Meeting 2
National Urban League, Group Meeting 2
The Salvation Army, Group Meeting 3
The Volunteers of America, Group Meeting 3

2:00 P.M.—5:00 P.M.

INFORMATION AND REFERRAL ROUNDTABLE

>*Presiding:* Aaron Sacks, Executive Director, Information and Volun-
>tary Services, Pittsburgh
>
>*Sponsor:* United Community Funds and Councils of America

2:00 P.M.—3:30 P.M.

STEPS TOWARD COMMUNITY CONTROL . . .

HEW AGENCIES

Presiding: Melvin A. Slawik, Wilmington, Del.

Sponsor: United Presbyterian Church, Health, Education and Welfare Association

VETERANS ADMINISTRATION AS A ROLE MODEL IN SOCIAL

POLICY: MEDICAL CARE AND INCOME MAINTENANCE

Presiding: Delwin M. Anderson, Director, Social Work Service, Veterans Administration, Washington

Speaker: Alton A. Linford, Professor, School of Social Service Administration, University of Chicago, Chicago

Sponsor: Veterans Administration

2:37 P.M.

FILM THEATER

Film: Anything for Kicks

Sponsor: NCSW Audio-visual Committee

2:48 P.M.

FILM THEATER

Film: A Human Condition

Sponsor: NCSW Audio-visual Committee

3:18 P.M.

FILM THEATER

Film: Those Who Stay Behind

Sponsor: NCSW Audio-visual Committee

3:34 P.M.

FILM THEATER

Film: Thursday's Child

Sponsor: NCSW Audio-visual Committee

4:00 P.M.—5:30 P.M.

THE WHITE HOUSE CONFERENCE ON AGING—

PANACEA OR PLACEBO?

Presiding: Henry L. McCarthy, Chief, Division of Community Services, Illinois Department of Public Aid, Springfield

Speakers: Elias S. Cohen, Commissioner, Office of Family Services, Pennsylvania Department of Public Welfare, Harrisburg

Bernard E. Nash, Executive Director, American Association of Retired Persons–National Retired Teachers Association, Washington

George E. Davis, Executive Director, Commission on the Aging and Aged, State of Indiana, Indianapolis

Willis W. Atwell, Deputy Commissioner, Administration on the Aging, Social and Rehabilitation Service, Department of Health, Education, and Welfare, Washington

Cosponsors:
American Association of Homes for the Aging
American Association of Retired Persons
American Home Economics Association
American National Red Cross
American Public Welfare Association
Executive Council of the Episcopal Church
National Association for Statewide Health and Welfare, Group Meeting 1
National Association of Social Workers, Group Meeting 1
National Council for Homemaker Services
National Retired Teachers Association
The Salvation Army, Group Meeting 1
United Community Funds and Councils of America
United Presbyterian Health, Education, and Welfare Association
The Volunteers of America, Group Meeting 1

CHILD WELFARE LEAGUE OF AMERICA'S FIFTIETH ANNIVERSARY PROGRAM AND ANNUAL MEETING

Presiding: Joseph H. Reid, Executive Director, Child Welfare League, New York

Child Welfare—a View from the Bridge

Speakers: Leonard W. Mayo, Professor of Development, Colby College, Waterville, Maine; President International Union of Child Welfare
Urie Bronfenbrenner, Professor, Department of Psychology and Human Development and Family Studies, New York State College of Human Ecology, Cornell University, Ithaca, N.Y.

Sponsor: Child Welfare League of America, Group Meeting 1

THE INDIAN LOOKS AT THE FUTURE OF SOCIAL WELFARE IN AMERICA

Presiding: Ruth Muskrat Bronson, Field Representative, Save the Children Federation, Community Development Foundation, Tucson, Ariz.

Panelists: Josiah Moore, Education Coordinator, Papago Indian Reservation, Sells, Ariz.
Abbott Sekaquaptewa, Director, Community Action Program, Oraibi, Ariz.
Mrs. Leah Manning, Owyhee, Nev.

Sponsor: Community Development Foundation Save the Children Federation

SOCIAL STRUCTURAL CHANGE: A NEW MODEL FOR SOCIAL PLANNING

Presiding: Roland L. Warren, Professor of Community Theory, Florence Heller Graduate School for Advanced Studies in Social Welfare, Brandeis University, Waltham, Mass.

Speaker: Robert R. Mayer, Lecturer in Social Policy, Department of City and Regional Planning, University of North Carolina, Chapel Hill
Discussant: Mayer N. Zaid, Professor, Department of Sociology and Anthropology, Vanderbilt University, Nashville, Tenn.
Sponsor: Council on Social Work Education

FAMILY DEVELOPMENT: AN APPROACH FOR SERVICES IN FAMILY AGENCIES

Presiding: Reuben Hill, Professor of Sociology, University of Minnesota, Minneapolis
Discussants: Earl J. Beatt, Executive Director, Family and Children's Service, Minneapolis
Robert Batholow, Family Counseling Supervisor, Family and Children's Service, Minneapolis
Elam Nunnally, Family Development Consultant, Family and Children's Service, Minneapolis; Family Study Center, University of Minnesota, Minneapolis
Sherod Miller, Family Development Consultant, Family and Children's Service, Minneapolis; faculty member, Augsburg College, Minneapolis
Sponsor: Family Service Association of America, Group Meeting 1

A WASHINGTON PERSPECTIVE FOR STATE CITIZEN ORGANIZATIONS

Presiding: A. Rowland Todd, Executive Director, Wisconsin Welfare Council, Madison
Speaker: The Hon. Charles H. Percy, U.S. Senator, State of Illinois, Washington
Sponsor: National Association for Statewide Health and Welfare

DELIVERY OF SOCIAL WELFARE SERVICES TO THE POOR (Workshop)

Presiding: Mitchell I. Ginsberg, Commissioner, Human Resources Administration, New York
Speakers: Will Richan, Assistant Dean, School of Social Administration, Temple University, Philadelphia
Herbert Winston, Assistant Dean, School of Social Administration, Temple University, Philadelphia
Elaine Rothenberg, Assistant Dean, School of Social Work, Virginia Commonwealth University, Richmond
Alan Wade, Dean, School of Social Work, Sacramento State College, Sacramento, Calif.
Sponsor: National Association of Social Workers, Group Meeting 2

INSTITUTIONAL RACISM IN SOCIAL WELFARE (Workshop)

Presiding: Ada E. Deer, Director, Upward Bound, Wisconsin State University, Stevens Point, Wis.
Speakers: Roger Miller, Director of Research, School of Social Work, Smith College, Northampton, Mass.

Josephine Nieves, Director of Public Relations Studies, Brooklyn College, Brooklyn, N.Y.

Douglas Glasgow, Associate Professor, School of Social Welfare, University of California, Los Angeles

Sponsor: National Association of Social Workers, Group Meeting 3

MEETING MANPOWER NEEDS FOR DELIVERY OF SERVICES (Workshop)

Presiding: Sherman Merle, Interim Professor, School of Social Work, Catholic University of America, Washington; Chairman, Division of Professional Standards, National Association of Social Workers

Current Issues in Social Work Education

Speaker: Herbert Bisno, faculty member, University of Oregon; Visiting Professor, Fairleigh Dickinson University, Teaneck, N.J.

Sponsor: National Association of Social Workers, Group Meeting 4

THE ONE-PARENT FAMILY TODAY

Presiding: Mary Louise Allen, Executive Director, Florence Crittenton Association of America, Chicago

Speakers: Mrs. Camille E. Jeffers, Director, Model Cities Office of Child Service and Family Counseling, Atlanta, Ga.

Bernice Q. Madison, Professor of Social Work, Department of Social Work Education, San Francisco State College, San Francisco

Cosponsors:

Child Welfare League of America, Group Meeting 2

Family Service Association of America, Group Meeting 2

Florence Crittenton Association of America

National Council on Illegitimacy

National Urban League

The Salvation Army, Group Meeting 2

The Volunteers of America, Group Meeting 2

NEW FORMS OF COMMUNITY CONTROL: ACTUAL DEVELOPMENTS

Presiding: Lillie Lynem, faculty member, School of Social Service Administration, University of Chicago, Chicago

Community Control: Recent Developments and Current Issues

Speakers: Arthur Hillman, Director, National Federation of Settlements Training Center, Chicago

Louis V. Huber, Executive Director, United Church of Christ Neighborhood Houses, St. Louis

Rodney Sam Wead, Executive Director, United Methodist Community Centers, Omaha

Sponsor: National Federation of Settlements and Neighborhood Centers

COPING WITH CONFLICT

Presiding: William H. Robinson, Director, Department of Registration

and Education, State of Illinois, Chicago; Chairman, Section V, NCSW
Speaker: Herbert Rubinstein, Deputy Executive Director, Michigan
Welfare League, Lansing
Sponsor: United Community Funds and Councils of America–Association
of Volunteer Bureaus

6:30 P.M.

ASSOCIATION OF VOLUNTEER BUREAUS OF AMERICA
ANNUAL MEETING
Presiding: Mrs. Alexander B. Ripley, President, Association of Volunteer Bureaus of America, Los Angeles
Speaker: Mrs. Elizabeth D. Coontz, Director, Women's Bureau, Department of Labor, Washington
Sponsor: United Community Funds and Councils of America–Association
of Volunteer Bureaus

8:30 P.M.

SOCIAL ISSUES FORUM
Presiding: Wilbur J. Cohen, Dean, School of Education, University
of Michigan, Ann Arbor; President, NCSW
Sponsor: NCSW

Wednesday, June 3

9:00 A.M.—10:45 A.M.

GENERAL SESSION
Welfare Reform and Income Security Policies
Presiding: Wilbur J. Cohen, Dean, School of Education, University
of Michigan, Ann Arbor; President, NCSW
The Report of the President's Commission on Income Maintenance
Speakers: The Hon. Barbara Jordan, Senator, State of Texas, Houston;
member, President's Commission on Income Maintenance
Mrs. Eveline M. Burns, Professor, Graduate School of Social Work,
New York University; Professor Emeritus, Columbia University School
of Social Work, New York; Past President, NCSW

11:00 A.M.

FILM THEATER
Film: Marijuana
Discussant: Dr. C. R. Schuster, Associate Professor, University of Chi-
cago Hospitals, Departments of Psychiatry and Pharmacology, Chicago.
Sponsor: NCSW Audio-visual Committee

11:00 A.M.—10:00 P.M.

CAUCUS
Sponsor: National Welfare Rights Organization

11:15 A.M.—12:45 P.M.

INCOME MAINTENANCE: WHERE WE ARE AND WHERE
WE ARE LIKELY TO GO
> *Presiding:* Wayne Vasey, Professor, School of Social Work, University
> of Michigan, Ann Arbor; Past President, NCSW
> *Speaker:* Alvin L. Schorr, Director, Brandeis University, Income Main-
> tenance Project, Washington

Sponsor: Division

THE GOOD, THE BAD, AND THE UGLY: A STUDENT'S
VIEW OF THE FIELD WORK EXPERIENCE
> *Presiding and moderator:* Herman Leon, Director of Special Projects
> and Development, Jewish Board of Guardians, New York
> *Panelists:* Mrs. Harriet Yurchak, casework student, Graduate School of
> Social Work, University of Nebraska, Lincoln
> Vere Dudgeon, casework student, Smith College School of Social Work,
> Northampton, Mass.
> Mrs. Betty A. Kirby, casework student, Graduate School of Social Work,
> University of Denver, Denver
> Mrs. Lynn Wickler, casework student, Graduate School of Social Work,
> University of Maryland, Baltimore

Sponsor: Section I (Casework), Group Meeting 1

NEW APPROACHES TO SERVICE DELIVERY: PROGRAM AND
PLANS OF THE COMMUNITY SERVICES ADMINISTRATION,
SOCIAL AND REHABILITATION SERVICE, DEPARTMENT OF
HEALTH, EDUCATION, AND WELFARE
> *Presiding:* Steven A. Minter, Director, Cuyahoga County Welfare
> Department, Cleveland
> *Speaker:* Stephen P. Simonds, Commissioner, Community Services
> Administration, Social and Rehabilitation Service, Department of
> Health, Education, and Welfare, Washington
> *Discussants:* Mrs. Aminda Wilkins, Assistant Deputy Commissioner and
> Director, Community Relations, New York City Department of Social
> Services, New York
> Mrs. Jennette Washington, Eastern Regional Representative, National
> Welfare Rights Organization, New York

Sponsor: Section I (Casework), Group Meeting 2

SOCIAL WORK AND DAY CARE
> *Presiding:* Thomas C. Taylor, Director, National Capital Area Child
> Day Care Association, Washington

Day Care for the Young Child: What Is the Social Worker's Role?

Speaker: Mrs. Sharon Kempf, Assistant Professor, School of Social Work, Catholic University of America, Washington

Day Care: a Mental Health Intervention

Speaker: Ira A. Gibbons, Acting Dean, School of Social Work, Howard University, Washington; former Director Social Service Office, Bureau of Head Start, Office of Child Development, Department of Health, Education, and Welfare

Sponsor: Section I (Casework), Group Meeting 3

ENHANCING THE QUALITY OF LIFE IN RURAL AMERICA

Speaker: Tomas Atencio, Specialist in Rural Services, Dixon, N. Mex.

Sponsor: Section I (Casework), Group Meeting 4

BLACK IDENTITY AND SOCIAL WORK

Presiding: Ann L. Fredd, Social Work Supervisor, Dr. Martin Luther King Family Center, Chicago

Emerging Social and Emotional Perspective of Black People in America and the Black-white Crisis: a Psychosocial Assessment

Speaker: Christopher G. Narcisse, Assistant Professor, Jane Addams Graduate School of Social Work, Chicago

Sponsor: Section I (Casework), Group Meeting 5

PREVENTIVE AND TREATMENT APPROACHES WITH LOW-INCOME FAMILIES

Presiding: Sam Negrin, Director, Department of Development, National Association of Social Workers, New York

Preventive Intervention with Low-Income Parents in a School Setting

Speaker: Norma Radin, Assistant Professor, School of Social Work, University of Michigan, Ann Arbor

The Development of School Social Work Practice Theory

Speaker: Frank F. Maple, Jr., Associate Professor, School of Social Work, University of Michigan, Ann Arbor

Discussants: Sharon Newton, Ypsilanti, Mich.

Marcella C. Egenes, Consultant for School of Social Work, Indiana Department of Public Institutions, Indianapolis

Cosponsors:

Section I (Casework), Group Meeting 6

Section II (Group Work), Group Meeting 1

ROLE THEORY FOR GROUP WORK

Presiding: Alan Connor, Assistant Professor, School of Social Work, University of Michigan, Ann Arbor

Speaker: Ronald A. Feldman, Associate Professor, George Warren Brown School of Social Work, Washington University, St. Louis

Discussant: Irving Miller, Professor, School of Social Work, Columbia University, New York

Sponsor: Section II (Group Work), Group Meeting 2

THE ADMINISTRATION'S INCOME MAINTENANCE PROPOSALS

Presiding and speaker: Edward Newman, Commissioner, Rehabilitation

Services Administration, Social and Rehabilitation Service, Department of Health, Education, and Welfare, Washington
Discussants: Robert Leighty, Director, Planning and Research, Pennsylvania Department of Public Welfare, Harrisburg
Hulbert Jones, Director, Domestic Hunger Programs, National Council of Churches of Christ in the U.S.A., New York
Sponsor: Section III (Community Organization and Methods of Social Action), Group Meeting 1

DELIVERY OF MEDICAL CARE

Presiding: Mrs. Ferne K. Kolodner, Community Planning Staff, Social Security Administration, Department of Health, Education, and Welfare, Baltimore
Speaker: Arthur E. Hess, Deputy Commissioner, Social Security Administration, and Staff Director, Task Force on Medicaid and Related Programs, Department of Health, Education, and Welfare, Baltimore
Discussant: Sol Levine, Chairman, Department of Behavioral Sciences, School of Hygiene and Public Health, Johns Hopkins University, Baltimore; Director, Center for Urban Studies, Baltimore
Richard Wilbur, M.D., Assistant Executive Vice President, American Medical Association, Chicago
Sponsor: Section III (Community Organization and Methods of Social Action), Group Meeting 2

EMERGING ROLES IN PLANNING AND ACTION

Presiding: John E. Tropman, Assistant Professor, School of Social Work, University of Michigan, Ann Arbor
Panelists: Harold D. Craft, Assistant Director, Employee Consultation Center, J. L. Hudson Co., Detroit
Lloyd Davis, Manager, Model Neighborhood Demonstration Program (MUND), Baltimore
Nancy Amidei, professional staff member, Select Commission on Nutrition and Human Needs, Washington
John L. Earlich, Assistant Professor, School of Social Work, University of Michigan, Ann Arbor
Sponsor: Section III (Community Organization and Methods of Social Action), Group Meeting 3

SOCIAL RESEARCH AND SOCIAL ADVOCACY

Presiding: Edward O'Donnell, Professor, School of Social Work, Catholic University of America, Washington
Speaker: Peter Rossi, Professor, Department of Sociology, Johns Hopkins University, Baltimore
Sponsor: Section IV (Social Research), Group Meeting 1

MASS VIOLENCE

Presiding: Robert Langer, Associate Executive Director, Health and Welfare Council of Metropolitan St. Louis, St. Louis
Speakers: John Spiegel, Professor, Florence Heller Graduate School

for Advanced Studies in Social Welfare, Brandeis University, Waltham, Mass.

Enrico Quarantelli, Professor, Department of Sociology, Ohio State University, Columbus, Ohio

Sponsor: Section IV (Social Research), Group Meeting 2

DRUG ADDICTION

Presiding and discussant: Robert Peterson, M.D., Drug Abuse Section, National Institute of Mental Health, Bethesda, Md.

Social Constraints on the Treatment of Heroin Addiction

Speaker: Charles B. Arnold, M.D., Professor, Department of Community Health, Albert Einstein College of Medicine, Yeshiva University, New York

Narcotics Addicts—Utilization of Service

Speaker: David N. Nurco, Baltimore

Sponsor: Section IV (Social Research), Group Meeting 3

EMPLOYMENT OF MOTHERS AS A CULTURAL AND ECONOMIC PHENOMENON

Presiding: Mrs. Sally McMahan, Executive Director, Association for Family Living, Chicago

Speaker: Mrs. Myra Sullivan, Assistant Director of Field Operations, Cook County Department of Public Aid, Chicago

Sponsor: Section V (Administration)

SOCIAL WORK EDUCATION TODAY—PERSPECTIVES AND PROMISE FOR INTERNATIONAL EXCHANGE

Presiding: Henry B. Ollendorff, Secretary General, Council of International Programs for Youth Leaders and Social Workers, Cleveland

Speaker and moderator: Mary Louise Somers, Professor, School of Social Service Administration, University of Chicago, Chicago

Panelists: Kathleen Flaherty, student, School of Social Work, University of Illinois, Chicago

Balgrim Ragoonanan, student, School of Social Work, University of Illinois, Chicago

Gilbert Santiago, student, School of Social Work, George Williams College, Downers Grove, Ill.

Patrick Moriarty, student, School of Social Work, George Williams College, Downers Grove, Ill.

Thomas Hopkins, student, School of Social Work, Loyola University, Chicago

K. T. Hopkins, student, School of Social Work, Loyola University, Chicago

Angelis De Leon, student, School of Social Work, Loyola University, Chicago

Jorje Valenzala, student, School of Social Service Administration, University of Chicago, Chicago

Ida Levi, student, School of Social Service Administration, University of Chicago, Chicago

Charline McCutcheon, student, School of Social Service Administration, University of Chicago, Chicago
Sponsor: U.S. Committee of NCSW

12:37 P.M.

FILM THEATER
Film: Black and White and Shades of Grey
Sponsor: NCSW Audio-visual Committee

12:48 P.M.

FILM THEATER
Film: Education and the Mexican-American
Sponsor: NCSW Audio-visual Committee

1:45 P.M.

FILM THEATER
Film: Flowers on a One-Way Street
Sponsor: NCSW Audio-visual Committee

2:00 P.M.—3:30 P.M.

NEW TOOLS FOR MAKING SOCIAL POLICY
Presiding: Alton A. Linford, Professor, School of Social Service Administration, University of Chicago, Chicago
Speaker: Howard E. Freeman, Morse Professor of Urban Studies, Florence Heller Graduate School for Advanced Studies in Social Welfare, Brandeis University, Waltham, Mass.; sociologist, Russell Sage Foundation
Discussants: Genevieve W. Carter, Director, Regional Social Welfare Research Institute, School of Social Work, University of Southern California, Los Angeles
Norman V. Lourie, Deputy Secretary for Public Welfare, Pennsylvania Department of Public Welfare, Harrisburg
Sponsor: Division

SERVICE DELIVERY AND SEPARATION OF FINANCIAL AID
Presiding: Maurice A. Harmon, Director, Baltimore Department of Social Service, Baltimore
Speaker: Mrs. Fredericka D. Williams, Acting Chief, Office of Service Development, Community Services Administration, Social and Rehabilitation Service, Department of Health, Education, and Welfare, Washington
Discussants: Mrs. Clara A. Hamilton, District Supervisor, Rockingham County Department of Welfare, Portsmouth, N.H.
Paul A. LeVecque, Director, Division of Adult and Financial Service, Department of Health, Education, and Welfare, State of Maine, Augusta

William N. Coffey, Welfare Field Representative, Department of Public Welfare, State of Louisiana, Baton Rouge
Sponsor: Section I (Casework), Group Meeting 1

BLACK IDENTITY AND SOCIAL WORK
Presiding: Raymond W. Fannings, Director, Group Home Program, Illinois Children's Home and Aid Society, Chicago
Race: Is It an Issue in Casework Treatment?
Speaker: Leon W. Chestang, Director, Casework Service, Child and Family Services, Chicago
Sponsor: Section I (Casework), Group Meeting 2

THE CHANGING ROLE OF WOMEN: ITS IMPACT ON PRACTICE
Presiding: Mrs. Lynn Wikler, student, School of Social Work, University of Maryland, Baltimore
Speakers: Rose Terlin, Chief, Economic Status and Opportunities Division, Women's Bureau, Department of Labor, Washington
Dr. Jo Anne Gardner, Center Associate, Learning and Research Development Center, University of Pittsburgh, Pittsburgh

INNOVATIONS IN CASEWORK PRACTICE THROUGH SPECIAL PROJECTS
Presiding: Merlin Taber, Professor, Jane Addams Graduate School of Social Work, University of Illinois, Urbana
An Innovative Model Designed to Deliver Medical and Social Services to the Poverty-ridden Consumer on a Pre-Crisis Basis
Speaker: Mrs. Merna Alpert, Field Unit Instructor, Lincoln Hospital, Albert Einstein College of Medicine, Yeshiva University, New York
Closing a Policy-Services Gap in Service for the Aging
Speaker: Theodore Ernst, Associate Professor and Associate Dean, School of Social Work, State University of New York, Buffalo
Services to Improve Family Living on AFDC
Speaker: Harris Chaiklin, Professor, School of Social Work, University of Maryland, Baltimore
Sponsor: Section I (Casework), Group Meeting 4

ROLE PLAY: A TOOL FOR THE PRACTITIONER
Presiding: James Whittaker, faculty member, School of Social Work, University of Minnesota, Minneapolis
Speaker: Edmond T. Jenkins, faculty member, School of Applied Social Sciences, Case Western Reserve University, Cleveland
Discussant: Martin Sundel, Assistant Professor, School of Social Work, University of Michigan, Ann Arbor
Sponsor: Section II (Group Work), Group Meeting 1

NEW APPROACHES TO WORK WITH OLDER ADULTS
Presiding: Herbert H. Shore, Executive Director, Dallas Home and Hospital for Jewish Aged, Dallas
Uses of Groups in Work with Older Adults
Speaker: Mary M. Seguin, trainee and doctoral student, Gerontology

Center, University of Southern California School of Social Work, Los
Angeles

Multiple-Group Memberships with Institutionalized Geriatric Patients
Speaker: Beryl L. Carter, Assistant Professor, School of Social Work,
University of Michigan, Ann Arbor
Discussant: Louis Lewy, Professor, School of Social Work, Boston University, Boston
Sponsor: Section II (Group Work), Group Meeting 2

THE PRACTITIONER ROLE IN SOCIAL WORK GROUPS:
A BROAD-RANGE MODEL OF INTERVENTION
Presiding: Donald J. Watkins, Executive Director, Area Service Association, Ferndale, Mich.
Speaker: Norma C. Lang, Instructor in Social Work, School of Applied
Social Sciences, Case Western Reserve University, Cleveland
Discussant: Charles Garvin, Assistant Professor, School of Social Work,
University of Michigan, Ann Arbor
Cosponsors:
Section II (Group Work), Group Meeting 3
Section III (Community Organization and Methods of Social Action), Group
Meeting 1

IMPLICATIONS OF THE DISABILITY STUDY
Presiding: Edward Newman, Commissioner, Rehabilitation Services Administration, Social and Rehabilitation Service, Department of Health,
Education, and Welfare, Washington
Disability and Social Planning: Policy and Program Implications of the
Social Security Disability Survey
Speaker: Bernard Popick, Director, Bureau of Disability Insurance,
Social Security Administration, Department of Health, Education, and
Welfare, Baltimore
Discussants: Lawrence Haber, Office of Research and Statistics, Directory
of Disability Studies, Social Security Administration, Department of
Health, Education, and Welfare, Baltimore
Monroe Berkowitz, Director, Bureau of Economic Research, Rutgers
University—the State University, New Brunswick, N.J.
Sponsor: Section III (Community Organization and Methods of Social Action), Group Meeting 2

FEDERAL REGIONAL COUNCILS AS SOCIAL PLANNING
INSTRUMENTS
Presiding: C. F. McNeil, Executive Director, National Assembly for
Social Policy and Development, New York
Speaker: Melvin B. Mogulof, Associate Professor, Department of Social Work Education, San Francisco State College, San Francisco
Discussant: Dan MacDonald, Executive Director, Health and Welfare
Council of Metropolitan St. Louis, St. Louis
Sponsor: Section III (Community Organization and Methods of Social Action), Group Meeting 3

NEW TECHNOLOGIES FOR PLANNING AND ACTION
Presiding: Jack Rothman, Professor, School of Social Work, University of Michigan, Ann Arbor
Panelists: Andrew Orlin, Project Coordinator, Management Information System, Health and Welfare Association of Allegheny County, Pittsburgh
Harvey Bertcher, Associate Professor, School of Social Work, University of Michigan, Ann Arbor
Yeheskel Hasenfeld, Instructor, School of Social Work, University of Michigan, Ann Arbor
Henry Wallace, Senior Instructor, Center for Programmed Learning, University of Michigan, Ann Arbor
Sponsor: Section III (Community Organization and Methods of Social Action), Group Meeting 5

BARRIERS TO EMPLOYMENT OF THE POOR AND/OR
MINORITY GROUP MEMBERS
Presiding: Irving Spergel, Professor, School of Social Service Administration, University of Chicago, Chicago
Speaker: Dr. Catherine Chilman, Dean of Academic Affairs, Hood College, Frederick, Md.
Discussants: Harold M. Baron, Center for Urban Studies, Northwestern and Associated Colleges, Evanston, Ill.
Earl L. Durham, Assistant Professor, School of Social Service Administration, University of Chicago
Sponsor: Section IV (Social Research), Group Meeting 1

EARLY SOCIAL WORK INTERVENTION WITH
YOUNG FAMILIES
Presiding: Dr. Josephy Lagey, School of Social Work, New York University, New York
A Report on the Findings of the Rutgers Family Improvement Project: Implications for Program and Policy
Speaker: Ludwig L. Geismar, Professor, Graduate School of Social Work, Rutgers—the State University, New Brunswick, N.J.
Cosponsors:
Section IV (Social Research), Group Meeting 2
Section I (Casework), Group Meeting 5

PARAPROFESSIONALS AND NEW CAREERS IN SOCIAL
WELFARE ADMINISTRATION: MYTH OR REALITY?
Presiding: Mrs. Dorothy Bird Daly, Dean, School of Social Work, Catholic University of America, Washington
New Careers: a Dynamic Approach to Manpower in the Human Services
Speaker: Jane Lee Hamman, Planning Associate, United Community Chest and Council, Syracuse, N.Y.
Employment of Paraprofessionals: a Challenge to Administrators
Speaker: John M. Riley, Associate Professor, School of Social Work,

University of Michigan, Ann Arbor (paper coauthored with Phillip A. Fellin, Professor, School of Social Work, University of Michigan)
Sponsor: Section V (Administration)

4:00 P.M.—5:30 P.M.

ANNUAL MEETING OF NCSW MEMBERS
  Presiding: Wilbur J. Cohen, Dean, School of Education, University of Michigan, Ann Arbor; President; NCSW
Sponsor: NCSW

8:30 P.M.

GENERAL SESSION
The Colonial Mentality in American Institutions Today
Planners of, and participants in, this session represent the blacks, La Raza, National Federation of Student Social Workers, the National Welfare Rights Organization, and American Indians
Black Point of View
  Speaker: Bill Thompson, Economic Opportunity Council, Reading, Pa.
La Raza Point of View
  Speakers: Julia Ruiz, Psychiatric Social Worker, Tempe, Ariz.
  Margarita Olivieri, Catholic Charities, New York
  Francisco Torres Rivera, School Social Worker, University of Puerto Rico High School
Representatives of National Federation of Student Social Workers
  Speaker: Adolph Sanchez
Representatives of National Welfare Rights Organization
  Speaker: Mrs. Johnnie Tillman, Chairman, National Welfare Rights Organization, Los Angeles
Representatives of American Indians
  Steve Fast Wolf, Chairman, Native American Committee of Chicago
  Russell P. Means, Director, Cleveland American Indian Center, Cleveland

Thurdsay, June 4

9:00 A.M.—10:45 A.M.

THE LAW AS A POSITIVE FORCE FOR SOCIAL CHANGE
  Presiding: John F. Larberg, Senior Staff Consultant, National Assembly for Social Policy and Development, New York; Chairman, Combined Associate Groups, NCSW
  Speaker: The Hon. Brooks Hays, Director, Ecumenical Institute, Wake Forest University, Winston-Salem, N.C.
Sponsor: Combined Associate Groups

11:00 A.M.

FILM THEATER
Film: Feeding and Function Pleasure in the First Year of Life
Sponsor: NCSW Audio-visual Committee

11:00 A.M.—10:00 P.M.

CAUCUS
Sponsor: National Welfare Rights Organization

11:15 A.M.—12:45 P.M.

GETTING READY FOR THE LATER YEARS
Presiding: Fred Faassen, President, American Association of Retired Persons, Zion, Ill.
Speakers: Woodrow W. Hunter, Acting Codirector, Institute of Gerontology, University of Michigan–Wayne State University, Ann Arbor
Donald L. Bowman, Director, Institute for Preretirement Planning, Drake University, Des Moines, Iowa
Bruce Roach, Manager, Preretirement Counseling Program, Chrysler Corporation, Centerline, Mich.
David Jeffreys, Director of National Affairs, American Association of Retired Persons, National Retired Teachers Association, Washington
Cosponsors:
American Association of Retired Persons
Family Service Association of America, Group Meeting 1
National Retired Teachers Association

ROLE AND RELATIONSHIP OF LAWYER AND SOCIAL
WORKER IN NEGLECT AND ABUSE CASES
Presiding: Emil M. Sunley, Dean, Graduate School of Social Work, University of Denver, Denver
Speaker: Earl J. Beatt, Executive Director, Family and Children's Service, Minneapolis
Discussants: The Hon. Lindsay Arthur, Judge, Juvenile Court, Hennepin County, Minneapolis
Edward J. Kosciolek, Program Supervisor, Child Service Division, Hennepin County Welfare Department, Minneapolis
Cosponsors:
American Humane Association, Children's Division
American Legion, Child Welfare Division
American Public Welfare Association
Child Welfare League of America. Group Meeting 1
National Council on Crime and Delinquency

COMMUNITY SERVICE CENTER: A CONCEPT TAKES ON LIFE
Presiding: Donald E. Brieland, Associate Dean, School of Social Service Administration, University of Chicago, Chicago

Speakers: Hubert Jones, Executive Director, Roxbury Community Service Center, Boston

Clinton McKay, Director, the Woodlawn Project, Chicago

Cosponsors:

Child Welfare League of America, Group Meeting 2

Florence Crittenton Association of America, Group Meeting 1

AGENCY ADMINISTRATION: RATIONALIZATION OR REAL CHANGE

Presiding: William Maxwell Mason, Assistant Professor of Sociology, Graduate School of Business, University of Chicago, Chicago

Speaker: Walter L. Walker, Vice President for Planning, School of Social Services Administration, University of Chicago, Chicago

Panelists: Paul Fromm, President, Family Institute of Chicago, Oak Park, Ill.

The Rev. Coyd Taggart, Director, Lake Bluff–Chicago Homes for Children, Chicago

Cosponsors:

Child Welfare League of America, Group Meeting 3

Florence Crittenton Association of America, Group Meeting 2

National Council for Homemaker Services

SETTING STANDARDS FOR THE B.A. SOCIAL WORKER

Presiding: Donald L. Feldstein, Senior Consultant on Undergraduate Education, Council on Social Work Education, New York

Speaker: Mrs. Erma Meyerson, Professor, School of Social Work, University of Pittsburgh, Pittsburgh; Chairman, Special Committee on Undergraduate Education

Sponsor: Council on Social Work Education

A COMMUNITY PLANS FOR ITS OWN DAY CARE NEEDS

Presiding: Mrs. Evelyn Zisserson, Assistant Director, Children's Services, Chicago Committee on Urban Opportunity, Chicago

Community Development

Panelist: Mrs. Helen Gordon, Portland, Oreg.

Volunteer

Panelist: Mrs. Sally Wertheim, National Council of Jewish Women, Beechwood, Ohio

Social Agency

Panelist: Mrs. Evelyn Zisserson, Assistant Director, Children's Services, Chicago Committee on Urban Opportunity, Chicago

Parent

Panelist: Mrs. Sylvia Harris, Head Start Parent Advisory Committee, Chicago

Illinois Department of Mental Health, Chicago

Panelist: Bertha Swindel

Community Involvement

Panelist: Mrs. Peter Sauer, Director, Bank Street at Morningside, N.Y.

Cosponsors:
Day Care and Child Development Council of America
National Council of Jewish Women

ATTITUDES OF SOCIAL WORKERS IN WORK WITH
THE AGED AND THEIR FAMILIES
> *Presiding:* Mrs. Frances H. Scherz, Director of Casework, Jewish Family and Community Service, Chicago
> *Speakers:* Liese Lee Haag, Assistant Administrator, Jewish Family and Community Service, Northern District Office, Chicago
> Mrs. Ruth Hyman, social worker, Jewish Family and Community Service, Chicago
> Mrs. Mary Slawski, caseworker, Jewish Family and Community Service, Chicago

Sponsor: Family Service Association of America, Group Meeting 2

ISSUES FACING STATE ORGANIZATIONS OPERATING
CONFERENCES
> *Presiding:* Mrs. Tina G. Howell, Executive Director, Massachusetts Conference on Social Welfare, Boston

Sponsor: National Association for Statewide Health and Welfare

LEADERSHIP TRAINING PROGRAM FOR SOCIAL
WORKERS IN MENTAL HEALTH
> *Presiding:* Goerge W. Magner, Project Director, National Association of Social Workers Leadership Training, Chicago

Sponsor: National Association of Social Workers

DISCRIMINATION AND ADOPTION PRACTICES:
ADOPTION OVERVIEW
> *Presiding:* Mrs. Marion Mitchell, Supervisor of Adoption, Chicago Child Care Society, Chicago
> *Speaker:* Anne T. Faletto, Supervisor, Community Resources Planning Specialist, Wisconsin Department of Health and Social Services, Madison

Cosponsors:
Child Welfare League of America, Group Meeting 4
Family Service Association of America, Group Meeting 3
Florence Crittenton Association of America, Group Meeting 3
National Council on Illegitimacy
National Urban League, Group Meeting 1
The Salvation Army
The Volunteers of America

MINORITY GROUP ECONOMIC DEVELOPMENT
IN NEIGHBORHOODS
> *Presiding:* Walter L. Smart, Associate Director, National Federation of Settlements and Neighborhood Centers, New York

Increasing the Employment Options for Unemployed and Underemployed
People through Social Involvement with Industry

Speaker: Mrs. Juliet F. Brudney, Executive Director, Settlement House Employment Development, New York

Making Tax Consumers into Tax Producers through Economic Development

Speakers: Antonio Tinajero, Catholic Conference Division for the Spanish-speaking, San Antonio, Texas

Halloway C. Sells, Jr., Executive Director, Seven Hills Neighborhood Houses, Cincinnati

Cosponsors:

American Jewish Committee

National Federation of Settlements and Neighborhood Centers

COALITIONS: FUTURE DIRECTIONS

Presiding: M. Leo Bohanon, Director, Midwestern Regional Office, National Urban League, St. Louis; member, National Board, NCSW

Speaker: Matthew Holden, Professor of Political Science, University of Wisconsin, Madison

Panelists: Robert Hill, National Director, Coalition for a Black Count Census Project

George R. Coker, Executive Director, Urban League of Gary, Ind.

Sponsor: National Urban League, Group Meeting 2

IS FAMILY PLANNING FOR THE *NOW* GENERATION?

Presiding: Russell H. Richardson, Southeast Regional Director, Planned Parenthood–World Population, Atlanta, Ga.

Panelists: Frederick S. Jaffe, Director, Center for Family Planning Program Development, Planned Parenthood–World Population, New York

Mrs. Helen Stanford, Mid-Atlantic Regional Director, Planned Parenthood–World Population, Philadelphia

Leah Potts, Director, Pregnancy and Abortion Counseling Service, San Francisco–Alameda County Planned Parenthood, Oakland, Calif.

Benjamin F. Lewis, Executive Director, Planned Parenthood Association, Chicago Area

Sponsor: Planned Parenthood–World Population

11:42 A.M.

FILM THEATER

Film: Do They Really Want Me?

Sponsor: NCSW Audio-visual Committee

12:10 P.M.

FILM THEATER

Film: None of My Business

Sponsor: NCSW Audio-visual Committee

12:42 P.M.

FILM THEATER
Film: Six Homes/Six Houses
Sponsor: NCSW Audio-visual Committee

1:09 P.M.

FILM THEATER
Film: Exploring the Treatment of Alcoholism
Sponsor: NCSW Audio-visual Committee

1:36 P.M.

FILM THEATER
Film: A Nice Kid like You
Sponsor: NCSW Audio-visual Committee

2:00 P.M.—3:30 P.M.

IN TRIPLE JEOPARDY:—OLD, POOR, AND IN A
MINORITY GROUP
    Presiding: Laplois Ashford, Executive Director, Chicago Urban League, Chicago
    Speakers: John H. Bell, Director, Senior Citizens' Mobile Service, YMCA of Metropolitan Chicago, Washington Park YMCA, Chicago
    Frank Carranza, American Association of Retired Persons–National Retired Teachers Association, Project Late Start, Brownsville, Texas
    Sharon Fuji, Director, Coordinated Comprehensive Services for the Aging Project, Seattle Model Cities, Seattle, Wash.
    Albert E. Abrams, Assistant Director, Office of Economic Opportunity, Washington
    Eugene H. Molenauer, Regional Representative, American Association of Retired Persons–National Retired Teachers Association, Toledo, Ohio
Cosponsors:
American Association of Retired Persons, Group Meeting 1
American Public Welfare Association, Group Meeting 1
Family Service Association of America, Group Meeting 1
National Assembly for Social Policy and Development, Group Meeting 1
National Association of Social Workers, Group Meeting 1
National Retired Teachers Association
National Urban League, Group Meeting 1

CONVERSATION ON PROTECTIVE SERVICES FOR CHILDREN
    Speaker: Norman Paget, Executive Director, Children's Aid Society, Buffalo, N.Y.
Sponsor: Child Welfare League of America, Group Meeting 1

CONVERSATION ON THE CHANGING SCENE
> *Speaker:* Joseph H. Reid, Executive Director, Child Welfare League of America, New York

Sponsor: Child Welfare League of America, Group Meeting 2

INCOME MAINTENANCE: CONTEMPORARY POLICY AND LONG-RANGE STRATEGY
> *Speaker:* Ben W. Heineman, Chairman of Board, Chicago and Northwestern Railroad Co., Chicago

Sponsor: Child Welfare League of America, Group Meeting 3

TREATMENT OF CHILDREN IN GROUP CARE: WHAT DO WE KNOW?
> *Speaker:* Morris F. Mayer, Executive Director, Bellefaire, Cleveland

Sponsor: Child Welfare League of America, Group Meeting 4

WELFARE MOTHERS: MODERN VARIATIONS ON AN OLD THEME
> *Presiding:* Milton D. Speizman, Professor, Graduate Department of Social Work and Social Research, Bryn Mawr College, Bryn Mawr, Pa.; Chairman, Social Welfare History Group
> *Speaker:* Blanche D. Coll, Historian, Social and Rehabilitation Service, Department of Health, Education, and Welfare, Washington
> *Discussant:* Gary A. Lloyd, Associate Professor, School of Social Work, Tulane University, New Orleans

Cosponsors:
Council on Social Work Education
Social Welfare History Group

THE DAY CARE CENTER AS LOCUS FOR SOCIAL WORK EDUCATION AND RESEARCH
> *Presiding:* Mrs. Doris C. Philips, Associate Professor and Director, Hilltop Child Care Center, George Warren Brown School of Social Work, Washington University, St. Louis

Sponsor: Day Care and Child Development Council of America

ENRICHMENT OF FAMILY AGENCIES' SERVICES TO THE AGING
> *Presiding:* Thomas A. Grubbs, Caseworker in Charge, Service for the Aged, Family Service Bureau, United Charities of Chicago, Chicago

Social Work Team with Aging Family Service Clients
> *Speaker:* Leonore Rivesman, Project Director, Family Service Association of America, New York

Group Counseling of the Elderly
> *Speaker:* Mrs. Rose Klitzner, Director of Special Services, Jewish Family Service, Los Angeles

Cosponsors:
American Association of Retired Persons, Group Meeting 2
American Foundation for the Blind

Family Service Association of America, Group Meeting 2
National Council on the Aging

ANNUAL MEETING, NATIONAL ASSOCIATION FOR STATEWIDE
HEALTH AND WELFARE
   Presiding: Cecil S. Feldman, President, National Association for State-
   wide Health and Welfare, Harrisburg, Pa.
   Discussant: Rowland Bishop, Executive Secretary, National Association
   for Statewide Health and Welfare, Columbus, Ohio
Sponsor: National Association for Statewide Health and Welfare, Group
   Meeting 1

DELINQUENCY PREVENTION THROUGH COMMUNITY
SERVICES
   Presiding: Sherwood Norman, Director, Youth Correctional Services,
   National Council on Crime and Delinquency, New York
   Speakers: Marta Valle, Commissioner, Human Resources Administra-
   tion, Youth Services Agency, New York
   Edgar W. Flood, Director, Oakland County Youth Assistance Program,
   Pontiac, Mich.
   William A. Lofquist, Director, Juvenile Services Bureau, Forsythe
   County, Winston-Salem, N.C.
Cosponsors:
American Humane Association, Children's Division
National Association of Christians in Social Work
National Council on Crime and Delinquency
The Volunteers of America, Group Meeting 1

EMERGING PATTERNS OF SERVICE FOR
UNMARRIED PARENTS
   Presiding and discussant: Ursula M. Gallagher, Specialist on Adoptions
   and Unmarried Mothers, Children's Bureau, Office of Child Develop-
   ment, Department of Health, Education, and Welfare, Washington
The Use of the Associate in Casework with Unmarried Mothers
   Speaker: Helen A. O'Rourke, Supervisor of Alice Hunt Center,
   Children's Services, Cleveland
Overview of the Problem of Illegitimacy and the School-Age Pregnant Girl:
the Minneapolis Response
   Speaker: Mrs. Helen C. Tyler, Assistant Director, School Social Work,
   Minneapolis Public Schools
Cosponsors:
Child Welfare League of America, Group Meeting 5
Family Service Association of America, Group Meeting 3
Florence Crittenton Association of America
National Council on Illegitimacy
National Urban League, Group Meeting 2
The Salvation Army, Group Meeting 1
The Volunteers of America, Group Meeting 2

REALISTIC FAMILY DAY CARE FOR THE URBAN
DAY CARE CONSUMER
> *Presiding:* Mrs. Mary N. Hilton, Deputy Director, Women's Bureau,
> Department of Labor, Washington
> *Speaker:* Arthur C. Emlen, Associate Professor, State University of
> Social Work, Portland, Oreg.; Director, Field Study of the Family Day
> Care System

Day Care Neighbor Service
> *Speakers:* Mrs. Alice H. Collins, Director, Day Care Neighbor Service,
> Field Study of the Neighborhood Family Day Care System, Portland,
> Oreg.
> Mrs. Audrey Pittman, Assistant Professor, School of Social Administra-
> tion, Temple University, Philadelphia

Sponsor: National Federation of Settlements and Neighborhood Centers

ON THE WAY HOME FROM THE FORUM
After the Conference, What?
> *Presiding:* Mrs. Capt. Dan Boyer, Planning Council, Salvation Army,
> St. Louis

Sponsor: The Salvation Army, Group Meeting 2

THE NATIONAL PROGRAM FOR VOLUNTARY ACTION
> *Presiding:* Albert Boyd, Executive Director, Lansing Chamber of
> Commerce, Lansing, Mich.

Clearinghouse, Office of Voluntary Action
> *Speaker:* Helga Roth, Director, Clearinghouse, Office of Voluntary Ac-
> tion, Washington

Goals and Objectives
> *Speaker:* Mrs. Alexander B. Ripley, President, Association of Volun-
> teer Bureaus of America, Los Angeles

Sponsor: United Community Funds and Councils of America–Association
of Volunteer Bureaus

STEPS TOWARD COMMUNITY OWNERSHIP (Workshop)
> *Presiding:* Melvin A. Slawik, Wilmington, Del.

Sponsor: United Presbyterian Health, Education, and Welfare Association

SOCIAL ACTION WORKSHOP: PLENARY SESSION
> *Presiding:* John J. Affleck, Assistant Director for Community Services,
> Department of Social Welfare, Providence, R.I.; Vice Chairman, Sec-
> tion III, NCSW

The Community Services Administration and Social Action
> *Speaker:* Stephen P. Simonds, Commissioner, Community Services Ad-
> ministration, Social and Rehabilitation Service, Department of Health,
> Education, and Welfare, Washington

Welfare Rights Organization, Social Action, and the Community Services
Administration
> *Speaker:* George A. Wiley, Director, National Welfare Rights Organiza-
> tion, Washington; member, National Board, NCSW

Cosponsors:
American Public Welfare Association, Group Meeting 2
National Assembly for Social Policy and Development, Group Meeting 2
National Association for Statewide Health and Welfare, Group Meeting 2
National Association of Social Workers, Group Meeting 2
Section III (Community Organization and Methods of Social Action)

2:10 P.M.

FILM THEATER
Film: The Captive
Sponsor: NCSW Audio-visual Committee

2:39 P.M.

FILM THEATER
Film: The Forgotten American
Sponsor: NCSW Audio-visual Committee

3:45 P.M.—5:30 P.M.

LOBBYING AND SOCIAL WORK (Social Action Workshop 1)
   Presiding: Steve Holloway, Assistant to the Dean, School of Social Work, State University of New York, Stony Brook, N.Y.
   Speaker: Maryann Mahaffey, Associate Professor, School of Social Work, Wayne State University, Detroit
Cosponsors:
American Public Welfare Association
National Assembly for Social Policy and Development
National Association for Statewide Health and Welfare
National Association of Social Workers
Section III (Community Organization and Methods of Social Action)

BEYOND ADVOCACY: TOWARD A NEW CONCEPT OF
COMMUNITY ORGANIZATION PRACTICE (Social Action Workshop 2)
   Presiding: John A. Conley, Assistant Professor, Graduate School of Social Work, University of Pittsburgh, Pittsburgh
   Speaker: Paul A. Kurzman, doctoral candidate, New York University, New York
Cosponsors:
American Public Welfare Association
National Assembly for Social Policy and Development
National Association for Statewide Health and Welfare
National Association of Social Workers
Section III (Community Organization and Methods of Social Action)

THE ROLE OF THE SOCIAL WORKER AS ADVOCATE
(Social Action Workshop 3)
   Presiding: Mrs. Opal C. Jones, Executive Director, Neighborhood Adult Participation, Huntington Park, Calif.

Speaker: Brooks Truitt, Consultant, California State Department of Social Welfare, Los Angeles

Cosponsors:

American Public Welfare Association

National Assembly for Social Policy and Development

National Association for Statewide Health and Welfare

National Association of Social Workers

Section III (Community Organization and Methods of Social Action)

A CONSERVATIVE STRATEGY FOR SOCIAL WELFARE

PLANNING IN THE 1970s (Social Action Workshop 4)

Presiding: Mrs. Ferne Kolodner, Community Planning Staff, Social Security Administration, Department of Health, Education, and Welfare, Baltimore

Speaker: Harold H. Weissman, Assistant Executive Director, Mobilization for Youth, New York

Cosponsors:

American Public Welfare Association

National Assembly for Social Policy and Development

National Association for Statewide Health and Welfare

National Association of Social Workers

Section III (Community Organization and Methods of Social Action)

THE POSITIVE VALUES OF SOCIAL CRISIS IN THE

DEVELOPMENT OF COMMUNITY ORGANIZATION

METHODS AND PRACTICES (Social Action Workshop 5)

Presiding: James F. Workman, Baltimore Urban Coalition, Baltimore

Speaker: Edward P. Dutton, Associate Professor of Social Work, Fresno State College, Fresno, Calif.

Cosponsors:

American Public Welfare Association

National Assembly for Social Policy and Development

National Association for Statewide Health and Welfare

National Association of Social Workers

Section III (Community Organization and Methods of Social Action)

4:00 P.M.—5:30 P.M.

COMMUNITY MENTAL HEALTH IN AN URBAN SETTING:

AN EVOLUTIONARY APPROACH

Presiding and moderator: Dr. Thomas McGee, Director, Mental Health Division, Chicago Board of Health, Chicago

Panelists: Mrs. Faye Price, Regional Director, Mental Health Division, Chicago Board of Health, Chicago

Dr. Stanley Rothstein, Director, Southeast Mental Health Center, Mental Health Division, Chicago Board of Health, Chicago

William J. O'Brien, Chairman, Community Mental Health Board, Chicago

The Rev. Francis Chiaramonte, Vice Chairman, Community Mental Health Board, Chicago
Othello Ellis, board member, Community Mental Health Board, Chicago
Sponsor: Community Mental Health Board of Chicago, Mental Health Division, Chicago Board of Health

"REACTING AMERICANS" IN A TIME OF ANXIETY
Presiding and discussion leader: Arthur Hillman, Director, Training Center, National Federation of Settlements and Neighborhood Center, Chicago
Speakers: Mrs. Judith Magidson Herman, Coordinator, American Jewish Committee, National Project on Ethnic America, New York
Glenn Olson, Executive Director, Alta Social Settlement, Cleveland
Cosponsors:
American Jewish Committee
National Federation of Settlements and Neighborhood Centers

ON THE WAY HOME FROM THE FORUM
Sponsor: The Salvation Army

6:30 P.M.—8:30 P.M.

BLACK CAUCUS
Sponsor: National Association of Black Social Workers

8:00 P.M.

THE MAN NOBODY SAW: Plays for Living Production
Moderator: Paul Neal Averill, publisher, *Birmingham Eccentric*, Birmingham, Mich.; President, Family Service Association of America
Panelists: William B. Shuster, Corporate Manager of Minority Affairs, Atlantic Richfield Co., New York
Beverly D. Gardner, Affirmative Action Coordinator, Products Mid-Continent, Atlantic Richfield Co., Chicago
Sponsor: NCSW Audio-visual Committee

8:30 P.M.—10:00 P.M.

TOWARD THE GREAT CITY: THE NEED FOR
FREEDOM *WITH* ORDER
(Howard F. Gustafson Memorial Lecture)
Presiding: Clyde L. Peterson, attorney, Indianapolis; Chairman, Advisory Committee of Howard F. Gustafson Memorial Fund
Speaker: The Hon. Richard G. Lugar, Mayor, City of Indianapolis; Vice President, National League of Cities
Cosponsors:
Indianapolis Howard F. Gustafson Memorial Committee
National Association of Social Workers
NCSW

Friday, June 5

9:00 A.M.—10:45 A.M.

THE NEIGHBORHOOD: SOCIAL POLICY AND SOCIAL ACTION

Presiding: Cecil S. Feldman, Executive Director, Community Services of Pennsylvania, Harrisburg; President, National Association for State-wide Health and Welfare

Speakers: William H. Robinson, Director, Illinois Department of Registration and Education; Chicago; Chairman, Section V, NCSW

Daniel M. Fox, Research Fellow, Institute of Politics, Kennedy School of Public Administration, Harvard University, Cambridge, Mass.

Sponsor: Division

THE USE OF SUBPROFESSIONALS IN AN INTENSIVE FAMILY SERVICE EFFORT WITH MULTIPROBLEM FAMILIES

Presiding: L. Jay Conrad, Field Instructor, Multnomah County Juvenile Court, Portland, Oreg.

Speaker: Kenneth D. Viegas, Chairman, Community Service Program, University of Oregon, Eugene

Discussants: Herbert Bisno, faculty member, University of Oregon, Eugene; Visiting Professor, Fairleigh Dickinson University, Teaneck, N.J.

Mrs. Margaret Hayes, Second Vice Chairman, National Welfare Rights Organization, Newport News, Va.

Sponsor: Section I (Casework), Group Meeting 1

IMPLICATIONS OF RECENT RESEARCH RESULTS FOR SOCIAL WORK PRACTICE WITH THE AGING

Presiding: Mrs. Roberta Brown, State Commissioner of Aging, Department of Social Services, District of Columbia, Washington

Speakers: Mrs. Marie Latz Blank, Social Work Consultant, Division of Mental Health Programs, Mental Health of the Aging Section, National Institute of Mental Health, Department of Health, Education, and Welfare, Bethesda, Md. (Paper read by Mrs. Bernice McIntosh, Chief, Training Division, Department of Social Services, District of Columbia, Washington)

Mrs. Elaine Brody, Philadelphia Geriatric Center, Philadelphia

Sponsor: Section I (Casework), Group Meeting 2

ETHNIC PATTERNS OF DRUG ABUSE AND NARCOTIC ADDICTION IN THE UNITED STATES

Speaker: Martin Ortiz, Director, Center of Mexican-American Affairs, Whittier College, Pasadena, Calif.

Sponsor: Section I (Casework), Group Meeting 3

INTEGRATING THE FUNCTIONS OF THE SOCIAL WORK PRACTITIONER (Authors' Forum)

Presiding: Max Casper, Assistant Professor, School of Social Work, Syracuse University, Syracuse, N.Y.

Group Work in Community Organization Settings
> *Speaker:* Andrew Dobelstein, Assistant Professor, School of Social Work, University of North Carolina, Chapel Hill

The Social Group Worker as a Consultant
> *Speaker:* Robert Chazin, Associate Professor, School of Social Sciences, Fordham University, New York

Let X Times Y = Group Work, Specifically in General Hospitals Serving Patients for Short-Term Periods
> *Speakers:* Harry Alpert, Assistant Director of Social Sciences, Brooklyn Hospital, Brooklyn Cumberland Medical Center, Brooklyn, N.Y.
> Mrs. Merna Alpert, Field Unit Instructor, Lincoln Hospital, Albert Einstein College of Medicine, Yeshiva University, New York

Cosponsors:
Section II (Group Work), Group Meeting 1
Section III (Community Organization and Methods of Social Action), Group Meeting 1

INNOVATION IN THEORY AND PRACTICE
(Authors' Forum)
> *Presiding:* Mrs. Janice Schopler, Professor, School of Social Work, University of North Carolina, Chapel Hill

The Educational *vs.* the Therapeutic Approach to Helping Processes
> *Speaker:* John J. Horwitz, Professor, San Francisco State College, San Francisco

Social Action and the Development of a Residential Change Program for Youthful Offenders
> *Speaker:* Sidney M. Rosen, Assistant Professor, School of Social Work, University of Hawaii, Honolulu

A Preventive Attack on Delinquency
> *Speaker:* Jules Mondschein, Assistant Professor, Graduate School of Social Work, University of Denver, Denver

Cosponsors:
Section II (Group Work), Group Meeting 2
Section III (Community Organization and Methods of Social Action), Group Meeting 2

PATERNALISM AND ITS IMPACT AND INFLUENCE UPON DELIVERY OF SERVICES TO THE DISADVANTAGED
> *Presiding:* Howard E. Prunty, Consultant, Child Welfare League of America, New York
> *Panelists:* Hisashi Hirayama, caseworker, Family Service Association of Bucks County, Pa.
> Chris C. Ruiz, Chairman, Mexican-American Studies Department, East Los Angeles College, Los Angeles
> Leticia Romero, Counselor, Seek Program, City College of New York, New York
> Don Stovall, Counselor, Youth Conservation Services, Department of Public Welfare, Philadelphia
> Mrs. Evelyn Blanchard, Social Work Board of Education, Bureau of Indian Affairs, Pueblo Agency, Albuquerque, N. Mex.

Sponsor: Section III (Community Organization and Methods of Social Action), Group Meeting 3

CAN A PHILOSOPHY OF A PLURALISTIC SOCIETY SERVE AS AN IMPETUS FOR SOCIAL ACTION?

Speaker: James M. O'Kane, Assistant Professor, Department of Sociology, Drew University, Madison, N.J.

Discussants: Walter L. Walker, Vice President for Planning, School of Social Service Administration, University of Chicago, Chicago

Mrs. Hannah Best, Albuquerque, N. Mex.

Sponsor: Section III (Community Organization and Methods of Social Action), Group Meeting 4

KINDS OF PEOPLE

Presiding: Ernest F. Witte, Dean, School of Social Professions, University of Kentucky, Lexington

Panelists: Ernest Fred Anderson, Assistant Professor, School of Social Work, San Diego State College, San Diego, Calif.

Morris L. Eisenstein, Executive Director, United Community Centers, Brooklyn, N.Y.

Sanford Kravitz, Dean, School of Social Work, State University of New York, Stony Brook, N. Y.

Sponsor: Section III (Community Organization and Methods of Social Action), Group Meeting 5

SOCIAL, PSYCHOLOGICAL, AND HEALTH ASPECTS OF FAMILY PLANNING

Presiding: Philip M. Hauser, Director, Population Research and Training Center, Chicago

Social and Psychological Aspects of Family Planning

Speaker: Oliver Moles, Social Research Specialist, Office of Economic Opportunity, Washington

Organization of Health Services for Family Planning

Speaker: Charles B. Arnold, M.D., Professor, Department of Community Health, Albert Einstein College of Medicine, Yeshiva University, New York

Sponsor: Section IV (Social Research), Group Meeting 1

CHARACTERISTICS OF AFDC FAMILIES

Presiding: Dr. Merlin Taber, Jane Addams Graduate School of Social Work, University of Illinois, Urbana

Speaker: Samuel M. Meyers, Research Associate, Bureau of Social Science Research, Washington

Discussants: Sidney E. Zimbalist, Research Director, Welfare Council of Metropolitan Chicago, Chicago

Ginger Mack, WRO Chairman, Chicago

Clinton McKay, Director, Woodlawn Service Project, Chicago

Sponsor: Section IV (Social Research), Group Meeting 2

9:00 A.M.—11:15 A.M.

CAUCUS
Sponsor: National Welfare Rights Organization

11:15 A.M.—12:45 P.M.

CLOSING GENERAL SESSION
Social Welfare in the 1970s: Three Significant Voices
  Invocation: Rabbi Seymour J. Cohen, Anshe Emet Synagogue, Chicago
  Presiding: Wilbur J. Cohen, Dean, School of Education, University of
  Michigan, Ann Arbor; President, NCSW
  Moderator: Studs Terkel, author, social observer, and broadcasting
  personality, Chicago
  Panelists: The Hon. Roman C. Pucinski, U.S. Representative to Con-
  gress from 11th District of Illinois, Washington
  The Rev. J. Archie Hargraves, Associate Professor of Urban Missions,
  Chicago Theological Seminary; Chairman, Black Center for Strategy
  and Community Development, Chicago
  David Friedman, member, Young Americans for Freedom; former As-
  sociate Editor, *Harvard Conservative;* graduate student in theoretical
  physics, University of Chicago, Chicago
  Cha Cha Jiminez, Chairman, Young Lords, Puerto Rican Youth Group,
  Chicago
Introduction of NCSW President for 1970–71
Sponsor: NCSW Public Relations and Development Committee

Appendix B: Business Organization of the Conference for 1970

THE NATIONAL CONFERENCE ON SOCIAL WELFARE is a voluntary association of individual and organizational members who have joined the Conference to promote and share in discussion of the problems and methods identified with the field of social work and immediately related fields.

NCSW OFFICERS

President: Wilbur J. Cohen, Ann Arbor, Mich.
First Vice President: Werner W. Boehm, New Brunswick, N.J.
Second Vice President: W. T. McCullough, Cleveland
Third Vice President: Mrs. Albert Werthan, Nashville, Tenn.
Secretary: Andrew Juras, Salem, Oreg.
Treasurer: William S. Guthrie, Columbus, Ohio
Past President: Arthur S. Flemming, St. Paul, Minn.
President-elect: Margaret E. Berry, New York
Executive Secretary: Joe R. Hoffer, Columbus, Ohio

NCSW NATIONAL BOARD
(includes officers listed above)

Term expires 1970: Bertram M. Beck, New York; Lisle C. Carter, Jr., Ithaca, N.Y.; David R. Hunter, New York; Morris Hursh, St. Paul, Minn.; Rabbi David Jacobson, San Antonio, Texas; Dewey C. Lawrence, Detroit; Robert Short, Cleveland; George A. Wiley, Washington

Term expires 1971: Donald D. Brewer, Athens, Ga.; Mrs. Wayne Coy, Washington; Franklin M. Foote, M.D., Hartford, Conn.; Mrs. Ruth I. Knee, Chevy Chase, Md.; Mrs. Henry Steeger, New York; Fred H. Steininger, Atlanta, Ga.

Term expires 1972: Alexander J. Allen, New York; Elmer L. Andersen, St. Paul, Minn.; Robert M. Ball, Washington; Charline J. Birkins, Denver; Robert S. Burgess, Providence, R.I.; Philip Hauser, Chicago; Darwin Palmiere, Ann Arbor, Mich.

Representative from NCSW Committee on Public Relations and Development: John H. McMahon, New York

Representative from National Association for Statewide Health and Welfare: Lowell Iberg, New York

Representative from Health and Medical Care Services: Leona Baumgartner, M.D., Boston

Chairman, U.S. Committee of ICSW: Kenneth W. Kindelsperger, Louisville, Ky.

Chairman, Advisory Committee on Program Scope, Content and Participation: M. Leo Bohanon, St. Louis

Legal Consultant: Rudolph Janata, Columbus, Ohio

NCSW COMMITTEE ON NOMINATIONS

Chairman: Wilbur J. Schmidt, Madison, Wis.

Term expires 1970: Dean A. Clark, M.D., Pittsburgh; Fern M. Colborn, Mill Run, Pa.; James R. Dumpson, New York; Katherine Hudson, London, England; Mrs. Annie Lee Sandusky, Washington; Wilbur J. Schmidt, Madison, Wis.; Harry T. Sealy, Cleveland

Term expires 1971: Mildred Arnold, Washington; Melvin A. Glasser, Detroit; Arthur Hillman, Chicago; Raleigh C. Hobson, Baltimore; Mildred Sikkema, Honolulu; Sue W. Spencer, Nashville, Tenn.; Roy C. Votaw, Sacramento, Calif.

Term expires 1972: Mark Battle, Washington; Maurice P. Beck, Lansing, Mich.; Clark W. Blackburn, New York; William J. Brown, Hartford, Conn.; Malvin Morton, Chicago; Sebastion C. Owens, Denver; Mrs. David Whitman, Winchester, Mass.

NCSW COMMITTEE ON PUBLIC RELATIONS AND DEVELOPMENT

Chairman: John H. McMahon, New York

Vice Chairman: Mrs. Alice Adler, New York

Term expires 1970: Lt. Commissioner John Grace, New York; Mary Helen Merrill, Washington; Guichard Parris, New York; Bernard Postal, New York; the Very Rev. Msgr. Thomas J. Reese, Wilmington, Dela.; Julian Rivera, New York; Preston R. Wilcox, New York

Term expires 1971: Helen Christopherson, New York; Mrs. Virginia Doscher, Chicago; Herbert S. Fowler, Washington; Mrs. Frances A. Koestler, Brooklyn, N.Y.; Paul Mendenhall, New York; Philip E. Ryan, Washington

Term expires 1972: Mrs. Adele Braude, New York; Mrs. Elma Phillipson Cole, New York; Frank Driscoll, New York; Mrs. Elly Robbins, New York; Layhmond Robinson, New York; William C. Tracy, New York

Consultant: Harold N. Weiner, New York

Ex officio: William S. Guthrie, Columbus, Ohio

NCSW TELLERS COMMITTEE

Chairman: Merriss Cornell, Columbus, Ohio

NCSW EDITORIAL COMMITTEE

Chairman: Arthur Katz, Lawrence, Kans.

Members: Delwin M. Anderson, Washington; Kathryn Close, Washington; Jeanette Hanford, Chicago; Rachel Marks, Chicago; Jay Roney, Baltimore

NCSW CENTENNIAL COMMITTEE

Chairman: C. Virgil Martin, Chicago

U.S. COMMITTEE OF ICSW

Chairman: Kenneth W. Kindelsperger, Louisville, Ky.
Vice Chairman: C. Virgil Martin, Chicago
Secretary: Martha Branscombe, Washington
Treasurer: James R. Dumpson, New York
Representatives of National Organizations: American Council of Voluntary Agencies for Foreign Service, Eugene Shenefield, New York; American Public Welfare Association, Raleigh C. Hobson, Baltimore; Council on Social Work Education, Katherine A. Kendall, New York; National Assembly for Social Policy and Development, Mrs. Michael Harris, New York; National Association of Social Workers, Kurt Reichert, New York; Department of Health, Education, and Welfare, Dorothy Lally, Washington
Members-at-Large
Term expires 1970: Dr. Ammu Menon Muzumdar, Pine Bluff, Ark.; Henry S. Ollendorff, Cleveland; Sanford Solender, New York; Mrs. Jayne B. Spain, Cincinnati; Mary Switzer, Washington; Phyllis Teicher, New York; Anne Wilkins, Austin, Texas
Term expires 1971: Mrs. Julius Alexander, Miami; Henry S. Maas, Berkeley, Calif.; Dr. Juan Ramos, Chevy Chase, Md.; Alvin L. Schorr, Washington; Edward J. Sette, New York; Malcolm B. Stinson, Los Angeles; George Wiley, Washington
Term expires 1972: Ellen E. Bullock, Washington; Margaret Hickey, St. Louis; William M. Mitchell, Washington; Dr. Ruben A. Mora, New York; Mrs. Aida G. Pagan, San Juan, Puerto Rico; Mrs. Annie Lee Sandusky, Washington; John B. Turner, Cleveland
Liaison: NASW–European Unit, Ruby B. Pernell, Cleveland; New England Committee, Pearl M. Steinmetz, Boston; NCSW Program Committee, Henry S. Ollendorff, Cleveland; NCSW, Werner W. Boehm, New Brunswick, N.J.
Subcommittee Chairman: Membership Committee, Ellen Winston, Raleigh, N.C.; Nominating Committee, Nelson Jackson, New York; U.S. Program Participants, John McDowell, New York; Dorothy Lally, Washington; U.S. Exhibit, Mary Helen Merrill, Washington; U.S. Report, Norman Lourie, Harrisburg, Pa.; Members of Committee of Representatives, ICSW, Ellen Winston, Raleigh, N.C.; and Stephen P. Simonds, Washington; Officers of ICSW (residing in the U.S.), Charles I. Schottland, President, ICSW, Waltham, Mass.; Kenneth W. Kindelsperger, Assistant Treasurer General, Louisville, Ky.; Mrs. Kate Katzki, Secretary General, New York

NCSW COMMITTEE ON PROGRAM

Chairman: Wilbur J. Cohen, Ann Arbor, Mich.
Members-at-Large
Term expires 1970: Dean A. Clark, M.D., Pittsburgh; Thomas Moan, Eugene, Oreg.; Howard E. Prunty, New York

Term expires 1971: M. Leo Bohanon, St. Louis; Robert N. Hilkert, Philadelphia

Term expires 1972: Joseph H. Douglass, Washington; Howard Samuel, New York

Representatives of National Social Welfare Organizations: American Public Welfare Association, Joseph H. Louchheim, New York; Council on Social Work Education, Patricia Stickney, New York; National Assembly for Social Policy and Development, John F. Larberg, New York; National Association of Social Workers, Sam Negrin, New York; National Association for Statewide Health and Welfare, Cecil S. Feldman, Harrisburg, Pa.; National Federation of Student Social Workers, Don Gilbert, Syracuse, N.Y.; National Health Council, Peter G. Meek, New York; National Welfare Rights Organization, Bert DeLeeuw, Washington; La Raza, Julian Rivera, New York

Liaison from NCSW Audio-visual Committee: Mrs. Ann P. Booth, New York

Liaison from NCSW Committee on Combined Associate Groups, John F. Larberg, New York

Liaison from NCSW Public Relations Committee, Helen Christopherson, New York

Liaison from U.S. Committee, ICSW: Henry S. Ollendorff, Cleveland

President-elect: Margaret E. Berry, New York

Past President: Arthur S. Flemming, St. Paul, Minn.

NCSW SECTIONS

SECTION I. CASEWORK

Chairman: Virginia Tannar, Washington

Vice Chairman: Mrs. Catherine C. Hiatt, Washington

Members: Arthur Berliner, Fort Worth, Texas; Leon Chestang, Chicago; John Clark, Washington; Louise d'A. Fairchild, Dallas; Merle M. Foeckler, Athens, Ga.; Peter Gaupp, Dallas; Effie L. Hudson, Oklahoma City; Will Scott, Greensboro, N.C.; Eva Stewart, Washington; Harry Tanner, Dallas; Mrs. Lennie-Marie P. Tolliver, Norman, Okla.; Mrs. Lynn Wikler, Hyattsville, Md.; Marjorie B. Wright, Tulsa, Okla.

SECTION II. GROUP WORK

Chairman: Paul H. Glasser, Ann Arbor, Mich.

Vice Chairman: Mrs. Margaret E. Hartford, Cleveland

Members: Gene Aronowitz, Chicago; Phyllis L. Bare, Chicago; Andrew Curry, San Francisco; Mrs. Thelma Eaton, Los Angeles; Goodwin Garfield, New York; Alex Gitterman, New York; Robert Glass, New York; Sue Henry, Denver; Morris Levin, Chicago; Clyde E. Murray, Chicago; Catherine Papell, Garden City, N.Y.; Charles Sells, Cincinnati; Donald J. Watkins, Ferndale, Mich.

SECTION III. COMMUNITY ORGANIZATION AND SOCIAL ACTION

Chairman: Elmer J. Tropman, Pittsburgh

Vice Chairman: John J. Affleck, Providence, R.I.

Members: Dr. Hobart Burch, Bethesda, Md.; Robert Caulk, San Diego,

Calif.; Morton E. Coleman, Pittsburgh; Harold Demone, Boston; David E. Epperson, Pittsburgh; Herman Gallegos, San Francisco; Charles Guzetta, New York; Leon L. Haley, Pittsburgh; Opal Jones, Huntington Park, Calif.; Mel King, Boston; Mrs. Ferne Kolodner, Baltimore; Dr. Edward Newman, Washington; Howard E. Prunty, New York; Robert Richards, San Diego, Calif.; Kenneth M. Storandt, Cocoa Beach, Fla.; James F. Workman, Baltimore

SECTION IV. SOCIAL RESEARCH

Chairman: Catherine S. Chilman, Frederick, Md.
Vice Chairman: Harold C. Edelston, Baltimore
Members: Andrew C. Billingsley, Berkeley, Calif.; Scott Briar, Berkeley, Calif.; Philip Hauser, Chicago; Saul Kaplan, Chicago; Joseph C. Lagey, New York; Robert Langer, St. Louis; Perry Levinson, Washington; Lawrence E. Nicholson, St. Louis; Dr. Juan Ramos, Chevy Chase, Md.; Irving Spergel, Chicago; Malcolm Stinson, Los Angeles; Merlin Taber, Urbana, Ill.; Gilbert Ware, Washington; Jack Weiner, Bethesda, Md.

SECTION V. ADMINISTRATION

Chairman: William H. Robinson, Springfield, Ill.
Vice Chairman: Charles X. Sampson, New York
Members: Chauncey Alexander, New York; S. J. Axelrod, M.D., Ann Arbor, Mich.; Harold Boysaw, Chicago; Nora Cartwright, Chicago; Lawrence T. Cooper, San Marino, Calif.; Joseph L. Farrell, Lansing, Mich.; Ralph L. Goff, Los Angeles; Emeric Kurtagh, Detroit; Ben S. Meeker, Chicago; William T. Patrick, Jr., Detroit; Mrs. Patricia Rabinowitz, Ann Arbor, Mich.; Harold Richmond, Chicago; James White, Chicago

NCSW DIVISION COMMITTEE

Chairman: Lowell Iberg, New York
Ex officio: Wilbur J. Cohen, Ann Arbor, Mich.
Members: Bertram M. Beck, New York; Duane Beck, Atlanta, Ga.; Genevieve Carter, Los Angeles; James R. Dumpson, New York; Cecil S. Feldman, Harrisburg, Pa.; Andrew Freeman, Philadelphia; David R. Hunter, New York; Alfred Kahn, New York; Alvin Schorr, Washington; Sanford Solender, New York; Fred H. Steininger, Atlanta, Ga.; Roland Warren, Waltham, Mass.; Henry Weber, Washington; Corinne M. Wolfe, Washington

NCSW AUDIO-VISUAL COMMITTEE

Chairman: Mrs. Ann P. Booth, New York
Vice Chairman: Ted O. Thackrey, New York
Consultants: Sumner Glimcher, New York; Rohama Lee, New York; Robert Mitchell, New York
Members
Term expires 1970: Robert Finehout, New York

Term expires 1971: Mrs. Janet S. Brown, New York; Robert Lewis Shay-on, Philadelphia; Daniel J. Ransohoff, Cincinnati

Term expires 1972: Dr. N. H. Cooper, Brooklyn, N.Y.; Lt. Col. Belle Leach, New York; Jack Neher, New York; Daniel O'Connor, Washington; Mrs. Marie Stewart, New York; William Tracy, New York

NCSW TASK FORCE FOR SOCIAL ISSUES FORUM AND ANNUAL MEETING OF MEMBERS

Chairman: Rabbi David Jacobson, San Antonio, Texas
Vice Chairman: Mrs. Ruth I. Knee, Chevy Chase, Md.
Secretary: Thomas C. Moan, Eugene, Oreg.
Members: Elmer L. Andersen, St. Paul, Minn.; Robert M. Ball, Washington; Robert S. Burgess, Providence, R.I.; Lowell Iberg, New York; Mrs. Albert Werthan, Nashville, Tenn.; George A. Wiley, Washington

COMMITTEE ON COMBINED ASSOCIATE GROUPS

Chairman: John F. Larberg, New York
Vice Chairman: David Jeffreys, Washington
Term expires 1970: AFL-CIO, Department of Community Services, Leo Perlis, Washington; American Jewish Committee, Mrs. Ann Wolfe, New York; American Social Health Association, Earle Lippincott, New York; National Health Council, Peter Meek, New York; National Jewish Welfare Board, Alfred Dobruf, New York; Salvation Army, Col. Jane E. Wrieden, New York

Term expires 1971: American Home Economics Association, Mrs. Natalie Preston, Brooklyn, National Association for Statewide Health and Welfare, Corinne M. Callahan, Albany, N.Y.; Social Work Vocational Bureau, Henry Stern, New York

PROGRAM CHAIRMEN OF ASSOCIATE GROUPS

AFL-CIO, Department of Community Services: Leo Perlis
American Association of Homes for the Aging: Lester Davis
American Association of Retired Persons: David Jeffreys
American Council for Nationalities Service: Gloria Seavers
American Foundation for the Blind: Harold G. Roberts; Dorothy Demby
American Friends Service Committee: Frank J. Hunt
American Home Economics Association: Mrs. Natalie Preston; Mrs. Lillie C. Scott
American Humane Association, Children's Division: Vincent DeFrancis
American Immigration and Citizenship Conference: Mrs. Sonia D. Blumenthal
American Jewish Committee: Mrs. Ann Wolfe
American Legion—National Child Welfare Division: Fred T. Kuszmaul
American National Red Cross: Mary Helen Merrill
American Public Welfare Association: Benjamin O. Hendrick
American Social Health Association: Earle Lippincott

Anti-Defamation League of B'nai B'rith: Oscar Cohen
Army Community Service Headquarters, Department of the Army: Lt. Col. Frank F. Montalvo
Association for Voluntary Sterilization: Janice Kaye; John R. Rague
Association of the Junior Leagues of America: Kathryn Oliphant
Big Brothers of America: Thomas E. O'Brien
Child Study Association of America: Otis B. Turner; Lillian Opatoshu
Child Welfare League of America: Helen D. Stone
Community Development Foundation: Mrs. Ruth Levine
Conference of Social Workers in State and Territorial Mental Health Programs: Margaret C. Schilling; Edward L. Davis
Council of Jewish Federations and Welfare Funds: Charles Zibbell
Council on Social Work Education: Patricia J. Stickney
Day Care and Child Development Council of America: Mrs. Jean H. Berman
Executive Council of the Episcopal Church: Mrs. Charles S. Monroe
Family Service Association of America: William G. Hill
Florence Crittenton Association of America: Helen Johnstone Weisbrod
Goodwill Industries of America: Robert E. Watkins
International Social Service, American Branch: Sidney Talisman
National Assembly for Social Policy and Development: John F. Larberg
National Association for Mental Health: Douglas Waterstreet
National Association for Statewide Health and Welfare: Corinne M. Callahan
National Association of Christians in Social Work: Donald Hageman
National Association of Housing and Redevelopment Officials: Mrs. Dorothy Gazzolo
National Association of Social Workers: Sam Negrin
National Committee on Employment of Youth: Eli E. Cohen
National Conference of Jewish Communal Service: Morton I. Teicher
National Council for Homemaker Services: Mrs. Florence Moore
National Council of Jewish Women: Mrs. Helen Powers
National Council of the Churches of Christ in the U.S.A.: John McDowell
National Council on Alcoholism: Yvelin Gardner
National Council on Crime and Delinquency: Robert E. Trimble
National Council on Illegitimacy: Mrs. Gertrude McLean
National Council on the Aging: Marjorie A. Collins
National Council, YMCAs: John W. Copeland
National Easter Seal Society for Crippled Children and Adults: Mrs. Rhoda Gellman; Jane Shover
National Federation of Settlements and Neighborhood Centers: Mrs. Elizabeth C. Day
National Health Council: Peter G. Meek
National Jewish Welfare Board: Alfred Dobrof
National Legal Aid and Defender Association: Mayo H. Stiegler
National Public Relations Council of Health and Welfare Services: Harold N. Weiner
National Retired Teachers Association: David Jeffreys

National Urban League: Manuel A. Romero
Planned Parenthood–World Population: Samuel Taylor
The Salvation Army: Col. Jane E. Wrieden
Social Work Vocational Bureau: Henry B. Stern
Travelers Aid Association of America: Paul W. Guyler
United Cerebral Palsy Association: Ernest Weinrich
United Community Funds and Councils of America: Lowell E. Wright
United HIAS Service: Ralph Bergel
United Methodist Church: Mona Kewish
United Presbyterian Health, Education, and Welfare Association: Jeanne Kleman
United Seamen's Service: Mrs. Lillian Rabins
Veterans Administration: Claire R. Lustman; Sidney Hirsch
The Volunteers of America: Lt. Col. Belle Leach
YWCA of the U.S.A.: Mrs. Wenonah Bond Logan

Index

Papers presented at the 97th Annual Forum may also be found in *Social Work Practice, 1970,* published by Columbia University Press: